90 0320... 06

KW-283-867

PERSPECTIVES ON ECONOMIC INTEGRATION AND BUSINESS STRATEGY IN THE ASIA–PACIFIC REGION

Also by Sam Dzever

INDUSTRIAL BUYING BEHAVIOUR

Perspectives on Economic Integration and Business Strategy in the Asia–Pacific Region

Edited by

Sam Dzever
Professor of Management
I.A.E., Université de Poitiers
France

and

Jacques Jaussaud
Associate Professor in Management
I.A.E., Université de Poitiers
France

First published in Great Britain 1997 by
MACMILLAN PRESS LTD
Houndmills, Basingstoke, Hampshire RG21 6XS and London
Companies and representatives throughout the world

A catalogue record for this book is available from the British Library.

ISBN 0–333–69182–2

 First published in the United States of America 1997 by
ST. MARTIN'S PRESS, INC.,
Scholarly and Reference Division,
175 Fifth Avenue, New York, N.Y. 10010

ISBN 0–312–17275–3

Library of Congress Cataloging-in-Publication Data
Perspectives on economic integration and business strategy in the Asia
-Pacific Region
p. cm.
Papers presented at Euro-Asia research conference, held in Nantes
and Poitiers, France in November 1994 and 1995 respectively.
Includes bibliographical references and index.
ISBN 0–312–17275–3 (cloth)
1. Asia—Economic integration—Congresses.   2. Investments,
Foreign—Asia—Congresses.   3. Corporations—Asia—Congresses.
I. Dzever, Sam, 1956–   . II. Jaussaud, Jacques, 1957–
HC412.P47 1997
337.1'5—dc21   96–44474
                                                                              CIP

Editorial matter and selection © Sam Dzever and Jacques Jaussaud 1997
Text © Macmillan Press Ltd 1997

This book is printed on paper suitable for recycling and made from fully managed and
sustained forest sources.

10   9   8   7   6   5   4   3   2   1
06   05   04   03   02   01   00   99   98   97

Printed and bound in Great Britain by
Antony Rowe Ltd, Chippenham, Wiltshire

Contents

Preface
(Professor Michel Kalika, Director, IAE – The University of
Poitiers)   vii

List of Contributors   viii

Editors' Introduction
(Sam Dzever and Jacques Jaussaud)   xi

PART I: Analysis of the Economic Integration Process in the
          Asia–Pacific Region

1 Trade and Specialization in the Asian Area
   (Sandra Palméro)   3

2 Economic Integration in East Asia: Situation and Perspectives
   (Catherine Figuière)   24

3 Japanese Trade with East Asia and Business Cycles:
   a Historical Perspective (1875–1993)
   (Jean-Pascal Bassino)   38

4 The EU Antidumping Policy Towards Asia
   (Matthias Niyonzima)   62

PART II: The Position of China

5 China and India: Economics and Performance
   (Indru T. Advani)   79

6 China's Integration into the Regional Economy
   (Shaun Breslin)   92

7 Foreign Direct Investment in China and the Economic
   Integration of East Asia
   (Yunnan Shi)   121

8 China: an Evaluation of Political Risk
   (Maria Weber)   144

9   Chinese Macroeconomic Reforms and the Japanese Model:
    Implications for Japanese Companies
    (Robert Taylor)   157

10 Industrial Procurement Practices of Taiwanese Firms in the
    Chinese Market
    (Sam Dzever)   172

PART III: Business Strategy in Selected Countries

11 Asian Economic Integration and the Role of Japanese
    Corporate Networks: the Case of the Electronics Industry
    (Christian Milelli)   189

12 Cooperation and Strategic Alliances with Japanese Companies
    (Jacques Jaussaud)   208

13 Japan as a Base for Establishing Markets throughout Asia:
    The Case of French Industrial Glue Manufacturers
    (Christine Di Domenico and Sami Slim)   218

Index   246

Preface

The current rate of economic growth in the Asia–Pacific region represents an important challenge to political leaders, managers of business enterprises, and researchers. It calls on management scientists to become quickly and fully aware of the implications of this macroeconomic evolution for business strategy in the region. A thorough understanding of these developments, from a research point of view, should provide the necessary basis for designing appropriate curricula for training future managers of business enterprises in the region, as well as for solving practical problems connected with managing in this area.

It was the recognition of this challenge that led the two institutions, IAE–Université de Poitiers, and Groupe ESC Nantes Atlantique, to join forces in 1994 to organize an annual Euro–Asia research conference. The papers presented in this volume, under the editorship of Sam Dzever and Jacques Jaussaud, represent a selection of research communications presented at the 1994 and 1995 conferences.

I hope that readers will find these contributions useful in enhancing their understanding of current developments in the Asia–Pacific region.

Professor Michel Kalika
Directeur,
IAE – Université de Poitiers
France

List of Contributors

Indru T. Advani, a French national, was born and raised in that part of undivided British India which is now called Pakistan. After graduating from Imperial College, London, Advani spent several years in Asia (the last fifteen in the People's Republic of China) as the senior executive of a European conglomerate. He has retired from active service and now occupies the post of Honorary *Délégué Général of Comité France – Chine* in Paris, where he lives.

Jean-Pascal Bassino is Associate Professor of Economics at Paul Valéry University (Vauban Campus), Nîmes, France. He is also a Research Fellow at **CEFI** (*Centre d'Economie et de Finances Internationales*), a CNRS – associated research unit at Château Lafarge, France. Dr Bassino has published widely in the area of economic and financial analysis of Asian countries.

Shaun Breslin is Lecturer in Chinese Politics at the University of Newcastle upon Tyne and Deputy Director of the Newcastle East Asia Centre. His research focuses on Chinese and comparative politics, in which he has a number of publications.

Christine Di Domenico is Lecturer in Economics at Lyon Graduate School of Management (Groupe ESC – Lyon), France, where she is in charge of research and elective courses concerning Asia.

Sam Dzever is Professor of Marketing and International Business at IAE, The University of Poitiers, France. His research focuses on industrial marketing and business strategy in the Asia–Pacific region. His publications include *Le Comportement D'Achat Industriel* (Industrial Buying Behaviour) (Economica, Paris, 1996).

Catherine Figuière is Lecturer in Economics at *Université Pierre Mendès – France* in Grenoble. She is also a Researcher at the *Institut d'Asie Orientale de Lyon*. Her research focuses on Japanese economic and business life. Her publications include 'A French Analysis of the Japanese Economy: a History of Ideas', *Journal of Contemporary Asia* (Forthcoming, 1997).

Jacques Jaussaud is Associate Professor of Management at IAE, The University of Poitiers. His research interests are in the areas of business strategy and human resource management (with a particular focus on Japan and Asian countries). He has published widely in these areas and is the editor of the French management journal, *Japon In Extenso*.

Christian Milelli is a CNRS Research Fellow at the *Centre de Recherche sur l'Entreprise Multinationale (FORUM)*, located at the University of Paris X, Nanterre. His research focuses on the strategy of multinational enterprises and the globalization of manufacturing operations. He has several publications in these fields, including *Les Firmes Multinationales* (with M. Delapierre) (Vuibert, Paris, 1995).

Matthias Niyonzima (Attorney at Law, Claes & Partners, Brussels) received his Ph.D. in Law at the University of Leuven, Belgium. He has taught commercial law, financial law, and international trade law at a number of universities in Europe and has several publications in these fields, including *La Clause de Monnaie Etrangère dans les Contrats Internationaux* (Bruylant, Brussels/Maklu, Antwerp, 1991).

Sandra Palmero is a Lecturer at the *Université de la Méditerranée Aix – Marseille II* (France). She is also a Researcher at CEFI URA CNRS, where she has worked on projects concerning Asian economic integration. She is particularly interested in institutional forms of integration and in the diffusion of technological innovation in these countries.

Yunnan Shi obtained his Ph.D. in Economics at the University of Rennes I (France), where he is now a faculty member in the Department of Economics. His research focuses on the economics of development (with particular reference to China), to which field he has contributed a number of publications.

Sami Slim is a Researcher at the Lyon Graduate School of Management (Groupe ESC Lyon), France.

Robert Taylor is Director of Chinese Studies at the University of Sheffield. He has taught at universities in Britain and overseas, and is the author of a number of studies of East Asia, including *Greater China in Japan* (Routledge, 1996).

Maria Weber is Professor of International Relations and Comparative Politics at Bocconi University, Italy. She is also Senior Research Leader at ISESAO (Institute of Economic and Social Studies for East Asia), Bocconi University. She has produced a number of publications on East Asia, including 'Regional Integration and Political Issues: The Case of ASEAN' (with A. Colombo) (*Quaderni ISESAO*, 1/1995).

Editors' Introduction

The current rates of economic growth in the Asia–Pacific region have been described as phenomenal. The World Bank estimates that by the year 2000 half the growth in the global economy will come from East and Southeast Asian countries. 'This growth will ensure that by the year 2000 one billion Asians will have significant consumer spending power and of these, 400 million will have average disposable incomes as high, if not higher, than their European or US contemporaries'[1]. Apart from Japan, almost all of the countries in the region (and in particular East Asian countries) have experienced average growth rates of above six per cent during the past few years, the most spectacular of these being the People's Republic of China (PRC) with annual growth of over 11% recorded during the last three or four years. These developments mark the growing impact of the region on the world economy. It has been estimated that average GNP growth per capita in East Asia between 1965 and 1990 was 5.5%[2], and (according to IMF) Asian GNP will have grown by 44% between 1990 and 1995.

But the rate of growth in the region is by no means evenly spread, and in order to obtain a more complete picture of these developments one needs to examine events in the individual countries closely. As research into the Asia–Pacific economies intensifies, scholars are faced with the need to re-examine past findings in the light of current developments. Japan, for example, is presently experiencing its worst post-war economic crisis – and past research findings that pointed to the Japanese model as an example to be emulated by other countries in the region with ambitions to attain rapid economic advancement might need to be carefully reassessed. China, long asleep, has finally awoken and is fast emerging as one of Asia's new economic giants. The Indian market, once shielded from foreign investment by a plethora of government regulations, is now being gradually opened up and the response of foreign firms to this policy change appears to be positive. With the liberalization of the economy, the Indian market is bound to emerge as one of the region's most important markets. (It must be added, however, that with the general elections of May 1996, which saw the Congress Party lose its majority in Parliament to the nationalist parties, it is difficult to predict just how this development might impact on foreign business in that country.)

The impact of Asian growth on the global economy is already clear. Japanese companies are rapidly expanding their market position in the region, and American companies, although relatively latecomers to the game, appear to have gained considerable ground in recent years and are poised to increase their market position throughout the region in the next few years. It is important to note, too, that US economic policy toward the Pacific Rim appears to have witnessed a significant change in direction in favour of certain of the countries in the region. Within the framework of Asia Pacific Economic Cooperation (APEC), the USA will continue to play an important role in the economic transformation now taking place in Asia. With the normalization of diplomatic relations between the USA and Vietnam, for example, American firms are expected to play an increasingly important role in the emerging market there. The Clinton administration, despite some hesitation, has recently renewed China's most favoured nation trading status with the United States, and American firms are establishing markets in the PRC as never before. A Chinese government survey of foreign countries with the highest investment in the PRC market in 1993 placed the USA in third position (with US$2068 million invested) after Hong Kong and Taiwan in first and second places respectively[3]. The same ranking placed Japan in fourth position (with a total of US1361 million invested). European Union (EU) countries that figured highly on the list were the United Kingdom (US$221 million) and France (US$141 million). The two EU countries occupied 9th and 10th positions respectively.

The position of Europe with respect to the developments in the region appears to be much more clearly defined. The main thrust of EU policy towards Asia is said to relate to economic matters. This is clearly outlined in the document 'Towards A New Asia Strategy', referred to earlier. Traditionally, much of Western Europe's relations with East Asia tended to focus on economic matters: a wide variety of bilateral trade agreements were signed between EU Member States and countries of the Asia–Pacific region, although Régnier et al.[4] argue that in the three decades after the Second World War Europe lost most of its ties (including economic ties) with East Asia, very easily letting the Americans, and then the Japanese, take charge of the markets there. A change emerged in late 1970 'with the increasing penetration of East Asian products in the European market, and from the mid-1980s the EC nations started to give East Asia higher priority'[5]. Europe's renewed economic interest in East Asia was generally within the framework of Trade and Cooperation Agreements. This policy has not changed significantly over the years, except that in more recent times greater emphasis has come to be placed on economic engagement rather than, for example, development cooperation. On the basis of the dramatic rise in the position of Asia in the global economy, the European Commission believes that the EU ought to accord the region a much higher priority than has hitherto been the case. In the executive summary of the document cited above, the Commission argues that:

'The Union needs as a matter of urgency to strengthen its economic presence in Asia in order to maintain its leading role in the world economy. The establishment of a strong, co-ordinated presence in the different regions of Asia will allow Europe at the beginning of the 21st century to ensure that its interests are taken fully into account there.' Furthermore, 'The success of Europe in taking advantage of the business opportunities in Asia largely depends upon decisions taken or not taken by the private sector. The Union's role is to pursue market-opening for both goods and services and to overcome obstacles to European trade and investment by encouraging a favourable regulatory environment for business in Asia. Active participation by European companies on Asian market ... can contribute to providing qualified jobs to European workers'[6]. And in order to achieve these objectives, 'the Union needs to adopt more proactive strategies: emphasising fuller, and increasingly targeted use of economic co-operation to promote European trade and investment'[7].

The preceding statements constitute the basic framework under which the EU-Asian economic relations will be developed. With regard to China, for example, Sino–European economic relations will take place at two levels: the institutional (i.e. governmental) level, and the private sector level.

At the institutional level, the reform process in the PRC's economy will impact on Sino–European economic relations in a number of ways, the most important of which will include a reappraisal of traditional European commercial policy towards that country. The EU document notes that emphasis will continue to be placed on trade liberalizations with China, as well as the continued opening-up of the market for European businesses. Furthermore, it will become increasingly important that the EU 'reinforces a nonconfrontational dialogue of equals' with the PRC in order to address questions of bilateral concern. In developing these relations, consideration will also be given to issues of a more global concern, such as the protection of the environment and human rights matters.

Other, more specific effects on Sino–European economic relations at the governmental level will include:

(1) the promotion of business cooperation between European companies and their Chinese counterparts;

(2) providing expertise and policy advice to the PRC government in order to help it 'set up the institutions, policies and laws to make a smooth transition. . .' to a market-based economic system;

(3) the enhancement of co-operation in the field of science and technology, as well as research and development;

(4) supporting European direct investment in the PRC with specific actions such as (for example) providing financial incentives for joint venture investments between European and Chinese enterprises;

(5) supporting trade promotion between the EU and the PRC.

At the private sector level, it is expected that there will be a significant increase in the total number of European firms successfully established in the PRC market. The present position of European firms in this market appears to be much weaker relative to, say, Japanese and American firms. It appears that so far the most successful European firms in the Chinese market have been large industrial concerns. There is thus a need to encourage small and medium-sized European firms to also look towards the PRC market. The increased opening-up of the market, coupled with specific policy initiatives on the part of the EU, will aid in helping smaller European firms gain access to this market. With the exception of certain industrial sectors, much of the PRC market is now open to international competition. And (as is generally the case with any competitive market), European firms that are unable to demonstrate innovativeness in product design and engineering as well as customer orientation will find it increasingly difficult to survive in this market. Succeeding in the PRC market generally requires a vigorous and sustained commitment on the part of foreign firms: in attempting to maintain a viable competitive position in this market, European firms will soon find that they are by no means an exception to this rule.

With this opening-up of the market, foreign firms are rushing to invest in China. The PRC government has clearly stated that developing the country's economy with the active participation of foreign enterprises is one of its priorities. To this end it has actively encouraged foreign investment by providing foreign firms with all sorts of favourable investment conditions, particularly in relation to setting up joint venture (JV) enterprises with local firms – the fundamental principle underlying the Chinese view of JV being that there should be *equity and mutual benefit* in the joint ventureship. The PRC government generally sees JVs as a way of earning foreign exchange by exporting goods produced under the agreement, in addition to acquiring foreign technical expertise and managerial know-how. A KPMG newsletter notes with regard to JVs that the law provides for the establishment of a limited liability company with foreign ownership of not less than 25 per cent, although there is no upper limit set. The foreign partner is expected to contribute capital, technology, and managerial expertise and the PRC partner contributes the land, building, and labour force:

'The foreign partner's investment will usually be a mixture of cash and equipment, whereas the PRC will usually contribute land and building. In addition, whilst the PRC partner provides the labour, the foreign partner will typically be expected to provide expert management and technical know-how'[8].

Five Special Economic Zones have been created with favourable investment conditions for foreign firms, which, together with the sixteen Open Coastal Cities, offer proof that the government wishes to attract as much foreign capital as possible into the economy. With the necessary conditions in place, three upsurges in foreign investment are said to have occurred in PRC's economy since the 1980s. The first was in 1984, the second in 1988 and the third in 1993. A government publication notes that in 1993 alone 83,000 new joint venture projects were approved comprising 'US$111,43 million subscribed in the agreement' and that 'real input' from foreign capital (i.e. the actual foreign capital committed in the agreements) amounted to US$26,023[9] million. And Warner (1994) estimates that there were approximately 20,000 JVs established in the PRC market in 1991. By 1993 the number had increased considerably to some 100,000[10]. This increase underlines the growing importance of China in the global economy.

Parallel with these developments has been the increased economic integration of the region. Intraregional trade between East and Southeast Asia has seen a considerable increase in recent years. The proportion of trade between the two regions in 1991 was comparable to that of NAFTA at 42 per cent. What is particularly striking about this increase is that it occurred quite 'naturally' rather than through formal trade arrangements. The significant increase in intraregional trade has also meant a decline in dependence on markets of the developed world (particularly North America and Europe).

What impact would the increasing importance of the Asia–Pacific region in the global economy – the effects of economic integration, resulting in a significant increase in intraregional trade and business, the emergence of formally protected markets such as China and India among the world's most important markets, developments in former Indochina, etc. – have on Euro-Asian trade and business? This question constituted the subject matter of the first and second Euro–Asia research conferences organized jointly by IAE, Université de Poitiers, France, and Groupe ESC Nantes Atlantique. The first conference was held in Nantes in November 1994 and the second in the following year in Poitiers. The conference has now become an annual event, with venues alternating between Nantes and Poitiers. The principal objective has remained that of providing an international forum for scholars who are actively engaged in research concerned with Euro–Asian business and economic relations to present the results of their most recent work and share a common experience with colleagues.

The present volume is a selection of papers presented at the 1994 and 1995 conferences. The papers are among the most recent empirical findings concerned with the analysis of the current economic transformation and business strategy in the Asia–Pacific region. Various themes have been addressed, ranging from an assessment of the environment to more specific issues related to the business and marketing strategies of firms operating in the region. The principal objective of the volume is to introduce to the reader the rapid economic transformation now taking place in the various countries of the region and the impact this might have on future Euro–Asian and international business. The volume is aimed at both the undergraduate (advanced level) and postgraduate student, as well as the general reader, and is intended as an important supplement to existing texts on international business and economics. Because of the geographical focus of the book, it is expected that students using it will already have completed introductory courses in international business and management and have familiarized themselves with the basic concepts.

The volume is divided into three parts:

Part I: Analysis of the Economic Integration Process in the Asia–Pacific Region (four papers)

Part II: The Position of China (six papers)

Part III: Business Strategy in Selected Countries (three papers).

THE PAPERS

Sandra Palmero traces the phenomenon of economic integration in Asia during the period 1984–1993, using appropriate statistical indicators. She analyses the growth in intraregional trade of each country within the region and then calculates comparative advantage indicators in selected industrial sectors of each country studied. The comparative advantage of Japan in relation to certain industrial sectors is accompanied by gains by the 'four dragons'. The author explains that this is the result of the increasing economic integration in the region.

Catherine Figuière analyses the different dimensions of the processes of regional economic integration in Asia. Using the work of François Perroux as the frame of reference, Figuière underlines the importance of the role played by Japan in Asia as the 'producer of norms'. Japan has increased its foreign direct investment activities in the region in recent years, while at the same time intensifying its bilateral trade relations with these countries.

Using appropriate statistical indicators, Jean-Pascal Bassino analyses the phenomenon of Asian economic integration during the period 1870–1994. His analysis emphasizes the importance of the role played by Japan in the process. He shows the relationship between Japan's macroeconomic business cycle and the dynamics of trade it maintains with its principal trading partners in the region.

Matthias Niyonzima's contribution is concerned with an examination of the European Union's (EU) antidumping regulations with particular reference to Asia. He notes that the EU has placed economic sanctions on several Asian countries in recent years for dumping a variety of products on the European market. The most recent cases (1994) involve textile products from China, Indonesia, India, etc., and computer disks from Hong Kong and South Korea. The main conclusion is that the EU's antidumping rules are an expression of a general protective policy rather than aimed specifically at Asian countries. The EU regulations are in conformity with WTO criteria rather than discriminatory as to the national origin of the products.

Indru T. Advani draws a parallel between developments in China and in India. Both countries sought to consolidate their independence by adopting planned economic systems, but on the political front India chose parliamentary democracy while China opted for a socialist system. Both countries are presently in the process of liberalizing their economies. Advani argues that China has an advance of twelve years over India, since it has at its disposal the means to implement political decisions more rapidly. In this regard, the author notes, democracy might not always be the most efficient instrument for the rapid implementation of decisions requiring urgency.

Shaun Breslin distinguishes three groups of investors in China, each of which has different objectives. These are Japanese firms, firms from other Asian countries, and Western firms. He argues that Japan's importance as a trading partner for China should not be underestimated. Bilateral trade between the two countries increased by 30% in 1993 over 1992, and by a further 22% in 1994. But there have also been significant increases in foreign direct investment in China from other Asian countries in the last few years. Consequently, the country has been steadily pulled into a regional pattern of interlocking investment, trade, and production networks, reflecting the pattern of increased economic integration in the region.

Yunnan Shi analyses the development of foreign direct investment (FDI) in China since 1979, the year the Chinese government decided to launch its economic reform policy. The author distinguishes three types of FDI in the Chinese economy: joint ventures, contractual joint ventures, and wholly-owned foreign firms. Shi attempts to bring to light the link between the strategy of direct investment in China by multinational enterprises and economic integration in the region. The author concludes that FDI has conditioned the structure of foreign trade in China. It has favoured the integration of the Chinese economy in East Asia, and contributed to accelerating the pace of economic integration in the region.

An analysis of political risk in China constitutes the subject matter of Maria Weber's contribution. She traces the different phases of Chinese political development from 1949 through the present and proposes three possible medium-term political scenarios: consolidation of power, return to economic control, and the secession of the southern part from the rest of the country. The author argues that should the management of inflation require the Chinese government to adopt a more moderate reform policy (even detrimental to the southern region), the political risk would still be low. On the other hand, a higher political risk might emerge should the southern region require greater autonomy, as this would arouse strong reactions from the central government.

Robert Taylor observes in his contribution that the Chinese authorities have been greatly influenced by the Japanese in their effort to modernize and decentralize their economy. The government's recent creation of the Office of Trade and Economics and its reorganization of the State Planning Commission reflects correctly the Japanese model. (The respective Japanese equivalents of these organizations are the Ministry of International Trade and Industry (MITI) and the Economic Planning Agency). Recent fiscal reforms and price control policies have both been introduced after a careful study of the Japanese model, as is the case with reforms related to human resource management. Taylor concludes that the increasing interest of Japanese firms in establishing bases in the PRC market could be explained, in part, by the presence of the Japanese model already firmly established there.

The near-brutal intensity of global competition is the force driving an increasing number of firms to seek strategic alliances in foreign countries. Jacques Jaussaud's contribution focuses on a study of strategic alliances between Western and Japanese firms. In the 1990s (the years that have seen companies in difficulty owing to escalating wage costs, the appreciation of the yen, growth in interest rates and an end to the dynamism of Western technological duplication) Japanese firms have been studying carefully all kinds of proposal for alliances that might be useful in easing their current difficulty or reinforcing their competitive positions. As a result, the alliances they form tend to be rather diverse in nature. Jaussaud examines the precautions that are necessary for the definition of strategic alliances with Japanese enterprises.

Christine di Domenico and Sami Slim analyse the evolution of the glue industry on the international market. The authors maintain that the industry can benefit from the commercial and technological influence of Japan in its efforts to establish a viable presence in the Asia–Pacific markets. After analysing the dynamics of the industry on a global basis, the authors proceed to show how the Japanese archipelago can provide an excellent platform for the industry's expansion in the region, recommending that French glue manufacturers considering the Asian markets should try to form strategic alliances with Japanese firms.

Organizational procurement practices of Taiwanese firms in the PRC market constitute the subject matter of Sam Dzever's analysis. The paper is based on empirical data collected among 95 Taiwanese firms currently doing business in China. The procurement practices of these firms were studied in relation to factors such as the role of purchasing managers in the decision process relating to the purchasing of industrial products from foreign suppliers, the importance of different functional departments in the decision process, the importance of technical, commercial, and social factors in the decision process, and the effects of environmental factors such as market structure, economic, technology, and culture on the decision process. The overall implications of the findings for the industrial marketing strategies of foreign firms in the PRC market are discussed.

Christian Milelli provides an analysis of Asian economic integration and the role of Japanese corporate networks in the process, with particular reference to the electronics industry. The author argues that Japanese corporate networks are much older than, say, European and American ones and appear to have a better understanding of the economic integration process now taking place in Asia. The author provides evidence related to different phases of the establishment of Japanese firms in this industry in the Asian markets and points out that these firms have, however, come under increased competition in recent years from their American counterparts.

Sam Dzever
Jacques Jaussaud

Notes

1. See the document 'Towards A new Asia Strategy', Com. (94) 312 published by EU Commission, Brussels, 1994.

2. Ibid.
3. *Statistical Yearbook of China*, 1994.
4. Régnier, Philippe, Niu Yuanming, and Zhang Ruijun, 'Towards a regional 'Block' in East Asia: Implications for Europe', in *Issues & Studies*, March 1993.
5. 'Towards A New Asian Strategy' op. cit. pp 1–2.
6. Ibid., p 30.
7. Ibid.
8. KPMG China Newsletter, August 1993.
9. PRC Government Publication 'Top Ten Joint Ventures', New Star Publishing, Beijing 1993.
10. Warner, M., 'Economic Reform, Industrial Relations and Human Resources Management in the People's Republic of China in the Early 1990'. Paper presented at the conference 'The Future of China', INSEAD, Fontainebleau, France, 1994.

Part I:

Analysis of the Economic Integration Process in the Asia–Pacific Region

1 Trade and Specialization in the Asian Area

Sandra Palméro

1 INTRODUCTION

This paper analyses the evolution of the commercial relations of the following Asian countries: Japan, China, Korea, Hong Kong, Singapore, Taiwan, Vietnam, Brunei, Indonesia, Malaysia, the Philippines and Thailand. Our objectives will be:

(1) to show how this area, which appears to be the most dynamic in the economic growth field as well as in the international trade sphere, constitutes a coherent group of integrating countries in which Japan remains the commercial and financial centre of gravity;
(2) to show how this economic region withdraws into itself in its trade relations. (This closing-in became accentuated at the beginning of the 1990s for countries like Japan, which realized not only saw a relative decline in their foreign trade with the United States but also realized that their strength lay in domestic growth.

The coherence of the Asian area delineated above is based on a division of interest that can be best understood by way of an analysis of its different commercial flows. Japan imports petroleum and raw materials, and exports high-tech equipment; China exports low-value-added manufactured goods, playing on its comparative advantage, and imports equipment and technology from Japan and especially from the Four Dragons. Oil-producing and exporting countries like Indonesia and Brunei mainly import manufactured goods and equipment goods. Commercial flows in the area reflect fairly well the comparative advantages of each country in the context of a strong movement of delocalization.

2 ORIENTATION AND CENTRING OF EXCHANGES

The relative intensity of exchange indicators[1] facilitates a fairly precise understanding of the commercial relations that countries or groups of countries have between them. In the case that interests us, our first aim is to study the evolution of trade flows, exports and imports, in the Asian area between 1984 and 1993. We will do the same thing with regard to the trade dynamics of the Asian area relative to the United States and the European Union.

These indicators define economic proximity relations in commercial trade relations which cannot be clarified or visualized otherwise. If this economic proximity is accompanied by a geographic and cultural proximity which minimizes the cost of crossing space – the cost of access to a market in terms of human capital – we will probably be considering an integrating area. Our intensity indicators will represent this phenomenon all the better as the different countries are in an economic and dynamic complementarity.

Calculation method of the relative intensity of exchange indicators

These indicators are calculated to compare the place that a country occupies in the trade of a partner country compared to the place that the latter occupies in world trade.

The relative intensity of the export indicator of country i to country j (IDRX) is shown as

$$\text{IDRX} = \frac{\dfrac{X_{ij}}{X_i}}{\dfrac{M_j}{W}}$$

Where:

X_{ij} is the exports of country i to country j,
X_i, the world exports of country i,
M_j, the world imports of country j,
W, world trade,
X_{ij}/X_i, the importance of the exports of country i to country j in the total export of country i, and M_j/W, the importance of imports of country j in world trade.

In the same manner, the relative intensity of import indicator of country i to country j (IDRM) is shown as

$$IDRM = \frac{\dfrac{M_{ij}}{M_i}}{\dfrac{X_j}{W}}$$

Where:

M_{ij} is the imports of country i to country j,
M_i, the world imports of country i,
X_j, the world exports of country j,
W, world trade,
M_{ij}/M_i, the importance of the imports of country i to country j in the total imports of country i, and X_j/W, the importance of the exports of country j in world trade.

These indicators are equal to 1 when bilateral flows are strictly proportional to the importance of two partners in world trade. In other words, for all indicators above 1, the commercial exchanges are more than proportional to the importance of two partners in world trade: – given that the concerned nations entertain privileged commercial relations and for all indicators below 1, the exchanges are less than proportional to the importance of two partners in world trade, which means that the two countries do not have preponderant commercial relations.

We have applied this method to the analysis of the evolution and the orientation of Asian commercial exchanges for 1984 and 1993, firstly within the area, secondly with the United States, and finally with the European Union. The calculation of relative indicators of exchange for each country towards another group of nations gives the degree of implication of each country in the exchanges.

Change and geographic reorientation

Figures 1 and 2 respectively showing the relative intensities of exchanges of Asian countries within the region, the United States and the European Union in 1984 and 1993, clearly indicate that

(1) the Asian countries centralize their exchanges within the region. This is evident from a general comparison of these countries with respect to the first bisecting line, which means that imports and exports have a tendency to balance out in volume;
(2) the commercial relations of these nations for 1984 and 1993 remain significant, with relative levels of trade above 2.5. This means that intraregional exchanges are on average two and a half times more important than the economic importance of the region in world trade.

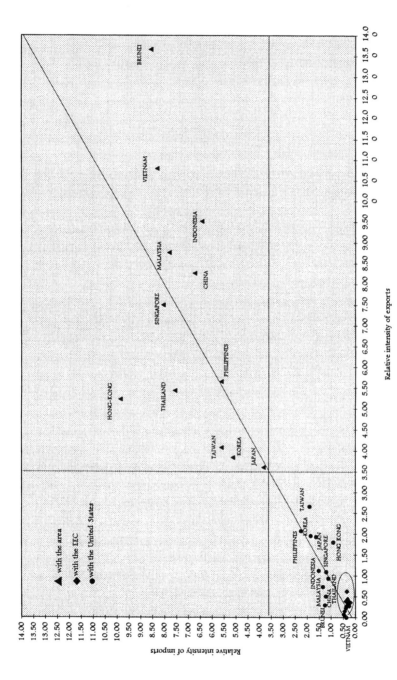

Figure 1.1. Relative intensity of exchanges in the Asian area for 1984

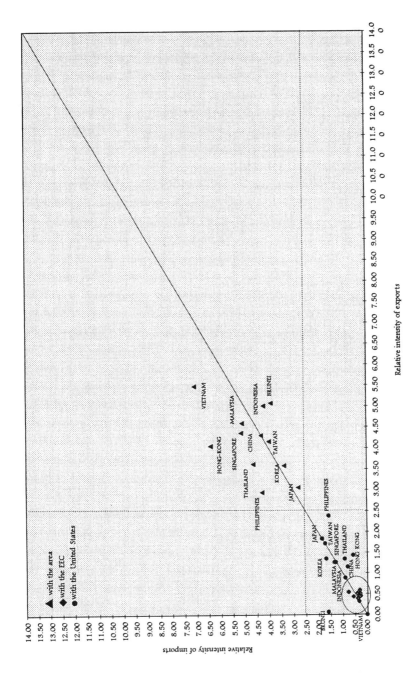

Figure 1.2. Relative intensity of exchanges in the Asian area for 1993

Asian trade for 1984 seems, for certain countries of the area, rather unbalanced – a phenomenon that is graphically shown by a scattering of nations here and there over the first bisecting line. All countries below this line had intensified their exports in the area – a factor which is more important than that related to their imports. Malaysia, Indonesia, China, Vietnam and Brunei significantly find the best openings in the Asian area. In the same way, the countries above the diagonal line have a relative intensity of exports in the area inferior to the relative intensity of imports. Japan, Korea, Taiwan, Hong Kong, Singapore and Thailand answer to this description and so consider the Asian area as their first source of supplies. With regard to Japan and the 'Four Dragons', this can only relate to imports of foodstuffs and basic manufactured goods. For Thailand, one of the first countries of the second wave of Asian industrialization, we can suppose that it favours economic development through imports of equipment and machines from countries in the area. As for the Philippines, there are equivalent relative intensities of exports and imports in the area.

With regard to relations with the United States, exchange links are relatively important, since the majority of Asian countries have, again, relative intensity indicators (for imports as for exports) between 1 and 3. But compared with the relative intensities of exchanges of countries of the area in the area, these appear to be less important. A certain number of Asian countries are still excluded because of the American market:

(1) Hong Kong (only from the point of view of imports)
(2) Brunei, Malaysia, Thailand and China (from the point of view of exports)
(3) and lastly Vietnam, which is principally oriented towards the Asian market.

As for Europe, the relative intensity of indicators of exchange are basically inferior to 1 for all Asian countries, which means that Asian commercial dynamics had nothing to do with the penetration of European markets in this period.

In 1993, important changes appear:

(1) All Asian countries centralize their exchanges in the area, and the indicators always stay above 2.5 for all the countries considered. It is very interesting to note that countries like Japan, Korea, Taiwan, which in 1984 were above the bisecting line, have now gone below it. This movement in relation to the first bisecting line stays quite marginal: it does not indicate a decreasing intensity of trade in the relationship of

Japan, Korea and Taiwan with the other Asian countries, but a balancing-out of the bilateral trade balances of Asian countries with these three nations. The fact that Vietnam, Malaysia and China have moved above the bisecting line shows that these countries are becoming industrialized, massively importing Asian plant and technical equipment – the continuation of their economic development staying very dependent on the area. We also notice that Brunei seems to keep itself outside this centralizing trend, even if it has made significant efforts in this field. Generally, those indicators which are weaker than 1984 for the Asian countries do not reflect a fall in commercial flows in the area but simply show that the volume of commercial exchanges from the area to the world has shown more rapid growth, which increases their importance in world trade.

(2) With regard to the American market, all levels of Asian trade decrease strongly – and since Asian trade has made much faster progress than American trade, it necessarily reflects a relative diversion of Asian products. This phenomenon indicates both a saturation of the American market and – perhaps more significantly – difficulties in penetrating it[2].

(3) In a symmetrical way, we observe a weak rise in levels of trade of Asian countries with the EEC, which seems to be linked to Asia's need to find new openings for its products.

A complementary explanation for the area's centralizing on itself can be found in the analysis of opening rates. Contrary to an idea that is too often accepted, the opening rate for external trade is not necessarily positively correlated with economic growth. The best proof of this is Japan which has taken the liberty of closing its frontiers more and more since its opening rate went from 12.09 in 1984 to 7.16%[3] in 1993, while maintaining a continued economic growth and a relatively low unemployment rate in comparison with other Western countries which generally support free trade. These numbers confirm the exactness of the analysis made by Maurice Allais, who argues that the European Union is centralizing on itself in protecting and setting up quotas for its markets[4]. In other words, Europe should do what the Asian area has been doing for years.

Moreover, it should be noted that when the opening rate of Asian countries increases, it essentially benefits the area. For example, China's opening rate rose from 8.5% in 1984 to 17.92% in 1993 – but if we calculate the corresponding rate for Europe, it only rose from 0.93% to 2.40%, which for the United States it increased from 1.03% to 2.53%. In contrast, it rose from 4.25% to 9.67% in the Asian area. This pattern of evolution is similar for all other countries.

This evolution cannot be consolidated, as we observed earlier, if this tendency depends on complementary beneficial trends in all countries in the area. Besides, the movement of certain Asian countries in 1993 above the first bisecting line with regard to relative levels of exchange shows the reallocation of resources in this direction.

3   THE DYNAMICS OF SPECIALIZATION

This phenomenon is again encountered when we study the evolution of comparative advantages and disadvantages by industrial sector for the different Asian countries considered here. For this purpose we have again taken (and extended up to 1993) the work that Gérard Lafay and Colette Herzog carried out from 1967 to 1986[5], for Japan, the 'Four Dragons', Indonesia, Malaysia, China, Thailand and the Philippines regrouped under 'other Asian countries'. We have also modified the sectors used before so as to have a comparable approach to that of Lafay and Herzog and to build up a picture of continuity since 1984.

The Calculation Method

To clarify the principles of construction of the comparative advantage indicator, an example is developed in the following table, which concerns the electrical industry in Indonesia in 1993. In this sector, exports X (1.33 billion dollars) are lower than imports M (2.63 billion dollars), so that the X − M balance in the relevant sector is negative (−1.30 billion dollars). We carry out the same calculation for Indonesian total exports and imports (with all sectors included). For 1993, we obtain a global positive X − M balance of about 8.50 billion dollars. In expressing these two balances in thousandths of gross domestic product Y (141.51 billion dollars) for the same year, we obtain respectively the numbers −9.18 and +52.92.

In Indonesian foreign trade, the relative importance g of the electrical sector is equal to 0.06 – that is to say, the ratio between the total exchanges of products in this sector (3.96 billion dollars) and the total exchanges of all goods (65.14 billion dollars). Hypothesising the absence of all comparative advantages or disadvantages, we may suppose that Indonesian surplus trade in 1993 is distributed among the different sectors according to their relative importance. So, the balance charged to the electrical sector will be: $z = 0.06 *$ $60.03 = 3.60$.

With specific reference to this theoretical balance z, it is advisable to calculate the contribution proper to the electrical sector. In 1993, the negative

Table 1.1 The Indonesian electrical industry in 1993

		Sector k	Total
(Y)	Gross domestic product (billions of $)		141.51
(X)	Exports (billions of $)	1.33	36.82
(M)	Imports (billions of $)	2.63	28.32
(X–M)	Balance (billions of $)	–1.30	8.50
(y)	Balance on GDP = 1000*(X–M)/Y	–9.17	60.03
(X+M)	Total exchanges (billions of $)	3.96	65.14
(g)	Importance of branch = (Xk+Mk)/ (X.+M.)	0.06	1.0
(z)	Theoretical balance = g * y (total)	3.60	60.03
(f)	Advantage or disadvantage = y – z	–12.77	0

relative balance y (−9.17) is widely inferior to the theoretical balance ($z = 3.60$). As a consequence, the electrical sector shows a deficit and brings a negative contribution to the Indonesian trade balance. This corresponds to a comparative disadvantage defined by the formula

$$f = y \sim z = \sim 9, 17 \sim 3.60 = \sim 12, 77.$$

Presentation of results

The four graphs on the following pages clearly reveal the complementarity of the principal industrial activities among the different countries of the area, according to their levels of development.

The most important point seems to be the fact that the Four Dragons have caught up with Japan in certain sectors such as the electrical and electronics industries, and have even overtaken her at the end of the period. For numerous product such as electronic components or basic electrical equipment, Japan is losing its comparative advantages over the Four Dragons, for two principal reasons: firstly, Japan is less competitive in labour costs, particularly with regard to unskilled labour; and secondly, being aware of this disadvantage, Japan prefers to concentrate on more carrier niches, generally in areas of high technology, where there is little competition from other Asian countries, and from which it will finally be able to derive important advantages.

So, by delocalizing a part of its activity, which is becoming less profitable as a result of competition – particularly with the Four Dragons – Japan firstly ensures the diffusion of technology to developing countries, which affords them more rapid economic development, and secondly controls, through joint ventures, the strategic policies of development of those countries which it supports. Note that the Japanese comparative advantage in the electrical sector rose from 5.1 in 1984 to 8.59 in 1993, while for the Four Dragons it rose from 0.5 to 12.4 during the same period. We can observe an important movement in electronics sector, since the Four Dragons' comparative advantage rose between 1984 and 1993 from 12.5 to 30.8, even as Japan lost about fifteen points in its comparative advantage (21.5 in 1984 and 6.08 in 1993) over the same period.

Often, we notice a correlation between the Japanese net loss of comparative advantage in a sector – or simply a relative decrease of comparative advantage – simultaneously with a net gain in comparative advantage for the Four Dragons in the same sector, or a relative increase in comparative advantage. This phenomenon can be observed in the mechanical industry, in motor vehicle production and in the iron and steel and metallurgical industries. In these three industrial sectors, Japan holds a significant comparative advantage in the region. This advantage seems to have decreased, however, between 1984 and 1993, since we can note a fall from 12.7 to 3.52 for the mechanical industry; from 3.8 to 1.59 for iron and steel and metallurgy, and from 25 to 13.23 for the motor industry. At the same time, the Four Dragons are experiencing a big improvement in these three industrial sectors. Their comparative disadvantages in the mechanical sector fell from −19.3 to −8.8 and for iron and steel from −9.8 to −0.5. As for motor vehicles, they preserve their comparative advantage which rises from 3.1 to 3.3. We can also note the important efforts that the Four Dragons have made in the chemical sector, where they have managed to increase their advantage from −25 to −5.7 in ten years, even while Japan maintained its comparative disadvantage around −1.3 without any significant improvement during this period.

As for the more upstream industrial activities, which of course need a plentiful labour force, Japan and the Four Dragons have more or less similar positions. For the food, energy and non-ferrous metal sectors, these countries are experiencing a chronic comparative disadvantage which essentially comes from a lack of natural resources. On the other hand, the countries of Southeast Asia are broadly better endowed and constitute the principal supply of food products as well as energy products for the area.

Obviously, trade contacts between the South Asian countries and the more developed countries of the region more often than not exchange basic consumers goods for manufactured goods. Moreover, for the wood-paper,

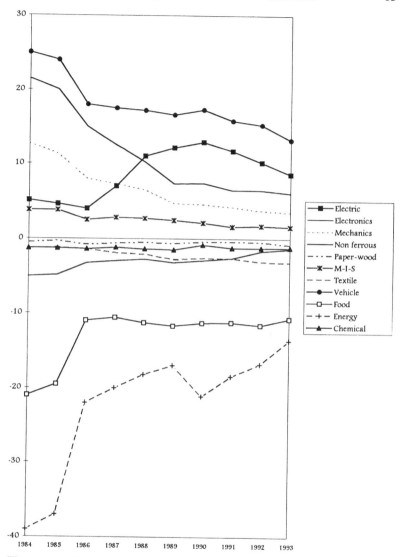

Figure 1.3. Comparative advantages and disadvantages of Japan by branch

textile, clothing and leather sectors, in which Japan (since the beginning of the 1970s) and the Four Dragons (since the end of the 1980s) have become less and less competitive, it seems that production has shifted to developing countries like Indonesia, China, Malaysia, Thailand and the Philippines. In

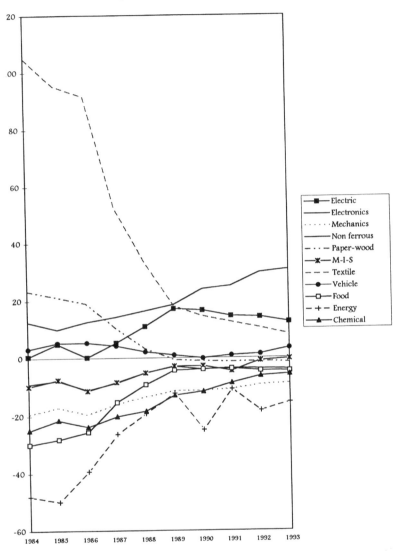

Figure 1.4. Comparative advantages and disadvantages of Four Dragons by branch

fact, the deterioration of comparative advantage for Japan and the Four Dragons in these areas has coincided with an improvement in comparative advantages in these very same areas for the South Asian countries. Here a phenomenon of complementarity is in play, through which a spread of

Table 1.2 Japan: Comparative Advantages

	1984	1985	1986	1987	1988	1989	1990	1991	1992	1993
Electric	5.1	4.6	4	7	11	12.14	12.92	11.70	10.17	8.59
Electronics	21.5	20	15	12.5	10.2	7.33	7.40	6.47	6.46	6.08
Mechanics	12.7	11.3	8	7.3	6.5	4.72	4.59	4.23	3.74	3.52
Non ferrous	-5.1	-4.9	-3.3	-3	-2.8	-3.24	-2.98	-2.66	-1.71	-1.40
Paper-wood	-0.5	-0.3	-0.8	-0.6	-0.49	-0.63	-0.41	-0.42	-0.45	-0.84
Metallurgy of iron and steel	3.8	3.8	2.5	2.8	2.7	2.46	2.11	1.61	1.73	1.59
Textile	-1.3	-1.2	-1.4	-1.9	-2.1	-2.78	-2.59	-2.66	-3.12	-3.17
Vehicle	25	24	18	17.5	17.2	16.60	17.31	15.80	15.25	13.23
Food	-21	-19.5	-11	-10.6	-11.3	-11.71	-11.34	-11.27	-11.65	-10.79
Energy	-39	-37	-22	-20	-18.2	-17.00	-21.16	-18.46	-16.82	-13.67
Chemical	-1.3	-1.3	-1.4	-1.2	-1.4	-1.50	-0.87	-1.28	-1.25	-1.21

Table 1.3 Four Dragons: Comparative advantages

	1984	1985	1986	1987	1988	1989	1990	1991	1992	1993
Electric	0.5	4.8	0.2	5.2	10.8	17.1	16.5	14.5	14.1	12.4
Electronics	12.5	9.8	12.5	14.2	16.4	18.5	24.0	25.1	29.7	30.8
Mechanics	-19.3	-17.1	-19.4	-15.8	-13.4	-11.4	-11.3	-10.7	-9.3	-8.8
Non ferrous	-9.02	-7.8	-11.1	-8.6	-5.1	-3.0	-4.0	-3.6	-3.7	-4.0
Paper-wood	23.4	21.2	19	10.3	3.2	-0.7	-1.1	-1.4	-1.2	-1.6
Metallurgy of iron and steel	-9.8	-7.5	-11.3	-8.4	-5.2	-2.9	-2.8	-4.6	-1.0	-0.5
Textile	105	95.2	91.5	52.3	33.4	18.0	14.5	12.4	10.3	8.0
Vehicle	3.1	5.2	5.3	4.2	2.1	0.9	-0.2	0.8	1.3	3.3
Food	-30	-28.2	-25.6	-15.3	-9.2	-4.4	-4.0	-3.8	-4.5	-4.6
Energy	-48.2	-50	-39.4	-26.4	-19.2	-12.3	-24.9	-10.8	-18.1	-15.4
Chemical	-25	-21.4	-23.7	-20.1	-18.3	-12.9	-11.6	-8.7	-6.3	-5.7

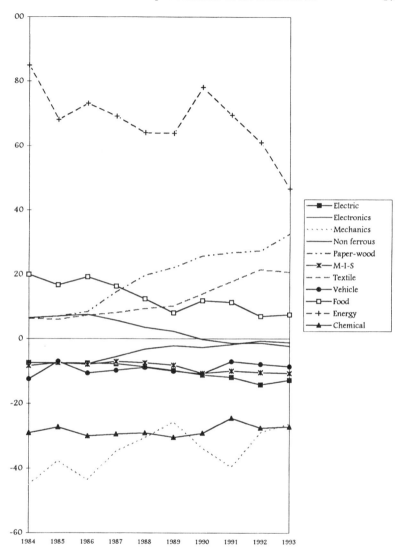

Figure 1.5. Comparative advantages and disadvantages of Indonesia by branch

technology takes place, enabling each country in the area to become gradually industrialized.

The process of regional integration is based *a priori* on a classical division of labour which in turn is based on the comparative advantages of each

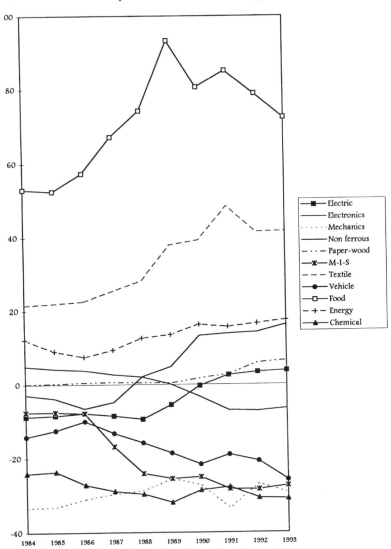

Figure 1.6. Comparative advantages and disadvantages of other Asian countries by branch

participant: the technologically most developed countries provide plant and contribute to the industrialization of the less developed countries, which use their comparative advantage (entirely based on low labour costs) for the development of their manufacturing industries.

Table 1.4 Indonesia: Comparative advantages

	1984	1985	1986	1987	1988	1989	1990	1991	1992	1993
Electric	-7.5	-7.5	-7.6	-7.8	-8.7	-9.80	-11.20	-11.87	-14.21	-12.83
Electronics	-7.5	-7.5	-7.8	-5.6	-3.2	-2.18	-2.64	-1.79	-0.68	-1.18
Mechanics	-45.01	-37.54	-43.6	-34.65	-30.5	-25.63	-33.65	-39.54	-28.93	-26.34
Non ferrous	6.5	7	7.5	5.68	3.5	2.25	-0.22	-1.38	-1.32	-2.30
Paper-wood	6.3	7	8.4	14.5	19.7	22.08	25.77	26.75	27.37	32.54
Metallurgy of iron and steel	-8.4	-7.5	-8	-7.1	-7.5	-8.20	-10.70	-10.00	-10.40	-10.66
Textile	6.3	6	7.3	8.1	9.4	10.19	13.94	17.80	21.52	20.64
Vehicle	-12.4	-7	-10.6	-9.8	-8.9	-10.01	-10.82	-7.07	-7.93	-8.61
Food	20	16.7	19.2	16.3	12.4	8.04	11.81	11.30	6.98	7.47
Energy	85	68	73	69	64	63.82	78.08	69.41	61.00	46.64
Chemical	-29	-27.3	-30	-29.5	-29	-30.44	-29.18	-24.46	-27.54	-27.19

Table 1.5   Other Asian countries: Comparative advantages

	1984	1985	1986	1987	1988	1989	1990	1991	1992	1993
Electric	-8.7	-8.4	-7.8	-8.5	-9.4	-5.5	-0.4	2.5	3.3	3.7
Electronics	-2.8	-3.8	-6.5	-4.8	2.1	4.8	13.2	13.8	14.1	16.1
Mechanics	-33.4	-33.1	-31	-29.6	-28.7	-25.5	-27.2	-33.5	-26.9	-29.3
Non ferrous	4.9	4.2	3.8	2.7	2	0.1	-3.3	-6.9	-7.2	-6.5
Paper-wood	0.1	0.3	0.5	0.6	0.5	0.4	1.7	2.7	5.8	6.5
Metallurgy of iron and steel	-7.5	-7.5	-7.8	-16.8	-24.1	-25.5	-25.1	-28.3	-28.4	-27.4
Textile	21.5	21.9	22.5	25.3	28.1	37.9	39.2	48.5	41.5	41.6
Vehicle	-14.2	-12.5	-10	-13.2	-15.8	-18.6	-21.6	-19.0	-20.8	-25.9
Food	53	52.5	57.3	67.2	74.2	93.28	80.62	85.15	78.81	72.39
Energy	12.2	9.1	7.5	9.4	12.6	13.50	16.20	15.60	16.50	17.40
Chemical	-24.1	-23.7	-27.2	-28.9	-29.7	-31.90	-28.62	-27.75	-30.75	-30.94

We must, however, have certain reservations as regards the relevance of the groupings of countries discussed here. For example, economic development levels within the Four Dragons, although superficially similar in numerous ways, are not really the same – and the splitting-up of the area into subgroups hides certain development disparities which are not insignificant. In fact, among the Four Dragons, Korea is the country closest to Japan, leaving Singapore, Hong Kong and Taiwan far behind in certain areas. This is the case for the motor vehicle sector, in which Korea had a comparative advantage in 1993 of about 12, at a time when Taiwan did not pass 7 and Singapore was suffering from a comparative disadvantage of about −16. It is the same for the iron and steel industry in which the Four Dragons collectively had a comparative disadvantage between 1984 and 1993 – but if we take each of these four countries one by one, the situation is more diversified: Korea showed a comparative advantage in this branch over the entire period, with a maximum in 1993 of 5.5, whereas Singapore had a significant comparative disadvantage which went from −31.7 in 1984 to −21.5 in 1993.

We meet this disparity in levels of development again – and still more clearly – in the less developed Asian countries, classified here as 'other Asian countries'. In fact, although Malaysia and Thailand have experienced a successful economic takeoff, Indonesia remains a 'classical' supplier of raw materials and the Philippines today are still marginalized[6]. For the electrical and basic electronics sectors, China, Malaysia and Thailand have quite important comparative advantages (around 15), even though Indonesia and the Philippines show a comparative disadvantage in these two areas, ranging from −5 for the latter to −12 for the former. It is quite clear that the positions of China, Malaysia and Thailand in these two areas arise globally from the delocalizations of the Four Dragons: principally from Hong Kong and Taiwan for China, and Singapore for Malaysia and Thailand[7]. This gap in comparative advantages or disadvantages for the electrical and basic electronics sectors points to interesting differences in levels of development among the Asian countries normally considered to be the least developed.

Our study shows that the commercial dynamism characteristic of the Asian area is not the engine of economic growth. On the contrary, the high potential of domestic growth appears to explain the levels of trade. Our conclusion (of course) goes against received wisdom, because this Asian area, where the opening rate is weak in comparison with those in other parts of the world, and where migratory flows are also unimportant, remains a model of growth and economic progress. It is curious that this phenomenon has not been better perceived by Western observers, who nevertheless often quote Asia and Japan as examples which the West must follow, for their regular and harmonious growth patterns and also for their low unemployment rate.

Notes

1. This technique of calculation of intensity stems from the work of Gérard Lafay and Colette Herzog, *Commerce International: La fin des avantages acquis*, Economica 1989, and has been recently taken up in a study by Isabelle Bensidoun and Agnès Chevalier, *Les échanges commerciaux euro-méditerranéens*, Economie Internationale, ñ 58, 1994.
2. This is illustrated by the recent commercial conflict between Japan and the United States in regard to the automotive industry.
3. The definition of 'opening rate' used here is: ((exports + imports)/2)/GDP.
4. *Combats pour l'Europe, 1992–1994*, Editions Clément Juglar 1994, pp 277 and following.
5. *La Fin des Avantaages Acquis*, op. cit..
6. Cf. Banque Paribas, *Tropismes asiatiques*, Conjoncture, April 1995.
7. Cf. Françoise Lemoine, Alix de Saint Vaulry et Mouhamadou Dramé, *Hong-Kong-Chine: un dragon à deux-tête*, Economie Internationale, No. 57, 1994.

REFERENCES

Allais Maurice, *Combats pour l'Europe, 1992–1994*, Editions Clément Juglar, 1994.
Balassa Bela, *The Theory of Economic Integration*, Grennwood Press, 1963.
Balassa Bela and Williamson John, *Les réussites du Sud-Est Asiatique dans le commerce mondial*, Economica, 1987.
Banque Paribas, *Tropismes asiatiques*, Conjoncture, April 1995.
Bensidoun Isabelle and Chevallier Agnès, *Les échanges commerciaux euro-méditerranéens*, Economie Internationanle, No. 58, 1994.
Bhagwati Jagdish, *Departures from multilateralism: regionalism and aggressive unilateralism*, The Economic Journal, December 1990.
Bhagwati Jagdish, *The world trading system at risk*, Harvester Wheatsheaf, 1991.
Bloom Martin, *L'évolution technologique et l'industrie électronique coréenne*, OCDE, 1992.
Bollard Alan and Mayes David, *Regionalism and the Pacific Rim*, Journal of Common Market Studies, No. 2, June 1992.
Bouteiller Eric, *Attirer un oiseau sur une branche*, Economie Internationale, CEPII, 1994.
Chaponnière Jean-Raphaël, *L'ASEAN: réussite politique, échec économique?*, Economie Internationale, CEPII, 1994.
Conroy Richard, *L'évolution technologique en Chine*, OCDE, 1992.
de Laubier Dominique, *Les implantations dans le sud-est asiatique: des craintes excessive?*, Economie Internationale, CEPII, 1994.
de Melo Jaime, Panagarlya Arvind and Rodrik Dan, *The new regionalism: a country perspective*, CEPR, Discussion Paper No. 715, September 1992.
de Saint Vaulry Alix, Dramé Mouhamadou and Lemoine Fran&coise, *Hong Kong–Chine: un dragon à deux t^etes*, Economie Internationale, CEPII, 1994.
de Laubier Dominique, *Les implantations dans le sud-est asiatique: des craintes excessives?*, Economie Internationale, No. 57, 1994.

Devereux Michael B. and Lapham Beverly J., *The stability of economic integration and endogeneous growth*, Quarterly Journal of Economics, 1994.

Espana Juan R. and Sengupta Jati K., *Exports and economic growth in Asian NICs: an econometric analysis for Korea*, Applied Economics, 1994.

Elek Andrew, *Trade policy options for the Asia-Pacific region in the 1990's: the potential of open regionalism*, American Economic Review, May 1992.

Fukasaku Kiichiro, Wall David and Wu Mingyuan, *La «longue marche» de la Chine vers une économie ouverte*, OCDE, 1994.

Fung K. C., *Economic integration as competitive discipline*, International Economic Review, No. 4, November 1992.

Guiheux Gilles, *Les conglomérats taiwanais*, Economie Internationale, No. 61, 1995.

Herzog Colette and Lafay Gérard, *Commerce International: La Fin des Avantages acquis*, CEPII, Economica 1989.

Hine Robert C., *Regionalism and the Integration of the World Economy*, Journal of Common Market Studies, No. 2, June 1992.

Jones Randall S. King Robert E. and Klein Michael, *L'intégration économique entre Hong-Kong, Taïwan et les provinces côtières de la Chine*, Revue économique de l'OCDE, No. 20, 1993.

Kim Duk-Choong, *Open Regionalism in the Pacific: a World of Trading Blocs?*, American Economic Review, May 1992.

Mytelka Lynn Krieger, *L'industrie du textile et de l'habillement: le modéle coréen en difficulté*, Economie Internationale, No. 61, 1995.

Lafay Gérard, *Dynamique de la spécialisation internationale*, Economica, 1979.

Lloyd Peter J., *Régionalisation et commerce mondial*, Revue Economique de l'OCDE, No. 18, 1992.

Maximin Bertrand, *L'enjeu de l'investissement direct international en Thailande: l'émergence d'un N.P.I. de la seconde génération*, Mondes en Développement, 1994.

OCDE, *De la croissance poussée par les échanges aux échanges poussés par la croissance: réévaluer l'expérience de développement des pays de l'Asie de l'Est*, 1993.

Rodrik Dani, *King Kong meets Godzilla: the World Bank and the East Asian miracle*, CEPR, Discussion Paper No. 994, April 1994.

Rollet Phillippe, *Spécialisation Internationale et Intégration Européenne*, Economica, 1990.

Sautter Christian, *Les préceptes du développement asiatique*, Economie Internationale, No. 57, 1994.

Schott Jeffrey J., *L'intégration économique de la région Asie-Pacifique*, Economie Internationale, CEPII, 1994.

Yamazawa Ippei, *Echanges et investissements dans la zone Asie-Pacifique*, Economie Internationale, CEPII, 1994.

Yamazawa Ippei, *On Pacific Economic Integration*, The Economic Journal, November 1992.

Wolf Charles and Weinschrott David, *International transactions and regionalism: distinguishing 'Insiders' from 'Outsiders'*, American Economic Association, No. 2, May 1973.

2 Economic Integration in East Asia: Situation and Perspectives[1]

Catherine Figuière

Current discussion about the future of international economic relations seems to centre on an alternative, widely noted by observers: globalization or regionalization. A broad consensus has developed which qualifies the 1980s as a stage of 'globalization' of trade and investments. This process, resulted, *de facto*, in the intensification of commercial flows between the three poles: the Americas, Western Europe and Eastern Asia. Exchanges of goods and services between the three poles globally increased, as well as direct and indirect investments.

The 1980s were mainly characterized by an explosion of foreign direct investments (FDI). FDI stock went up from a world total of 560 billion dollars in 1980 to 1,850 billion in 1990[2]. While the United States was still the leader in FDI in terms of stock, its annual flows were first equalled and then exceeded by those of Britain and Japan, and indeed by those of France.

It was, in fact, more precisely between 1985 and 1990 that foreign direct investments 'raced out of control', to slow down at the turning point of the two decades. FDI flows in the world as a whole increased from 55 billion dollars in 1980 to 58 billion in 1985, and then from 94 billion dollars in 1986 to 238 billion in 1990.

The 1985–1990 period is also noteworthy for evolving patterns of such FDI allocations. In the case of European foreign investments, one can notice the very sharp rise of the European Economic Community as an FDI destination of the three most important investing countries (Great Britain, Germany and France). The very quick growth in FDI then moved towards the centre of the area by itself. As for Japan, it chose to wait until the beginning of the 1990s to reorient the bulk of its investments and trade links towards Eastern Asia.

At the same time, from 1986 to 1993 the Uruguay Round discussions took place with the aim of instituting a 'single market' on a world scale. This historic Round ended with the creation of the World Trade Organization, which started operating on 1 January 1995 but will not prevent the rise of regional free-trade agreements which have been under discussion at the same time as the GATT negotiations. Indeed, the APEC (Asia-Pacific Economic Cooperation) was created in 1989, the NAFTA (North America Free-Trade Area) came into effect on 1 January 1994 and the ASEAN (Association of South-East Asian Nations) free trade zone will soon be created.

Our reading of these events leads us to a first conclusion: from the middle of the 1980s, tendencies towards globalization and towards regionalization have coexisted, at both the commercial and institutional levels. The question that now arises focuses on the nature of the regionalization trends: will they form a stage of development on the way towards 'worldwide capitalism'[3], or, at the opposite extreme, will they be a step on the path to its demise. Globalization would then constitute only a single phase of the 'great crisis'[4] of the advanced capitalist economies, and not its outcome. Regionalization would constitute the next stage in the dynamic of capitalism. The turning point of the 1980s and the 1990s might thus have set up a transitional period of coexistence between the remaining processes of globalization and the beginnings of regionalization.

It is within this framework that we must analyse the present reorientation of trade links and specify to what extent the sustainable intensification of trade flows between the countries in a named area can result in regional integration. If we are going to talk about regional economic integration, a network of sustainable relations, irreversible in the short or medium term, must at least be in place. More generally, we need to examine the nature of these relationships in order to define the precise domain of regional economic integration. Then we must discuss the first elements which lead us to put forward our hypothesis of a regional economic process in Eastern Asia.

1 THE ANALYSIS OF REGIONAL INTEGRATION

1.1 The Markers Given by the History of a 'Process'

Even though discussion of trends towards economic integration invariably gives rise to political argument, this integration does exist in reality. The analysis of all objective[5] processes of economic integration must begin with the 'important' flows between the nations in question: flows of goods and services, direct and indirect investments, official development assistance, etc. It is the reported increase of such and such a kind of flow inside a fixed geographical area that raises the question of the integration process.

However, attention must be focused on a kind of flow which has particular incidences. Generally, FDI flows inside a given area are often taken as the main indicator of envisaged integration[6]. Indeed, the FDI flows of each country in an area described as 'integrated' are principally oriented through this area. These crossing investment networks give rise to trade networks between the area members, which thus strengthen the integrated nature of their relations. The direct investment flows through foreign countries will then establish the first indicator of regional economic integration, which will result in the setting-up of a 'regional division of labour'.

Exchanges of goods and services can, on the contrary, be considered as a crucial indicator, because they come, so to speak, 'first': the geographical structure of trade prefigures the FDI one. In fact, the stages of the integration process are still specific and are determined by the moment and by the characteristics of the nations involved. However, the results of the process are similar. As Michel Aglietta has pointed out, for the process of integration to be complete it must occur in the financial, currency and goods and services markets[7]. For Aglietta, the process is carried out through the convergence of real interest rates and the stabilization of foreign exchange rates. These two factors lead to a similar structure of relative prices. The economic integration process will therefore have structural repercussions on the organization of each of the economies.

Thus, everything happens as if at a *t* date – before the integration process – the area was constituted with its components (the nations) all more or less independent of the others two by two. At the *t* date +1, once the integration process has been achieved, the area takes on a structure: interdependent relations of different kinds take place between the component nations. Such interdependence appears on the one hand in sustainable and important trade flows between the integrated components and on the other hand in structural changes in each component.

Insofar as each nation becomes integrated within the same unit, this new common environment will have similar influences. However, these repercussions are never the same, as the initial bases are different. In other words, the economic integration of an area seems to be a 'process of structural homogenization' of this area which proceeds in accordance with the features of each nation.

1.2   A 'Leading Nation' As a Catalyst of Integration

'Even if history doesn't serve the same dishes again, it doesn't miss out on good recipes'[8]. Historically, cases of advanced integration often point to the catalyst role of a particular country as the initiator of the process. The term 'leading economy' seems to be the most appropriate one to identify the economy which gives the initial impulse to the integration process. It is

eventually around that economy – and possibly in its interest – that a system of regional relations will be structured.

The idea of a leading unit – an *unité motrice* – has been closely defined by François Perroux: *'The unit which exerts on the other units some actions which change their dimensions as well as their growth rate, which distort their structures, which modify their organizational nature and which create or favour the economic process. Leading units act through the flows of goods, demanded and supplied, through investment flows and by inducing innovations'*[9]. Although this definition was initially applied to firms, industries, or industrial groupings, it seems nonetheless completely suitable for describing the role of an economy leading the process of regional integration.

Actually, a series of links emerges. First of all, the network of interdependent relationships that proceeds from integration is not symmetrical, insofar as whole nations do not include the network, either in the same way or to the same degree. We may qualify this relational network as one of 'asymmetrical interdependence'. From this asymmetry comes a hierarchy which places at the top the leading nation and which relatively penalizes some of its components.

Furthermore, the hierarchical organization of relationships shows itself in learning effects and in the freeze exerted by the leading nation on the other economies of the area. This means that the evolution of the leading economy will have an impact on the whole area. The learning effect feature depends here as much on the historical form of the integration process as on the place of each economy.

These effects are neither direct nor systematic – which prevents us from considering the integration links as mechanical. For example, a recession in the leading nation does not necessarily lead to recessions in the adjoining economies: it can, on the contrary, have a boosting effect on the other countries, insofar as it may encourage a movement in the flows of this economy towards the centre of the area.

Lastly, structural homogenization processes are initiated by the leading nation. History shows that one of the major characteristics of the leading economy is to produce organizational 'standards' – or references – both at the microeconomic and the macroeconomic levels. In other words, such a country has a tendency to influence its environment according to its own image, although in fields that are always specific to the historical process in progress.

It does not mean that the economies of the area are carbon copies of the leading economy (the relations being asymmetrical), but it can mean that common structural features can be identified in the organization of different national economies. The role of the State in the development of productive structures, the organization of wage structures or the forms of competition can constitute the long-term indicators of an area going through 'structural homogenization'.

If the beginning of the 1990s can indeed be seen to have constituted the turning-point between a stage of globalization and a stage of regionalization, one must try to understand the initial developments of this process of integration. It is important now to single out the mechanisms which foreshadow a regional integration process.

The hypothesis according to which international economic relations are being structured into three big regions is frequently advanced. In this case, the United States, the internationally dominant economy, has a leading economic role in its own area, in view of the recognized strong influence of American structures. It is not the same with Europe – already very homogeneous – which today would like to follow an integration process without any leading economy. Europe's historical legacy raises the problem of the role of Germany. Indeed, one can observe from current events in the European Community that Franco-German relations are, from day to day, characterized more and more by conflicting interests. The situation is admittedly comparable in Asia, considering the past role of Japan and its 'Greater Asia Co-Prosperity Sphere'. However, it is easier for a European observer to recognize Japan as a leading economy within the area, all the more so since a (relative) homogenization of national structures seems to have been take place[10].

2   EASTERN ASIA: THE FIRST INDICATIONS OF REGIONAL INTEGRATION

It is difficult to determine *a priori* which countries will be subject to economic integration. From the observable premises of East Asia's regional integration, the number of countries involved is still changing. The presence of China and the recent political evolutions in that country generate major uncertainties regarding the future of the area. A first overview can however be established from the density of the trade flows which place these economies in a proper regional framework: Japan, South Korea, Thailand, Singapore, Hong Kong, Taiwan, Malaysia, Indonesia, The Philippines and (possibly) China.

2.1   Japan, the Standards Producer

The evolution of economic relations between the countries of East Asia points to Japan as an essential producer of organizational standards – or as a 'development model' – within the area. Japan acquired this role well before regional integration began in earnest.

The Japanese economy was the first one to be developed as a capitalist economy (from 1868), while the industrialization of East and Southeast Asia came after World War II. If we take the most industrialized of these nations, South Korea[11], we notice signs of an advanced application of the Japanese development model[12].

This model assigns an important role to State action. Such a role, established during the period of industrialization, still exists in spite of the evolving forms of State intervention[13]. The Korean development process seems to borrow this model by applying it to a pattern of development which gives priority to industrial growth, while trying to preserve some national autonomy through its economic policy.

The Korean state is still very preoccupied with foreign trade on the one hand, and with foreign direct investments within its national territory on the other (like Thailand and Taiwan). A tight link exists between the evolution of foreign trade and the specialization of national industry, as well as in relation to the construction of heavy industries, whose development is actively promoted by the State. In regard to these heavy industries, the role played by imported technologies in the Japanese and Korean development processes is in every way comparable as well.

The Korean case has been defined as follows: '*The principal strength of this kind of State (lies) in the collaboration between bureaucracy and enterprises (...). The bureaucracy wants to guide the economy using (enterprises) as antennas*'[14]. Imitating Japan, the Korean state chooses the development actors in giving priority to important industrial groupings – the *chaebols*.

The internal structure of the big Korean[15] groups and their role in the industrialization process reveal some important similarities with the Japanese Zaibatsu[16] and also with the Taiwanese conglomerates[17]. The multi-sectorality of their activities, the family-based control of capital, the privileged relations that these groups maintain with the country's important banks and their integration with general trading companies all replicate a mode of industrial development already tested in Japan.

With regard to the general trading companies[18], it must be stressed that they have been intentionally set up to provide at the same time intermediary agencies for Korean foreign trade and for the groupings to which they belong[19]. In this context, the duplication of the Japanese model is at the same time voluntary and successful. Although Taiwan also tried to set up comparable structures to serve as intermediaries, for its foreign trade the project was not achieved with the same success as in South Korea.

The role of small and medium-sized enterprises in Korea's industrial structures also needs to be examined. Neglected over a long period, these enterprises have been receiving political support since the middle of the 1980s: the State, together with the largest *chaebol* enterprises, is now aware of the need to have an efficient subcontracting network within the national territory[20]. State support of small and medium-sized enterprises has been organized around the development of the large groups.

Beyond the case of South Korea, the presence of the State in the industrial policies of the economies of the area confirmes the role of the leading economy in setting standards. Chaponnière stresses that the Four Dragons have a common aim of fixing precise axes and acquiring the means to reach them. So they choose not only the activities they wish to develop but also the actors who will be the leaders. This reminds us of the methods of the industrialist Japanese State (the benefits of which seem to be recognized even by the World Bank[21]). Sautter mentions the example of the petrochemical industry, which was considered by the Japanese State as a key area during the 1950s and which received such benefits as important public loans to help set itself up: '*Once the race started, the role of the MITI was not to advance some candidatures, but to limit them (...) The MITI allowed only four groupings because, in its view, only the firms from the (ex-)Zaibatsu had command of enough technologies, sales revenue and financial networks to obtain the enormous financings for the new factories*'[22].

So Japan constitutes an implicit model – reference to which has had different degrees of success from one country to another – in regard to standards of organization, as significant for State involvement as for the role of industrial structures. Lee and Yamazawa notice differences between Japan and South Korea in the forms of State intervention. South Korea (in the 1980s) revealed more structural relationships in common with Japan before the Second World War than with the Japan of the 1980s, including direct State intervention and family-based control of capital in big industrial groupings.

2.2 The Intensification of Intra-area Flows

The recent intensification of intra-area trade flows sets up a second example whereby we can appreciate the 'overhang' state of the regional integration process in Asia. This speeding-up of integration seems however to be a negative reaction to a stage of recession in the leading economy in the area, which could well lead to the crumbling of the latter.

In fact, the situation of the Japanese economy between 1988 and 1993 was characterized by the relative stability of the yen between two *endaka*[23] stages, by a slowing-down of growth during the past two years, and by the maintenance of American pressures concerning foreign trade (Structural Impediment Initiatives were signed on the 28th of June 1990). The year 1989 was generally noted as the beginning of the Japanese recession: on one hand, the 'bubble economy' exploded in 1989[24], and on the other hand, the growth rates of the GFCF (Gross Fixed Capital Formation) and of the industrial production began to slow down[25].

Asian regional integration does not seem to suffer from the Japanese recession. Two Japanese reactions, on the contrary, tend to ratify the idea of a positive correlation between the area integration process and the Japanese reaction to the crisis. As the table shows, Japan has widely centred its FDI and its foreign trade (especially its exports) on Eastern Asia[26].

The recession of the early mid-1970s produced a reorientation of Japanese trade flows from Asia towards North America. Instead, the recession of the 1990s is characterized by an opposite process: Eastern Asia's share has grown in terms of both Japanese exports and imports. In 1993, the first nine partners of Japan in East Asia represented more than a third of the Japanese exports, and just less than a third of Japanese imports. All told, this amounts to ten points more than at the beginning of the 1980s.

The Japanese trade surplus with the area went on growing during a period characterized by a recession in the global trade surplus, linked to the rise of

Table 2.1. Trade partners of Japan in Eastern Asia (% of Japanese exports and imports)

	Japan exports to		Japan imports from	
	1988	1993	1988	1993
United States	33.8	29.2	22.4	23.0
Hong Kong	4.4	6.3	1.1	0.9
Taiwan	5.4	6.1	4.7	4.0
South Korea	5.8	5.3	6.3	4.9
China	3.6	4.8	5.3	8.5
Singapore	3.1	4.6	1.2	1.5
Thailand	1.9	3.4	1.5	2.7
Malaysia	1.2	2.7	2.5	3.2
Indonesia	1.2	1.8	5.1	5.2
Philippines	0.7	0.8	1.1	1.0
Asia Total	**27.3**	**35.8**	**28.8**	**31.8**

Source: Japan Tariff Association: '*The Summary Report: Trade of Japan*', several editions.

world-wide protectionism. One can note that only two countries achieved a trade surplus with Japan: China and Indonesia – both producers of raw materials (Indonesia is an oil producer). The Asian integration process seems to be activated by this effective rise of protectionism from the other regional areas which are taking shape.

This Asian 'movement to the centre' in Japan's trade is coupled with a parallel movement in the matter of (private) foreign direct investments. After two decades of growth, the annual flow of Japanese FDI was effectively reduced between 1989 and 1992. But the characteristics of the resumption of these flows from 1992 appear to be substantially relevant to the strategy of Japanese enterprises. Japanese FDI in Asia got going again from 1992, whereas flows through Europe and the United States would not start moving before 1993. Moreover, the part of Asia in Japanese FDI would increase from 12.2% in 1989 to 18.4% in 1993, while the United States and European elements in the annual flow decreased between 1989 and 1993. Concerning the ODA, the recession period of the Japanese economy has been characterized, just as in the matter of trade, by an 'Asian movement towards the centre' process, or also by a 're-Asianization' of Japan[27].

This movement towards the centre comes, in part, from the very high comparative profitability of Japanese FDI in Asia. These investments are still, indisputably, the most profitable (and were so even during the first *endaka* provoked by the Plaza Accords in 1985), while Japan's FDI in North America are by far the least profitable[28]. Combined with American pressure to equalize the balance of trade, the will to strengthen investments abroad at a recession stage of national economy logically leads Japanese enterprises to give priority to the most profitable areas in their strategy, giving more strength to the regional integration process around Japan.

The second factor which influences the destination of Japanese FDI is linked to the global economic situation of the Asian area, which now makes up the first pole of growth at a worldwide level and thus offers a potential outlet which cannot be neglected.

The evolution of the direct investments structure reveals the specificity of the Asian area in the strategy of Japanese enterprises: in 1993, 55% of these investments were in manufacturing industries, while financial services are today the principal leader of Japanese FDI in Europe and United States:

This specificity is strengthened if one considers the destinations of the sales of the Japanese enterprises' affiliates. While the affiliates based in Europe and the United States sell the most important part of their production on the local market (the foreign location and its regions), a significant part of the Japanese affiliates' production in Asia is allocated to the Japanese market (16% of this production from 1986)[29].

Situation and Perspectives 33

Table 2.2. Evolution of the part of manufacturing industries in Japanese FDI by areas (% of annual flows)

	1985	1993
World	19.2	30.1
North America	22.2	27.1
Europe	16.7	25.7
Asia	32.0	55.1

Source: Ministry of Finance, Japan.

All these factors lend strength to the hypothesis which states that Japanese FDI is based on two distinct strategies, depending on the relevant base area: FDI in Europe and United States is focused on local markets, whereas FDI in Asia coincides more with the logic of integration through the prioritization of long-term production, with market research staying very much at a lower level of interest.

Still about the long-term, Eastern Asia constitutes the first destination of Japanese Official Development Assistance (ODA): it received two-thirds of such assistance during the past fifteen years[30]. The main profit-making countries, such as Indonesia, are those which are important recipients of Japanese FDI and which have a high natural resource potential. The structure of this assistance reveals a low level of donations against an important proportion of linked loans. The Japanese policy on ODA thus logically lies within the global economic policy of Japan: the use of public funds emphasizes the importance of private investments abroad[31].

Nevertheless, some dimensions of the international economy are still at a distance from the Asian integration process. The United States still has a very significant investment presence within the area[32]: it is the most important investor (ahead of Japan) in the Philippines, in Singapore and in Taiwan[33]. Moreover, the US dollar remains the monetary reference of the area: fluctuations in foreign exchange rates in the countries of the area are not directed by movements of the yen but by those of the dollar[34].

Yet recent transformations need to be interpreted. The structure of debt in the countries of the area reveals an increase in the yen element against the dollar element since the beginning of the 1980s. The use of the yen as an invoice currency in Japanese foreign trade with the Asian area grew more than with the other regions (more especially in the payment of Japanese imports). Between 1983 and 1990, the proportion of Japanese imports coming from South-Eastern Asia payable in yen rose from 2% to 19%[35]. Besides, '*in Asia, the Central Banks of Malaysia and Thailand announced in April (1995) their intention to increase their part of reserves in yen. South Korea has recently reevaluated the won towards the dollar, while Thailand wants to change the composition of the reference basket of currencies by increasing the yen element against the dollar element (80% now)*'[36]. If it is still too early to think in terms of a real 'yen area', the question of the internationalization of this currency seems to have a substantial regional importance.

CONCLUDING REMARKS

In a geopolitically complex region, the question of future of the Asia area[37] points to a process of non-achievement. The conditions for a regional economic integration process to succeed are nevertheless combined in the long-term. The role of Japan as a standards provider hardly dates back to the end of the 1980s. Far from slowing down the process, the recent period, on the contrary, has seen a speeding-up in the establishment of these conditions. However, the geo-economic entity in question comes within the bigger entity of the worldwide economy. The integration of the area is, thus, strongly conditioned by global evolution. Consequently, the future of Asia as an integrated economic area depends at the same time on the internal evolution of the area and on the evolution of relations between this area and the rest of the world. A possible decrease in trade flows between the Asian and North American areas could constitute an indicator of the progress of Asian integration. If the regionalization of international economic relations is confirmed, there will remain one more unknown factor: will the world economy be satisfied with a closed tripolarity, or will it prefer the domination of a specific area – and which one?

Notes

1. Translated from French by Catherine Danion.
2. Dominique de Laubier (1993).
3. Charles-Albert Michallet (1985) *Le Capitalisme Mondial*, Presses Universitaires de France, Paris.
4. Robert Boyer (1986) *La théorie de la régulation: une analyse critique*, Agalma la Découverte, Paris, pp 64–68.
5. 'Objective' in the sense that the one political will declared is not enough.
6. G. Loulergue et F. Hatem (1994).

7. Michel Aglietta (1991) p 100.
8. 'Si l'histoire ne repasse pas les mêmes plats, elle ne se prive pas de quelques bonnes recettes'. Alain Cotta (1994) *'Un nouveau Président pour rien'*, Editions Fayard, Paris, p 176.
9. François Perroux (1961) p 50 of the 1991 edition.
10. Emphasis has been put on the observable permanencies in the process of regional integration. Nevertheless, one must stress that each process is in fact a combining of similarities and specificities. It may particularly be noted that political integration is in advance of economic integration in Europe, and that Eastern Asia reveals the opposite situation.
11. Catherine Figuière (1995).
12. These two countries already showed similarities before going through the industrialization process: both of them are latecomers to development (even if they are of different generations) and their natural resources are few. Thus, they both have had to face comparable constraints with the possibility of resorting to imported technologies, developed by advanced countries. On this topic, see C. H. Lee and I. Yamazawa (1990).
13. Catherine Figuière (1993a) pp 13–33, 250–283.
14. M. Blanc et J. R. Chaponnière (1990) p 803.
15. J. R. Chaponnière (1992).
16. The term *zaibatsu* qualifies the Japanese multisector groupings as they were financially structured before the second World War. See Catherine Figuière (1993 b).
17. Gilles Guiheux (1995).
18. About the role of trading companies, see K. Kojima and T. Ozawa (1984).
19. Karl J. Fields (1989).
20. Philippe Régnier (1992).
21. World Bank Report (1993) *'The East Asia Miracle: Economic Growth and Public Policy'*.
22. Christian Sautter (1973) p 196.
23. The Bank of Japan's interbanking foreign exchange rate in end of periods move this way: (1988) 126 yens for one dollar, (1989) 143, (1990) 135, (1991) 125, (1992) 125, (1993) 112.
24. 'Bubble economy': a term frequently used in he early 1990s to refer to the asset inflation, or the speculative and inflated wealth in securities and land in the 1986–89. Robert Hsu (1994) p 38.
25. So that in January 1995, the hypothesis of the beginning of a resumption of the Japanese economy (from 1992) was reasonably conceivable; the impact of the Mexican crisis during the winter 94/95, on the yen-dollar parity especially, make it difficult to forecast the end of this recession period.
26. The book of Michel Fouquin (1991) (CEPPI) 'Pacifique: le recentrage aisiatique', already drew up the constat of the existence of a long-term global process.
27. François Gipouloux (1993).
28. MITI's Statistics in G. Loulergue and F. Hatem (1994) p 412.
29. MITI's Statistics in F. Nicolas (1993) p 30.
30. *Accélérations*, (Mounthly publication of 'la Direction des Affaires Economiques et Fiancières' of the 'Crédit Lyonnais') June 1995.
31. Derek Healey (1991).

32. Catherine Figuière (1991).
33. L. Y. C. Lim and Pang Eng Fong (1991).
34. Foreign exchange rates evolutions (SDR). IMF's Statistics.
35. BIRD's Statistics.
36. Olivier Passet (1995) pp 36–37.
37. Catherine Figuière (1991).

REFERENCES

Aglietta, Michel (1991), 'L'ajustement international', *Cahiers Français*, No. 253, Oct–Dec.

Blanc, M. and Chaponnière, J. R. (1990), 'Les "Jeabuls" coréens à l'heure de la globalisation', *Revue Tiers Monde*, t.XXXI, No. 124.

Chaponnière, J. R. (1989), 'Les politiques industrielles des NPIA', *Les Cahiers Français*, No. 243, Oct–Dec., pp 46–47.

Chaponnière, J. R. (1992), 'Korea Inc. en transition', *Working Paper IREPD*, Grenoble, March.

Fields, Karl J. (1989), 'Trading Companies in South Korea and Taiwan. Two Policy Approaches', *Asian Survey*, Vol. XXIX, No. 11, Nov.

Fields, Karl J. (1989), 'Trading Companies in South Korea and Taiwan', *Asian Survey*, vol. XXIX, No. 11, Dec.

Figuière, Catherine (1991), 'Les enjeux de lazone Pacifique', *Etudes et Recherches de l'Iseres*, No. 70.

Figuière, Catherine (1993a), '*Les groupes multisectoriels japonais: un facteur de cohérences des structures productives nationales*'. Thèse, Université de Grenoble Pierre Mendès-France.

Figuière, Catherine (1993b), 'GMS et keiretsu: propos d'étape pour une typologie des groupes industriels japonais', *Japon in Extenso*, No. 30, Dec.

Figuière, Catherine (1995), 'Les origines des structures productives japonaises', in SFEJ, *Japon Pluriel*, Editions Philippe Picquier.

Fouquin, Michel *et al* (1991), '*Pacifique: le recentrage asiatique*', CEPII, Economica, Paris.

Gipouloux, François (1993), 'Fragmentation et recomposition des espaces économiques en Asie orientale: le Japon leader ou networker', *Ebisu*, No. 1, Apr–June.

Guiheux, Gilles (1995), 'Les conglomérats taïwanais', *Economie Internationale*, No. 61, 1er trimestre.

Healey, Derek (1991), '*Les exportations japonaises de capitaux et le développement économique de l'Asie*', OCDE, Paris.

Hsu, Robert (1994), '*The MIT Encyclopedia of the Japanese Economy*', MIT Press.

Kojima, K., and Ozawa, T. (1984), '*Les sociétés japonaises de commerce général. Leur rôle dans le développement économique*', OCDE, Paris.

Laubier, Dominique (1993), 'Une décennie d'expansion des investissements directs', *Economie Internationale*, No. 56, 4ème trimestre.

Lee, C. H., and Yamazawa, I. (1990), '*The Economic Development and Korea. A Parallel with Lessons*', Preager, New York.

Lim, L. Y. C., and Pang Eng Fong (1991), '*L'IDE et l'industrialisation en Malaisie, à Singapour, à Taïwan et en Thaïlande*', OCDE, Paris.

Loulergue, G., and Hatem, F. (1994), 'Intégration régionale en Asie', *Chroniques Economiques de la SEDEIS*, No. 12, Dec.

Nicolas, Françoise (1993), 'Les Japonais dans la course à la globalisation', in *'Les entreprises japonaises en Europe. Motivations et stratégies'*, Ed. Frédérique Sachwald, IFRI-Masson, Paris.

Passet, Olivier (1995), 'Le Japon: les doutes d'un créancier', *Revue de l'OFCE*, No. 54, July.

Perroux, François (1961), *'L'économie du XXe siècle'*, 1991 edition, PUG, Grenoble.

Régnier, Philippe (1992), 'Industrialisation de la Corée du Sud: à la recherche du rôle des petites et moyennes entreprises', *Symposium du GRESCO*, Paris, EHESS, 30–31 March.

Sautter, Christian (1973), *'Japon, le prix de la puissance'*, Ed. du Seuil, Paris.

3 Japanese Trade with East Asia and Business Cycles: a Historical Perspective (1875–1993)

Jean-Pascal Bassino[1]

1 INTRODUCTION

The economic integration of East Asia appears, at first glance, to be a new tendency related to the emergence of the Asia–Pacific region during the 1980s as the new centre of the world economy. We could, however, consider this integration as a long-term trend which was thwarted over some thirty years (from around 1945 to 1975) partly by exogenous shocks (wars) and institutional constraints (the political evolution of continental China, Korea and Vietnam) but also by the economic and technological superiority of the United States.

An analysis of the economic integration of the East Asian countries in a historical perspective inclines us to put most emphasis on the contribution of Japanese trade and local subsidiaries of Japanese industrial groups to this process. An approach focused on economic relations with Japan is justified by that country's role as the dominant commercial power (trade with Japan represents about 50% of international trade in the area) and as the main diffusion centre of transfer of technological and organisational innovations, either imported and adapted from the West or locally produced.

This does not, however, imply our support of any view of the present process as a Japanese attempt to revive the short-lived 'East Asian Co-prosperity Sphere'. The Second World War, in effect, brought about a deep break in the economic relations of East Asian countries that can be seen as a discontinuity in almost all statistical series. However, the present economic integration process is characterized both by the developing role of South Korea and Taiwan as secondary centres for the spread of innovation and by structural changes in international trade.

This paper is aimed at proposing an interpretation and a projection of Japanese trade with East Asian countries, both in a long-term perspective and in relation to Japanese business cycles. First of all, we will present an analysis of the long-term evolution of Japanese trade with the main East Asian countries and territories since the end of the 19th century. We will investigate dynamic patterns in bilateral trade with Korea, Taiwan, continental China (the People's Republic since 1949), Hong Kong, Singapore, Malaysia, Vietnam (Indochina before 1945), Thailand, Indonesia and the Philippines. Secondly, we will compare international trade series with Japanese macroeconomic business cycles[2].

2 EVOLUTION OF EAST ASIAN COUNTRIES IN JAPANESE INTERNATIONAL TRADE

Long-term analysis of East Asian countries in Japanese international trade should allow us to re-evaluate the magnitude of the recent concentration of world trade in this area, especially the current spectacular growth of Japanese trade with China[3]. In order to evaluate each East Asian country's or territory's share in Japanese trade, we will use two distinct standard indicators: on the one hand, the trade share indicator, measured as a ratio of each partner in the total Japanese international trade (in both cases, the sum of exports and imports); on the other hand, the Japanese bilateral opening rate, measured as the ratio of bilateral trade (exports and imports divided by two) to the Japanese GDP.

2.1 Evolution of the Relative Share of World Regions in Japanese International Trade

For a long-term analysis of the share of countries and territories, Japanese international trade with East Asia as a whole should be compared with the evolution of flows with Europe and North America, these three regions having comparable economic weight (Fig. 3.1). We could then propose a projection for 2005–2010 according to a hypothesis of evolution along long-term national trends that we may consider as representing a level of equilibrium.

The East Asian share in Japanese international trade increased steadily from the second part of the 20th century, starting from a relatively low level – around 20% during the 1870s – reaching around 40% in the 1930s and rising drastically at the eve of the Second World War to exceed 60%. At the same

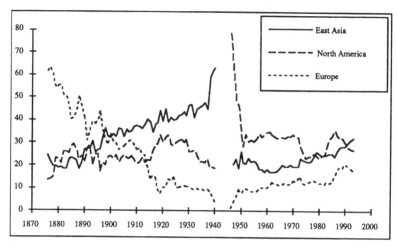

Figure 3.1 Relative share of East Asia, Europe and North America in Japanese international trade (1875–1993)

time, the North American share lay beyond 20%, reaching almost 30% during the 1920s. Accordingly, Europe's relative importance declined sharply between 1875 and 1920, from an hegemonic share of 60% to about 10%, stabilizing thereafter around this level.

The 1920s and 1930s correspond therefore to a first phase of East Asian economic integration with the Japanese economy that does not however lead to a global integration of the area. It seems significant that this integration occurred before the Sino-Japanese war and even before the military occupation of Manchuria. It does not only appear as a consequence of Japanese military imperialism but rather as the development of an exchange and co-operation process, even if sometimes with a very adversarial relationship, between geographically and culturally close countries and territories.

During the post-war period, the East Asian share fell sharply, as a result of the political independence of former Japanese colonies and of the United States' technological and economic superiority and influence in the area. It remained thereafter stable at about 20% until the 1970s and then increased steadily, reaching around 30% in the 1990s, overshooting the North American share for the first time since the war. Europe's share also tended to increase, but irregularly, from a low of no more than 10% in 1950 to around 20% in the 1980s and 1990s.

Long-term trade share evolution therefore shows a tendency to reduce exchanges with countries whose economic and technological relative influence is declining – Europe as a whole (and especially Great Britain and France) at the end of the 19th century, and perhaps the United States from the 1980s – favouring a contrary increase of trade with the most dynamic partners or countries at the technological frontier Germany and the United States at the beginning of the century or during the 1920s.

Japan's global technological advantage since the 1980s has induced a structural change. For the moment, Japan does not have the same kind of interaction with East Asian NIEs as it had with Western industrialized countries. Furthermore, in most areas of manufacturing, dynamic Japanese firms – until the 1980s essentially creative imitators of their Western competitors – are reaching closer to technological frontiers and in several cases are pioneering innovation.

2.2 Evolution of the Japanese Bilateral Opening Rate with East Asian Countries Before the 1950s

A historical study of the Japanese bilateral opening rate confirms these tendencies, while introducing restrictions and nuances related to the evolution of the magnitude of this indicator. Japan's global opening rate followed an upward trend, affected by fluctuations of strong amplitude, from 4% of the GDP in the 1880s to almost 20% in the 1940s (Fig. 3.2). After the war, the rate remained around 8% to 10% but a significant downward

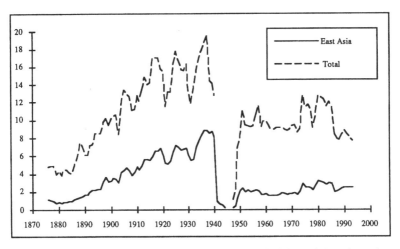

Figure 3.2 Total Japanese opening rate (including Colonial Empire) and opening rate with East Asia (1875–1993)

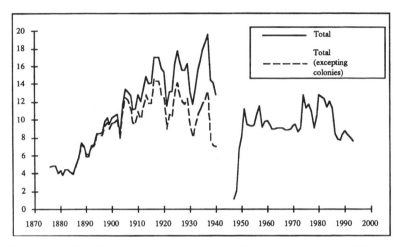

Figure 3.3   Total Japanese opening rate and opening rate with the colonial Empire (1875–1993)

tendency appeared at the beginning of the 1980s, mainly explained by the appreciation of the yen against the dollar.

Japan's relatively high opening rate during the 1920s and 1930s corresponds, given the pattern in the market share evolution already mentioned, to a strong increase of the opening of Japan towards East Asia, from an overall low of 1% in 1880 to more than 5% in 1914 and almost 9% in the 1930s. Considering bilateral data, this evolution results mainly from the expansion of trade within Japan's colonial Empire.

Excluding trade with Korea, Taiwan, Kwangtung and Manchuria (Fig. 3.3), for the period prior to 1940, we notice that, during the 1920s and 1930s, the opening rate outside Japan's colonial Empire, or the total opening rate after 1945, remained approximatively at the same level, around 8 to 10%, from the beginning of the century to the 1980s. Trade with Korea alone represented 3% of the Japanese GDP in 1940, against 1% in 1920. We can observe the same tendency for Taiwan and the North China colonies, Kwangtung and Manchuria (Fig. 3.4). For these last two territories, the opening rate doubled from less than 1% in 1920 to around 2% in 1940. Thus, the strong increase in the aggregate indicator for China considered as a whole is mainly explained by the annexation of Manchuria (Fig. 3.5). The relative decline of Hong Kong as a trade partner indicates a diversification of flows and the new predominance of North China[4].

With Southeast Asia also, the development of Japanese trade is sustained and characterised by wide fluctuations. However, relative to the flows in

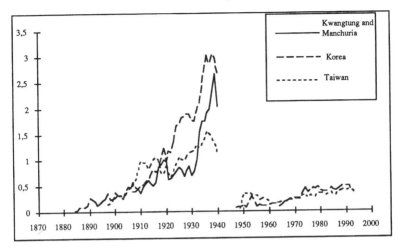

Figure 3.4 Japanese opening rate with the main colonial territories (1875–1940) and with South Korea and Taiwan (1945–1993)

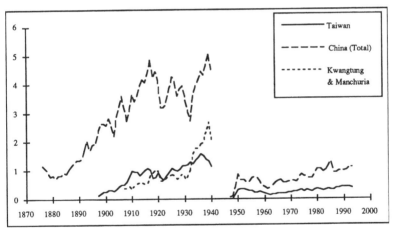

Figure 3.5 Japanese opening rate with China (as a whole; including Japanese and British colonial territories) and with Taiwan and Manchuria (1875–1993)

Northeast Asia, the global trade with the whole area remained modest, about the same as with Taiwan in 1940. This was partly a consequence of the Western colonial administrations' mistrust of Japanese motivations and intentions. The strongest increases in trade are observed with Thailand, politically independent even if very close economically to Britain, and with

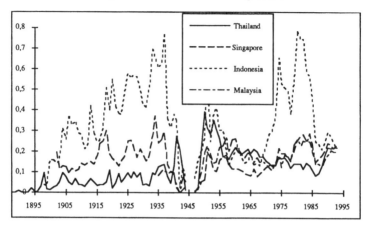

Figure 3.6   Japanese opening rate with the main trade partners in Southeast Asia (1890–1993)

Indonesia, the main trade partner of Japan in South-East Asia, half the global trade with this area (Fig. 3.6) being mainly due to crude oil exports.

Thus, Asian economic integration of the 1920s and 1930s concerned mainly North-East Asia dominated by Japan. It was, not, however a conventional colonial integration process like those promoted by France and Britain in order to build a colonial free trade area in the 1930s. As early as the 1920s, Japanese industrial groups, especially the so called *shinko zaibatsu* – new industrial groups closely related to the military and intelligence services – invested massively in Korea and then in Manchuria, setting up huge capital-intensive projects in mining and manufacturing including the high-technology activities of the moment, chemicals and metal processing. This massive inflow of productive capital may be noticed from the increase in Japanese machinery exports during these years and the resulting commercial deficit for Korea. We can observe the same tendency in Taiwan, even if at a reduced scale and with a concentration of investment in food processing activities (especially sugar).

These investments in mining and manufacturing resulted, as early as the 1930s, in a significant development of Japanese manufactured goods imports from these territories, both in volume and relative to global flows. Manufactured goods represented about 30% of Korean exports to Japan on the eve of the second World War. Various difficulties in availability and reliability of data and exogenous perturbations between 1940 and 1955 do not allow us to follow the whole trajectory, but its pattern until the 1990s corresponds to a logistic curve whose inflexion point would be around 1950.

The constitution of the imperial economic co-ordination structure called the 'East Asian Co-prosperity Sphere' quickly enabled Japan to control and rule the East Asian economies during the Second World War and therefore to extend economic integration, especially through the organisation of a yen bloc with stable currency rates. For South East Asia, however, the trend is toward bilateral integration with Japan rather than multilateral global integration, both during the war and after the war. The disorganization of trade and transport networks, the reconversion of Japanese export-oriented consumer goods manufacturing activities toward military production and other war destruction in Japan induced a collapse of the Japanese opening rate for around five years.

As early as the 1950s, however, the Japanese opening rate with East Asia reached pre-war level again, with strong contrasts between countries. Levels were much higher than in the 1930s with Thailand, the Philippines and Malaysia, and that can be considered to a certain extent as a legacy of the war. Levels were much lower for Singapore, Vietnam and Indonesia. In the two last countries, it was certainly due to economic conditions brought about by wars of independence. In the case of Singapore, it may have been a result of increasing direct trade with Malaysia, another legacy of the war.

Whatever the local specificities explaining these flows, bilateral Japanese trade with East Asian countries does not appear to be a result of Japan's integration in the US-dominated economic sphere. It is rather in line with the dynamics initiated in the 1920s and 1930s – with the development by Japanese industrial firms and general trading companies of networks, local subsidiaries and joint ventures in mining, forestry, agriculture, and also labour-intensive manufacturing (textile, assembly of electric consumer goods, bicycles, etc.).

2.3 Evolution Since the 1950s and Projections for Northeast Asian Countries

The Japanese opening rate with Northeast Asia declined sharply after the war to levels much lower than during the 1930s, in the case of Korea and Taiwan – but also China, and even Hong Kong. For these four economies, we observe a comparable volume of bilateral trade, around 0.2% of the Japanese GDP, but with an upward trend and wide fluctuations, especially in the case of China. During the 1980s and 1990s, the evolution is characterized by a tendency to stabilization and a convergence of opening rates toward a level of around 0.3% (in 1993, Korea: 0.36%; Taiwan: 0.37%; Hong Kong 0.29%; China 0.24%).

Given the demographic differential, Korea's and Taiwan's contribution to Japanese trade indicates how important geographical proximity and institutional closeness are, the colonial era's cultural legacy allowing Japan to go beyond political and nationalist disputes, especially with Korea. The weakness of trade with China relative to the population explains the constant effort made by Japanese politicians and businessmen, since the 1950s and the 1960s, to promote the activities of industrial groups and general trading companies in that country despite political instability and institutional constraints.

The recent and spectacular increase of Japan's opening rate with China, from 0.14% in 1986 to 0.24% in 1993, may be interpreted as the beginning of a long-term strongly upward trend. However, this 1993 level corresponds exactly to rates observed at the beginning of the 1980s and only indicates a recovery after the decline of the second half of the decade. Actually, Japan's opening rate with China fluctuated strongly after the war and the 1993 level is just above the respective maxima of the middle of the 1950s.

Since a great deal of Chinese foreign trade passes through Hong Kong, it appears necessary to evaluate the global evolution of Japanese trade with continental China (the People's Republic and Hong Kong). We obtain similar results, the 1993 level (0.53%) being the same as in 1984 and barely superior to the post-war maximal level of 1956 (0.44%). Considering China as a whole – the People's Republic, Hong Kong and Taiwan – we once more observe similar levels in the 1950s and the middle of the 1990s.

A projection of Japan's opening rates with East Asian countries should take into account both long-term evolution and recent trends, but also changes in the relative importance of multilateral trade between these countries, especially between Hong Kong, China (the People's Republic), Taiwan and Korea. Even if there is a diversification and a substitution from Japan to Korea as supplier of capital goods, the pre-war opening rate with China, including Hong Kong but excluding colonial territories (Kwangtung and Manchuria), around 1% to 1.5%, probably constitutes a good indicator of the potential and equilibrium level that may be reached in the medium term (2005–2010) unless there is no change in the political and institutional environment.

This would certainly induce a correlative decrease in the opening rate with North America, but it does not imply an inversion of the tendency towards an increase in the share with Europe, respectively 2.06% and 1.35% in 1993[5]. Considering that Japanese opening rates with Taiwan and Korea are at their equilibrium level, we could observe in the short term a convergence tendency of these three areas, North-East Asia, North America and Europe at around a 2% level.

2.4 Evolution Since the 1950s and Projection for South-East Asian Countries

The evolution of the Japanese opening rate with South East Asian countries, from 1950, is characterized by wide amplitude fluctuations around a global equilibrium level of approximately 1%, corresponding exactly to the 1992 and 1993 level. On these opening rate fluctuations, the upward phases correspond to the years of strong increase in the real prices of raw materials, such as crude oil. This means we should not necessarily interpret the strong increase of the opening rate between 1986 and 1993 (from 0.74 to 1.00%) as a trend for the following years, even if there are significant changes in the structural characteristics in this trade, notably in exports to Japan.

One of the most interesting recent trends in this area was a convergence tendency at the beginning of the 1990s around the level of 0.2% to 0.25% for the main countries, Indonesia, Malaysia, Thailand and Singapore (respectively 0.22%, 0.20%, 0.22% and 0.24% in 1993). As in the case of Northeast Asia, a relationship between population and Japanese trade does not seem to exist. The opening rate declined over the last twenty years with the main exporters of raw materials in the area, Indonesia and the Philippines: in the case of Indonesia, this was despite the demographic importance of this country, and in the case of the Philippines, it was probably due to political instability and to the relative failure in technology transfer to this country. The Japanese opening rate increased in the meantime with Thailand, the main emerging industrial power in the area, and remained stable with Malaysia and Singapore, which was certainly due to a shift from raw materials to manufacturing goods as dynamic exports in the former country and to a relative decline of manufacturing in the economic activity in the latter.

For a projection of opening rates with Southeast Asian countries, we should again take into consideration not only long-term evolution and equilibrium levels but also the potential development of trade, until now inhibited by political instability and institutional factors. In this case, we could suppose a validation of the convergence tendency for trade with the Philippines and above all Vietnam (respectively 0.08% and 0.02% in 1993) at a level comparable with those of other countries.

The increasing share of manufactured goods in Japanese imports from the area introduced a structural evolution from the situation of the 1960s and 1970s, when they were mainly raw materials and basic agricultural goods. This suggests a possible tendency towards an augmentation of the Japanese opening rate with the area comparable with the evolution that has taken place with China. A combination of these dynamics could lead in the medium term (five to ten years) at around 1.5% to 2%, corresponding to a level slightly higher than the historical maxima reached during the inter-war period (1.23% in 1925 and 1.62% in 1937).

3 RELATION BETWEEN JAPANESE BUSINESS CYCLES AND TRADE DYNAMICS

For a long-term analysis of the relationship between Japanese business cycles and trade dynamics, we hypothesise micro-economic behaviours of Japanese agencies that could explain this interaction; during the recessions in business cycles, Japanese firms explore new foreign markets and experiment with new foreign supply sources. We intend basically to investigate business cycles of about a seven to ten-year period, mainly related to innovations in manufacturing and infrastructure equipment or in process and organisations. This interpretation puts an emphasis on the relationship between business cycles and the structure of trade by country rather than by product, which is the approach usually adopted by scholars. The main exception concerns the upsurge of Japanese exports in the Middle East after 1974 which was extensively studied. This was a short-lived phenomenon, though one which above all had limited indirect effects.

It would also be useful to compare trade and investment data. In the face of a degradation of their performances during recessions, industrial and commercial firms may decide to reallocate their internal resources internationally by expanding their productive capacities in foreign countries or through delocalization. This could induce a structural shift in foreign trade, with a reduction of consumer goods exports, but also a decline in raw materials and intermediate goods imports and eventually a temporary increase in capital goods exports. Difficulties in collecting data on Japanese foreign investment by sector and by country before the 1950s[6], on the one hand, and on Japanese trade by product and country before the 1920s on the other constrain us to limiting the analysis to trade series by country since the 1870s.

3.1 Indicators of Cyclical Japanese Trade Behaviour

The opening rate by country and country's share in Japanese imports and exports does not allow an identification of a cyclical pattern in foreign trade since the amplitude in fluctuation is usually very narrow over a short period. We therefore use two other indicators: on the one hand, the relative trade balance (ratio of trade balance to GDP); on the other hand, the relative growth rate of Japanese exports (growth rate differential of Japanese exports and GDP).

The first indicator seems more suitable than the export-to-import ratio, since the measure of the amount of surplus or deficit relative to the size of Japanese economy makes a comparison by country more meaningful. A strong imbalance with a country may have no significant consequence as long as the trade is negligible. It should be useful to compare these data with the Japanese opening rate with each country or world region.

The second indicator is used to identify if (and also, in this case, when), during the phases of business cycles, an export growth rate higher than the GDP growth rate corresponds to a recession or an expansion. The growth rate differential enables us, in addition, to eliminate problems related to the conversion from current yen to constant yen series. Deflating data is in fact a hard task, since export price as well as import price indicators are available globally or by commodity and not by country. Difficulties in collecting trade series by country and by product before the middle of the century make it almost impossible to produce data without a significant risk of distortion in the results.

For the relative trade balance, short period fluctuations are small and negligible, but that is not true for the relative export growth rate on which inventory stock variation may have a significant impact. For the second indicator, it appears essential to filter out annual data with a three-year moving average in order to eliminate short period business cycles, mainly inventories stocks-related.

For these two indicators, an automatic selection procedure, a simple adaptation of a more sophisticated procedure elaborated by the NBER, enables us to identify turning points in these two series for each country. Years with values superior to those of the two previous and the two following years are considered as the turning points. These results are compared with the turning points of a synthetic index of major Japanese macro-economic indicators: GDP per head, consumption per head, money supply, interest rate, investment, etc. (cf. tables 3.1 and 3.2 in the appendix).

3.2 Cyclical Behaviour of Relative Trade Balances

The first interesting result concerns the relative trade balance evolution (Fig. 3.7). These time series seem to follow the same periodicity as main macroeconomic indicators. We notice, however, an advance until the 1920s and thereafter (when the trade balance becomes structurally negative) a tendency to a delay until the 1970s and 1980s. This phenomenon seems to confirm the fact, underlined by many scholars, that Japan's economic growth during these decades is driven more by internal demand than by external trade, the latter following the internal business cycles without giving any

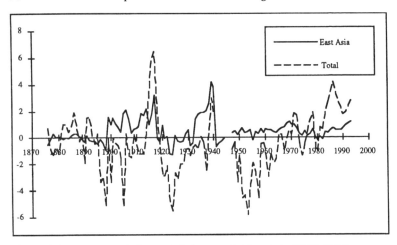

Figure 3.7   Japanese relative trade balance with East Asia (1875–1993)

significant impulse to the economic system. In fact, trade imbalance reaches a low at the eve of expansion and a peak at the eve of recession.

The situation is reversed at the beginning of the 1980s, which means at a moment when Japanese trade becomes structurally in surplus with a significant advance of the relative trade balance indicator to the synthetic index that even seems to evolve toward an opposition of phases. It is probably a consequence of the opening of the Japanese market to imported manufactured consumer goods.

The analysis of turning points for different world regions and East Asian countries suggests that relative trade balances fluctuate approximatively at the same pace as the Japanese macroeconomic synthetic indicator, but with an amplitude for East Asia as a whole that is not so wide as for the global relative trade balance indicator. While the tendency is to a delay for global trade, it is usually coincident for East Asian countries. We find the same break during the 1980s – but amplified, however, since the structural surplus increased continuously.

Concerning more specifically Southeast Asian countries, the bilateral trade balance was almost systematically delayed from the 1920s to the 1970s. The inversion of the tendency during the 1980s toward an advance is associated with the appearance of a global deficit for Japan until the beginning of the 1990s. Individual studies by country (Fig. 3.8) allow us to underline a contrast between traditional raw material suppliers (Malaysia and Indonesia), with a trade surplus toward Japan and an opposition in phases, and Singapore, whose trade, structurally in deficit with Japan, has a pattern of

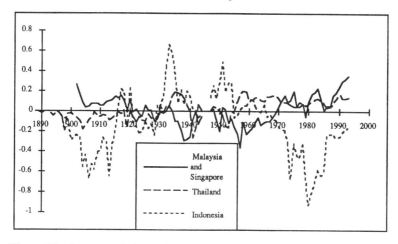

Figure 3.8 Japanese relative trade balance with Singapore and Malaysia, Thailand and Indonesia (1890–1993)

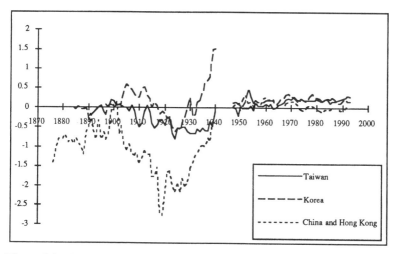

Figure 3.9 Japanese relative trade balance with Taiwan, Korea and China and Hong Kong (1875–1993)

evolution comparable with the other NIEs, particularly Korea and Taiwan (Fig. 3.9). However, we can observe for all East Asian countries a trend leading to a convergence in the relative size of bilateral trade and homogeneous cyclical patterns since the end of the 1980s.

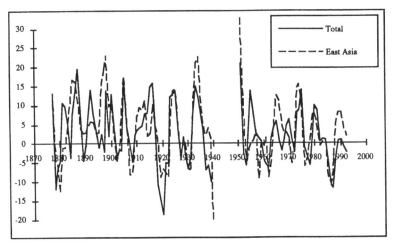

Figure 3.10 Relative growth rate of Japanese total exports to East Asia (1876–1992); three-year moving average

3.3 Cyclical Behaviour of the Relative Growth Rate of Japanese Exports

The relative growth rate of Japanese exports has fluctuated since the end of the 19th century with the same periodicity and globally in phase with the synthetic Japanese macroeconomic indicators, both in the case of total exports and of exports to East Asian countries. A study of three year-moving average filtered series of total exports shows a phase opposition during the 1950s and 1960s. This means that, during these decades, the relative growth rate of exports reaches a peak at the end of recessions and a trough at the end of expansions.

An analysis by country allows us to specify and to date the gap relevant to the relative growth rate indicator of total exports. For East Asia as a whole (Fig. 3.10), the relative growth rate of Japanese exports is superior to the total exports indicator at the end of the 19th century during successive phases which we could identify with the opening of regular Japanese shipping lines to these countries. Discontinuities in the trade growth rate with individual countries are a consequence of a long-term economic policy of subsidies to national shipping companies, particularly Mitsubishi and thereafter Nippon Yusen Kaisha, for the opening of new strategic lines. This is of special importance for Southeast Asia before the First World War and also may be during the inter-war period (Fig. 3.11).

After the war, also, the relative growth rate of exports fluctuated much

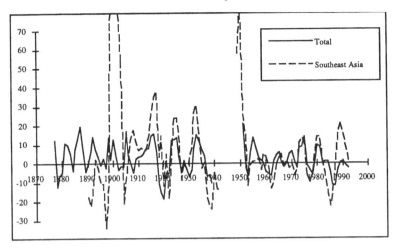

Figure 3.11   Relative growth rate of Japanese total exports to Southeast Asia
(1876–1992); three-year moving average

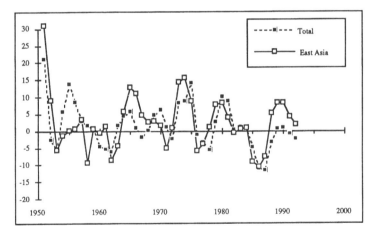

Figure 3.12   Relative growth rate of Japanese total exports to East Asia (1952–
1992); three-year moving average

more widely in the case of East Asian countries (Fig. 3.12) than for the global
flow of exports, particularly with peaks around 1965, 1973–1974 and 1990.
The study of specific countries indicates that in Korea (Fig. 3.13) and Taiwan
(Fig. 3.14) the indicator behaves in a specific way. The sequences of a strong
relative growth of export correspond to an opposition of phase with the

54 *Perspectives on Economic Integration*

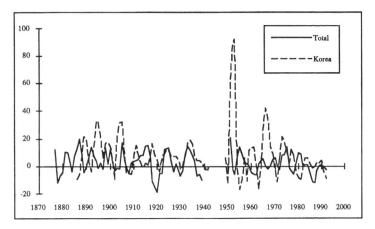

Figure 3.13 Relative growth rate of Japanese total exports to Korea (1876–1992); three-year moving average

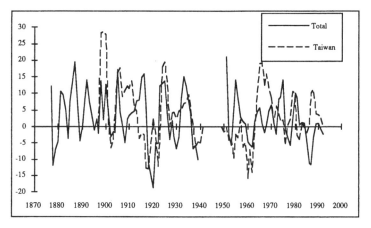

Figure 3.14 Relative growth rate of Japanese total exports to Taiwan (1876–1992); three-year moving average

relative growth rate of total exports.

In the case of Korea, this can be observed from the peaks of 1893, 1905, 1918, 1927 and after the war in 1960, 1966–1967 and 1976. The peak of 1952, however, coincides with the exporting of Japanese industrial products to the United Nations Forces during the Korean war and not to a real increase of trade between the two economies. In the case of Taiwan, peaks can be identified in 1890, 1895, 1918, 1927 and after the war in 1967

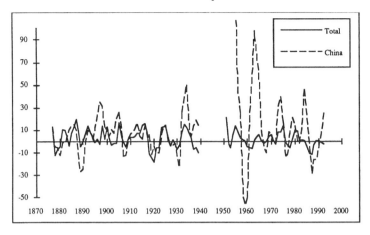

Figure 3.15 Relative growth rate of Japanese total exports to China (1876–1992); three-year moving average

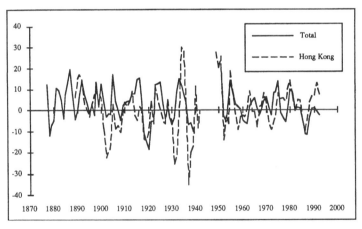

Figure 3.16 Relative growth rate of Japanese total exports to Hong Kong (1876–1992); three-year moving average

and 1987. These years usually correspond to the end of expansion, with Japanese firms exporting as an extension of the domestic effort. This phenomenon suggests a strong association of these two economies with the Japanese dynamics.

In the case of China, however (Fig. 3.15 and 3.16), despite the existence of a political cycle with essentially internal concerns, the fluctuation of the relative growth rate of exports is the same as for the indicator of total exports.

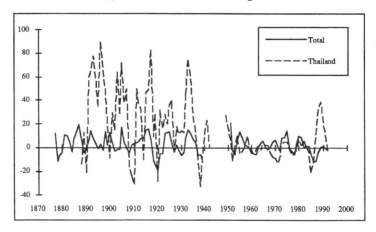

Figure 3.17 Relative growth rate of Japanese total exports to Thailand (1890–1992); three-year moving average

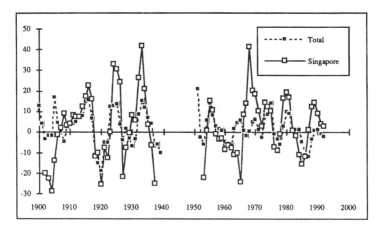

Figure 3.18 Relative growth rate of Japanese total exports to Singapore (1900–1992); three-year moving average

A similar pattern may be noticed for different Southeast Asian countries. The push in exports usually appears during the recession of Japanese business cycles, leading to an increase in the trend observed for total exports.

For the four main trade partners of Japan in South East Asia – Thailand, Singapore, Malaysia and Indonesia (Figs 3.17, 3.18, 3.19 and 3.20) – the peaks appear to indicate discontinuities in the opening of new markets for

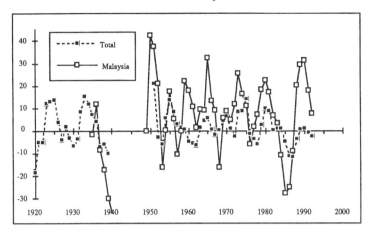

Figure 3.19 Relative growth rate of Japanese total exports to Malaysia (1935–1992); three-year moving average

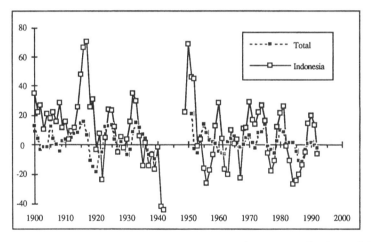

Figure 3.20 Relative growth rate of Japanese total exports to Southeast Asia (1900–1992); three-year moving average

Japanese exporters. They seem related to the opening of regular shipping lines by Japanese companies between the 1890s and the 1920s, and to the development of networks of Japanese trading companies and manufacturing firms' local subsidiaries during the 1920s and the 1930s.

For the same countries, peaks clearly higher than the indicator of total exports appear around 1970, 1980 and especially 1990. There is a strong contrast for this last peak, with very low levels observed for Japanese exports to North America and even Europe at the same time. This gap indicates the extent of the process of stimulating the economic integration of these countries on the Japanese pattern of economic dynamics, even if there is a wide differential in level or extent between Japan's and other East Asian countries' macroeconomic performance.

CONCLUSION

A long-term analysis of Japanese trade with East Asian countries inclines us to put in historical perspective the recent structural changes in international trade in this area and allows us to propose medium-term projections, relying on extrapolations and taking into account long-term equilibrium levels. Economic integration in East Asia appears therefore as a long-term trend, and the Second World War-related discontinuities as temporary deflections in these dynamics. It is, moreover, possible to identify a relationship between Japanese business cycles and the dynamics of trade or the phases of strong increase in trade flows.

   Japan certainly has a central role in the economic development process in East Asia since there was, from the inter-war period onwards, a surprisingly early spread of technologies and organizational innovations to Japan's colonial territories and also to China and Southeast Asia. Unlike other colonial powers, Japan adopted during the 1920s and the 1930s an industrialization-oriented colonial policy in Korea, Taiwan and North China whose impact on post-war economic development was probably under-estimated.

   A study by product or sector for each country and a comparison with direct Japanese investments, especially in mining and manufacturing in the area, should point to more accurate results. For example, Asian NIEs' economic dynamics may be characterized by a progressive evolution, from a pace following the American business cycles to fluctuations broadly similar to those of Japanese business cycles, with a significant but rather stable period of phases[7].

   We could also consider a correlative hypothesis according to which Asian countries' economic integration has, since the beginning of the century, depended positively on the role of manufacturing in the productive structure and in trade, and negatively on the contribution of mining and agriculture to exports.

   This would mean that economic integration works as a manifestation and consequence of a cultural and institutional capacity to import and adopt appropriate technologies rather than on the basis of a static specialization relying on sectoral comparative advantages. More precisely, the economic integration process could depend on a ratio of human capital to labour cost in manufacturing, human capital accumulation and dispersion in the population being considered as broad indication of capacity to adopt appropriate technologies. This hypothesis seems valid in the case of Korea and Taiwan since the 1920s and appears, in the contest of a research programme, likely to contribute to a better understanding of economic dynamics in East Asia.

Notes

1. Associate Professor of Economics at Paul Valéry University (Campus Vauban, 30021 Nîmes, France) and Researcher at the C.E.F.I. (Centre d'Economie et de Finances Internationales, CNRS Associated Research Unit n° 951, Château Lafarge, 13290 Les Milles, France).
2. Statistical data: Tokei Kyoku, 1986, Nihon Choki Keizai Tokei Soran (Historical Statistics of Japan), Tokyo, Tokeikyoku; Ohkawa K, Shinohara M. & Umemura M. eds., 1965–1988, Choki Keizai Tokei (Estimate of Long-Term Economc Statistics of Japan since 1868), 14 vol., Tokyo Toyo Keizai; Nihon Tokei Nenpo (Japan Statistical Yearbook) from 1985.
3. Fourquin M., Dourille-Feer E. & Oliverira-Martins J., 1991.
4. We can thereafter find, especially during the 1980s, the same attraction of North China for Japanese firms and trading companies. This appears clearly in the regional distribution of Japanese direct investment in China and the share of Beijing, Tianjin, Darian and other Manchurian or North East cities or provinces.
5. It should be mentionned that the Japanese opening rate with the United States is characterized by a significant decrease at the end of the 40s, from around 4% to 3%. It remained thereafter at a stable level before falling again in the 80s to its historical lowest level since the beginning of the century. In the case of Europe, a downward trend dominated between 1914 and 1940, from 3.5% to 1.5%, but was inversed after 1945 with a steady progression until the 90's.
6. First cases of Japanese foreign investment in manufacturing during the 1910s, in textile industry in China and Korea
7. Shinohara, M., 1982.

REFERENCES

Fouquin, M., Dourille-Feer, E. and Olivera-Martins, J. (1991), *Pacifique: le recentrage asiatique*. Paris, CEPII-Economica, La Documentation Fran&caise.
Fujino, S. (1965), *Nihon no keikijunkan*. Tokyo, Shobosha.
Hori, K. (1995), *Chosen Kogyoka no Shiteki Bunseki*. Tokyo Yuhikaku.
Ito, T., and Kruger, A. O. (1993), *Trade and Protectionism*. University of Chicago Press.

Ito, T., and Kruger, A. O. (1994), *Macroeconomic Linkage; Savings, Exchange Rates, and Capital Flows*. University of Chicago Press.

Ito, T., and Kruger, A. O. (1995), *Growth Theories in Light of the East Asian Experience*, University of Chicago Press.

Ko, S. (1979), *Taiwan Sotokufu*. Tokyo, Kyoikusha.

Koishi, O. (ed) (1994), *Nihon Teikokushugishi*. 3 vol., Tokyo, Tokyo University Press.

Ohkawa, K., Shinohara, M., and Umemura M. (eds) (1965–1988), *Choki Keizai Tokei (Estimate of Long-Term Economic Statistics of Japan since 1868)*. 14 vol., Tokyo, Toyo Keizai.

Okichi, A., and Inoue, T. (eds) (1983), *Overseas Business Activities*. Tokyo, University of Tokyo Press.

Osada, H., and Hiratsuka, D. (eds), *Business Cycles in Asia*, Institute of Developing Economies Occasional Papers Serie, No. 26.

Murakami, Y., and Kosai, Y. (1986), *Japan in the Global Community*. Tokyo, University of Tokyo Press.

Nakamura, R. (1993), *Nihon Keizai, sono seicho to kozo*. Tokyo, University of Tokyo Press.

Sakudo, Y. (1979), *Sumitomo Zaibatsu Shi*. Tokyo, Kyoikusha.

Shinohara, M. (1982), *Industrial Growth, Trade, and Dynamic Patterns in the Japanese Economy*. Tokyo, University of Tokyo Press.

Shinohara, M., and Lo, F. C. (eds), *Global Ajustment and the Future of Asian-Pacific Economy*. Paper and Proceedings of the Conference, Tokyo, 11–13 May 1988, Institute of Developing Economies Symposium Proceedings No. 9.

Sugihara, K. (1996), *Asia kan boeki no keisei to kozo (Formation et structure du commerce extérieur entre pays d'Asie)*. Tokyo, Minerva Shobo.

Takamiya, S., and Thurtley, K. (1985), *Japan's Emerging Multinationals*. Tokyo, University of Tokyo Press.

Togai, Y., and Yasuoka, S. (1979), *Mitsui Zaibatsu Shi*. Tokyo, Kyoikusha.

Tokunaga, S. (ed). (1992), *Japan's Foreign Investment and Asian Economic Interdependence, Production, Trade and Financial System*. Tokyo, University of Tokyo Press.

Udagawa, M., (1982), *Showashi to Shinko Zaibatsu*. Tokyo, Kyoikusha.

Yamashita, S., (ed). (1991), *Transfer of Japanese Technology and Management to the ASEAN countries*. Tokyo, University of Tokyo Press.

Yamamoto, K., and Igusa, K. eds., *Industrial Structure and Human Resource Development in the Asia – Pacific Region*. Institute of Developing Economies, March 1995.

Yamashita, Shoichi (ed). (1991), *Transfer of Japanese Technology and Management in the ASEAN countries*. University of Tokyo Press, 1991.

Yamazawa, I. (ed). (1995), *New Development of APEC*. Tokyo, Institute of Developing Economies.

Yamazawa, I., and Yamamoto, Y. (1979), *Foreign Trade and Balance of Payments*. Tokyo, Toyo Keizai Shinposha.

Yonekawa, S., and Yoshihara, H. (eds) (1987), *Business History of General Trading Companies*. Tokyo, University of Tokyo Press.

APPENDIX

Table 3.1 Turning points of relative trade balance cycles and of a synthetic indicator in Japanese macroeconomic business cycles

	East Asia	Europe	North America	China	Korea	Taiwan	Hong Kong	South-east Asia	Total	Syn. Ind Japan
min		1878							1878	
max		1882	1878	1881					1882	1878
min		1884	1882	1884					1884	1884
max	1891	1886	1886	1885		1886			1886	1888
min	1894	1890	1890	1888		1890			1890	1892
max	1896	1899	1896	1894	1899	1895	1891		1895	1896
min	1898	1900	1898	1897			1894	1900	1898	1901
max	1902	1903	1906	1901	1907	1905	1901	1902	1906	1905
min	1904	1905	1908	1907	1910	1910	1905	1906	1908	1907
max	1911	1909	1914	1912	1913	1912		1911	1909	1910
min	1913	1911	1915	1918	1916	1915	1911	1913	1912	1914
max	1917	1917	1920	1922	1918		1917	1917	1917	1918
min	1924	1924	1924	1924	1924	1924	1923	1924	1924	1922
max	1926	1927	1925	1927	1927	1930	1924	1925		1926
min	1928	1929	1931		1932		1932	1928	1931	1930
max	1933	1936		1934	1935		1936	1933	1935	1933
min	1941	1937		1936			1938	1938	1937	1937
max			1939			1940		1942	1939	1941
min								1944?		1945
max	1951	1950	1951	1952	1950	1948	1950	1951	1955	1951
min	1955	1953	1955	1955	1955	1955	1953	1957	1957	1955
max	1961	1958	1960	1960	1962	1963	1960	1961	1961	1960
min	1964	1964	1964	1966	1963	1964	1967	1966	1967	1965
max	1969	1966	1969	1970	1971	1969	1969	1972	1971	1969
min	1974	1967	1974	1975	1973	1974	1973	1974	1974	1972
max	1978	1977	1978	1978	1980	1978	1978	1978	1978	1977
min	1980	1979	1980	1982	1982	1982	1982	1980	1980	1981
max	1983	1986	1986	1983	1984	1986	1984	1983	1986	1984
min	1985	1990	1987	1985	1985	1989	1987	1985	1990	1987
max	1993	1992	1990		1992	1991	1992	1993?		1990
min										1994?

4 The EU Antidumping Policy Towards Asia

Matthias Niyonzima[1]

Any Asian company wishing to do business with the European Union (EU) must take account of EU law in general and EU antidumping rules in particular, having regard to table 4.1 below.

On the basis of this table, the following remarks can be made:

(1) The activities of an AC in the EU may include all or parts of the below-mentioned four basic functions of a company (production, sales, purchasing and administration); whatever function is performed, within the EU, EU law may affect the business activities of the AC concerned.

(2) EU law is the meeting-point of all activities relating to AC business activities with the EU.

Table 4.1 The business activities of Asian companies (AC) in the EU and the EU antidumping rules

	AC Sales (Export) to EU	→ EU antidumping rules may be applied
AC Production In EU	EU Law	AC Purchases (Import) From EU
	AC Administration (Management, marketing, accountancy, ...) in EU	

(3) ACs which are most affected by the EU antidumping rules are those involved in exporting to the EU.

(4) Significantly, there is an overwhelming number of ACs affected by the EU antidumping rules and practices, which raises the following question: is EU antidumping policy specifically targeted at Asia? This article seeks to address this particular issue.

Firstly, the article will examine the general features of the EU antidumping rules. Secondly, it will evaluate the administrative and procedural aspects of EU antidumping regulations with special reference to Asia. Thirdly, it will give an overview of the position of Asia in relation to EU antidumping measures; and, finally, it will address the question as to whether the EU has a specific antidumping policy targeted at Asia.

1   GENERAL PRESENTATION OF THE EU ANTIDUMPING RULES

Generally, antidumping laws provide for certain remedies which are made available to industries of a certain country or region injured by alleged 'unfair' international trade practices.

Dumping, according to EU regulations, is the export of goods to the EU at prices below the exporter's home market price or below the cost of production. There are other instances of unfair trade practices, such as government subsidization of exports, but dumping is by far the most commonly alleged unfair trade practice under EU rules, especially as regards products originating from industrialized Asian countries.

As a signatory of the GATT/WTO agreements, the EU is required to ensure that its antidumping rules are compatible with the GATT/WTO agreements in this field, in particular Article V of those agreements[2].

By the end of June 1992, there were 546 antidumping measures in effect among the signatories to the former GATT Antidumping Code. Most of those measures had been taken by the four major users of antidumping: the USA, the European Union, Canada and Australia[3]. Among the main target countries, there were, also by June 1992, the following: Hong Kong, Japan, Singapore and the Nordic countries. Nowadays other countries like the People's Republic of China and other Asian and Eastern European countries have joined the group of the main target countries.

It has to be borne in mind that even when antidumping rules are similar or the same, major differences in the administration and enforcement of those rules exist between different jurisdictions, due to the sizeable amount of discretion which is left to the responsible administration.

1.1 The 1994 WTO Antidumping Code

Until the early 1980s, antidumping was not generally perceived as a major issue in international trade. It appeared, however, during discussions on the reform of the Tokyo Round Antidumping Code, that antidumping was one of the most contentious issues in the Uruguay Round of Multilateral Trade Negotiations[4], which led to the birth of the World Trade Organisation (WTO) in 1994.

The new Antidumping Code (the WTO Antidumping Code) did not modify the basic foundations of the Tokyo Round Antidumping Code. However, it meets, on the one hand, certain US and EU demands for the multilateralization of some of their unilateral interpretations of the Tokyo Round Code. On the other hand, the New WTO Code outlaws some of the practices denounced by the target countries by, *inter alia*, setting certain minimum procedural safeguards and accepting minimum transparency requirements.

According to the 1994 GATT Antidumping Agreement[5], 'dumping' is putting a product into circulation in a country (or a group of countries) other than the country of origin of the product, at a price which is less than its normal value. Dumping is prohibited only if this causes material injury to a certain sector of the business community or when it slows down the creation of a new business sector. Under certain conditions, the disadvantaged country or group of countries may impose antidumping duties.

With regard to the determination of dumping, the new code introduced some innovations. For instance, it does greater justice to the fair comparison requirement by attaching more importance to differences affecting price comparability, including, *inter alia*, 'differences in conditions and terms of sale, taxation, levels of trade, quantities, physical characteristics, and any other differences which are also demonstrated to affect price comparability'.

Concerning the determination of injury, the new code has added a new element to the list of relevant economic factors to be taken into account when assessing the impact of the dumped imports on the domestic industry: this new element is 'the magnitude of the margin of dumping'.

The WTO Antidumping Code only establishes basic rules on dumped products. It then falls to the States or groups of States to apply those rules, should they consider that the use of antidumping measures are necessary to protect one or more of their industries.

1.2 The EC Antidumping Regulation

The transposition of the new WTO antidumping rules into EU law was done first by Council Regulation (EC) No. 3283/94 on 22 December 1994. This

Regulation was replaced by a new one, namely the Council Regulation (EC) No 384/96 of 22 December 1995 'on the protection against dumped imports from countries not members of the European Community'[6].

Whilst most of this new basic anti-dumping regulation corresponds to the WTO Antidumping Agreement, additional provisions have been introduced in the EU rules, especially on matters on which the WTO Agreement is silent or imprecise. The most recent EU rules were introduced in order to maintain the balance of rights and obligations 'which the GATT Agreement establishes ... that the Community takes into account of how they are interpreted by the Community's major trading partners'[7].

The EU antidumping rules (like all antidumping instruments) are protective in nature but, to the extent that they conform to the WTO rules, they are consistent with international law. They lead to the imposition of antidumping duties on products originating from countries outside the EU, especially Asia and Eastern Europe, when those products are believed to have been dumped.

According to the now applicable EU rules (and in accordance with the WTO general rules), certain conditions must be fulfilled before antidumping measures may be legitimately imposed[8]: the product must have been dumped (i.e. if its EU export price is less than the normal value of the like product), an EU industry must have been materially injured and the imposition of an antidumping duty must be in the interest of the EU.

(a) Determination of Dumping

With regard to the determination of dumping, the EC Regulation reproduces the WTO Code, e.g. in relation to the comparison of weighted average normal value of a product to individual export prices. The normal value is normally based on the prices paid or payable, in the ordinary course of trade, by independent customers in the exporting country. The dumping margin is the amount by which the normal value exceeds the export price. When dumping margins vary, a weighted average dumping margin may be established (ARTICLE 2, D, 12 of the EC Regulation).

(b) Determination of Injury

According to the EC Regulation, the term 'injury' generally means 'material injury to the Community industry, threat of material injury to the Community industry or material retardation of the establishment of such an industry' (Article 3, 1 EC Regulation).

With regard to the determination of injury, the language of the EC Regulation is again similar to that of the WTO Code. However, in examining the impact of dumped imports on EU industry, the EC Regulation contains an innovation, which is not in the WTO Code: one of the factors to be considered is 'the fact that an industry is still in the process of recovering from the effects of past dumping or subsidisation' (Article 3, 5 of the EC Regulation).

(c) Administrative and Procedural Aspects

EU antidumping measures are subject to judicial review; this means that the party which feels disadvantaged by any such measure (even non-EU companies) may bring the case before the European Court of First Instance in Luxembourg. This Court reviews the compatibility of the antidumping measures imposed with EU law.

At the EU administrative level, antidumping proceedings involve interaction between three institutions: the Council of Ministers, the Commission and the Advisory Committee[9]. The Commission is, however, the most important actor in the enforcement of EU antidumping rules: it takes the decision on whether or not to initiate a proceeding, conducts the investigation and, after consulting the Advisory Committee, can terminate the proceeding without taking any protective measures; it can also impose provisional duties and accept undertakings. Moreover, the Council of Ministers can only adopt final measures following a Commission proposal.

At the judicial level, the EC Court of Justice played an important role in the past in reviewing Commission and Council measures. This role is now shared with the Court of First Instance. Indeed, the Council, by decision 93/350/ECSC, EEC, EURATOM of 8 June 1993, enlarged the jurisdiction of the Court of First Instance by giving it jurisdiction to hear and determine at first instance all actions brought by legal and natural persons in antidumping matters.

By another decision, 94/149/ECSC of 8 March 1994, the Council fixed the entry into force of the above-mentioned decision with regard to antidumping cases at 15 March 1994, specifying that all actions brought by any natural or legal person in antidumping cases after that date are to be lodged before the Court of First Instance. Furthermore, cases already pending at the Court of Justice for which no preparatory note had yet been drawn up were transferred to the Court of First Instance[10].

The following are some antidumping and antisubsidy cases involving Asian companies, which were pending before the European Court of Justice in 1994[11]:

Case   223/91 Ajinomoto Co. Inc. v. Council (T-159/94)
Case 61/92   Sinochem Heilongjiang v. Council (T-161/94)

Case 75/92	Gao Yao (Hong Kong) Hua Fa Industrial Co. Ltd v. Council (judgment rendered on 07.07.94)
Case 10/93	Koyo Seiko v. Council (T-165/94)
Case 263/93	Koyo Seiko v. council (T-166/94)
Case C477/93	Shanghai Bicycle Corporation Group v. Council (T-170/94)

N.B. The bracketed references are to the relevant Court of First Instance registration number[12] of the case concerned.

2   ASIA AND THE EU ANTIDUMPING PROVISIONS

2.1   General Overview

By December 1994, the EC Commission had 151 antidumping and antisubsidy measures in force. Of these 151 measures, 124 were original measures and 27 were maintained following a review in accordance with Article 15 of Council Regulation 2423/88 (the former basic regulation in antidumping matters) and now Articles 14 and 15 of Council Regulation (EC) No. 384136 of 22 December 1995.

Of all the measures in force by the end of 1994, most were imposed on companies from Asian countries, more particularly the People's Republic of China with 26 measures, Japan with 16, South Korea with 12, Turkey with 8 and Taiwan with 6[13].

2.2   General Statistical Overview

In Table 4.2 above, the figures under the second heading ('Investigations initiated during the period') will be detailed in the following Table 4.3 in order to show the application of the EU antidumping rules to Asian countries in particular.

Table 4.3 shows that Asia is by far the main region against which the EU antidumping provision, starting in 1990, has been applied.

Table 4.4 shows the sectors which are most affected by the EU antidumping measures. The most industrialized countries of Asia, such as Hong Kong and South Korea, are more affected by measures relating to high-technology products (especially in the electronics sector) while their less industrialized neighbours like India and Pakistan are more concerned with measures affecting textiles and allied products.

Table 4.2   Antidumping and antisubsidy investigations during the period
1 January 1990–31 December 1994

	1990	1991	1992	1993	1994
Investigations in progress at the beginning of the period	60	59	46	57	51
Investigations initiated during the period	43	20	39	21	43
Investigations in progress during the period	103	79	85	78	94
Investigations concluded by:					
– imposition of definitive duty	18	19	16	19	19
– acceptance of price undertakings	9	3	–	–	2
– determination of no dumping	–	1	1	1	5
– determination of no subsidization	–	–	–	–	–
– determination of no injury	13	6	4	1	1
– other reasons	4	4	7	6	2
Total investigations concluded during the period	44	33	28	27	29
Investigations in progress at the end of the period	59	46	57	51	65
Provisional duties imposed during the period	23	19	18	16	25

Source: The EC Commission

2.3   Discussion in the Light of some Concrete Cases

EU antidumping measures affecting Asia are diverse in form and intensity.
What follows is an account of one case involving the investigation process
(the beginning of antidumping proceedings) and another involving a case
where a duty was imposed (the end of antidumping proceedings).

*(a)   Investigation Relating to Cotton Cloth from the People's Republic of
China, India, Indonesia, Pakistan and Turkey (1994)*

The notice of initiation of an antidumping proceeding was published in the
EC Official Journal on 20 January 1994, following a complaint lodged by
the Committee of Cotton and Allied Textile Industries of the EU
(Eurocoton), allegedly acting on behalf of a large proportion of Community
production.

According to the Commission, the complaint contained evidence of
dumping following a comparison of export prices to the EU and a national

Table 4.3   Investigations initiated, by country of export, during the period
1 January 1990–31 December 1994

Country of origin	1990	1991	1992	1993	1994
Albania	1	–	–	–	–
Argentina	1	–	–	–	–
Belarus	–	–	1	–	1
Brazil	4	–	1	1	–
Bulgaria	–	–	–	1	–
China P.R.	4	4	8	4	5
Croatia	–	–	–	–	1
Czech Republic	–	1	–	–	2
Egypt	2	1	–	–	–
Georgia	–	–	1	1	–
Hong Kong	–	–	1	–	–
Hungary	–	1	–	–	–
India	4	–	–	–	4
Indonesia	1	–	–	–	4
Japan	3	5	–	1	2
Kazakhstan	–	–	1	–	1
Korea (South)	5	1	3	2	–
Lithuania	–	–	1	–	1
Malaysia	–	–	2	2	2
Mexico	–	–	–	–	1
Norway	1	–	–	–	–
Pakistan	–	–	–	–	3
Poland	–	2	1	1	1
Rumania	–	–	1	–	–
Russia	–	–	3	1	3
Singapore	–	–	3	–	–
Slovakia	–	–	–	–	2
South Africa	–	–	2	1	–
Taiwan	1	2	1	1	1
Thailand	2	–	1	2	5
Trinidad & Tobago	1	–	–	–	–
Tunisia	–	–	1	–	–
Turkey	7	1	2	1	2
Turkmenistan	–	–	1	–	–
Ukraine	–	–	2	1	1
USA	1	–	1	1	1
USSR	2	1	–	–	–
Uzbekistan	–	–	1	–	–
Yugoslavia	3	1	–	–	–
	43	20	39	21	43

Source: The EC Commission

Table 4.4 Investigations initiated by product sector during the period
1 January 1990–31 December 1994

Product	1990	1991	1992	1993	1994
Chemical and allied products	8	4	10	5	3
Textiles and allied products	14	–	–	1	17
Wood and paper	–	1	–	–	–
Electronics	1	5	13	7	3
Other mechanical engineering	6	4	–	2	4
Iron and steel (EEC & ECSC)	9	6	3	–	7
Other metals	3	–	5	5	3
Other	2	–	8	1	6
	43	20	39	21	43

Source: The EC Commission

normal value based on the estimated production costs in each exporting country plus a profit margin, except in the case of the People's Republic of China. Since the latter is still considered by the EC Commission as a non-market economy, the normal value was established on the basis of the national value for India, which was claimed to be the most appropriate analogous country with a market economy[14].

With regard to injury, it was claimed that the market share of the cotton fabric imported from the countries concerned had risen from 14.4% in 1989 to 19.3% in 1992, whilst consumption in the EU had dropped over the same period. Moreover, it was alleged that the low prices of the imports in question had continuously undercut the prices charged by EU producers by between 22% and 38%. As a consequence, the EU industry was allegedly forced to align its prices downwards to levels insufficient to cover costs. Furthermore, employment in the EU was alleged to have decreased by 22% since 1988. The case was not settled in 1994.

(b) Microdisks From Hong Kong and South Korea (1994)

On 12 March 1994, provisional anti-dumping duties were imposed on imports into the EU of 3.5" microdisks originating from Hong Kong and South Korea. The proceeding was initiated on 18 September 1992, following a complaint lodged by the Committee of European Diskette Manufacturers (DISKMA). This was the second complaint involving 3.5" microdisks lodged by DISKMA. The first, concerning imports from Japan, Taiwan and the People's Republic of China, had been initiated in July 1991, with the imposition of provisional duties in April 1993 and definitive duties in October 1993[15].

Dumping   In the above-mentioned microdisks case, dumping margins were decided as ranging from 6.7% to 22.2% for co-operating producers in Hong Kong, while the corresponding margin for the sole cooperating producer in South Korea was set at 8.2%.

The highest dumping margin alleged by the complainant, 35.7%, was considered appropriate for provisional determination for non-cooperating producers in Hong Kong. For non-cooperators in South Korea, the dumping margin established for the sole cooperator, 8.2%, was considered appropriate.

Injury   After examining all the elements affecting EU industry, the Commission concluded in the said microdisks case that the EU industry under consideration was suffering material injury – e.g. despite expanding consumption, the EU industry's prices in the sector concerned fell by around 30% between 1989 and mid-1992.

Community interest   After weighing the various interests involved, the Commission concluded that the adoption of measures would re-establish fair competition by eliminating the injury caused by dumping and give the EU industry an opportunity to maintain and develop its presence in a rapidly evolving sector of technological importance. In addition, the component supply industry would derive a degree of security from the continued viability of the EU industry concerned.

Measures   In the microdisks case under consideration, the EC Commission imposed provisional dumping duties. For Hong Kong, provisional duties ranged from 6.7% to 25.7%; for South Korea, the duty rate was 8.2%. At the final stage, the EC Council adjusted these duties only very slightly. For Hong Kong, duties ranged from 6.?% to 27.4%; for South Korea, the duty rate was 8.1%. The definitive measures were published in the EC Official Journal of 11 September 1994.

3   TARGETING ASIA OR NOT?

On the basis of the foregoing analysis, it appears strikingly that there is a considerable number of EU antidumping measures against Asian products. The question which comes to mind is the following: is Asia targeted by the EU? In order to answer this question, the author met with officials of the EC Commission and of some Asian Embassies in Brussels.

3.1   The Position of the EC Commission

According to the EC Commission, it does not target ASIA. The EU rules conform to the WTO rules and the objectivity of their implementation is guaranteed by EC courts. Moreover, the initiation of antidumping procedures usually follows a request by a particular EU industry or group of industries; the Commission does not act on its own initiative.

3.2   Asian Views

No Asian official could clearly establish that EU antidumping policy was specifically targeted at Asia. However, there is a general feeling among Asian officials that Asia is not always fairly treated, that the EC Commission could be arbitrary in applying the general rules and that the EU rules are an expression of too protectionist a policy, resulting from a fear of competition. This feeling of unfair treatment was clearly summed up as follows:

> While it cannot be said that antidumping suits are primarily targeted at East Asian NIC products, it can be deduced from an analysis of the European Commission's promulgations and from the established jurisprudence that from the viewpoint of their application, the antidumping regulations as they exist today are well tailored to reduce competition from NIC firms whose manufactures have acquired a competitive edge over similar products from European companies.[16]

Moreover, Asian officials consider that the antidumping procedure in the EU is less transparent than the US model. This lack of full transparency is allegedly supposed to facilitate arbitrariness. There are differences in   the views of the various Asian countries as shown by the chart in Fig. 4.1.

			– Special position – Non-WTO member
– Close to the position of JAPAN			– Not considered as a market economy in determining dumping margins
			– Wants to be recognised as a market economy
The Four Tigers (HONG KONG, S. KOREA, SINGAPORE and TAIWAN)		P.R. CHINA	
Others (India, Pakistan, ...)	common hostility to EU antidumping rules	JAPAN	– Complex position because of the strong penetration of the EU market
			– Supports the exporters' views within the WTO
– Position close to the one of ASEAN		ASEAN (Malaysia, The Phillippines, Singapore, Thailand, Vietnam, Brunei and Indonesia)	– Finds the EC Commission arbitrary in its antidumping attitude
			– common views within the WTO
			– feels the EC Commission's antidumping practices are not fair

Figure 4.1   The differing perspectives of Asian countries

(a)   Japan

The position of Japan is complex. On the one hand, Japanese companies based in Europe are also protected by the EU antidumping policy. On the other hand, Japan fears that its other companies may become victims of arbitrariness in the implementation of EU legislation. Japanese feelings about this issue were clearly summed in a recent Report:

> Given the European Union's past history of rampant abuse in this area, there are legitimate fears that abuse may continue in discretionary items even if practices as prescribed by the European Union implementing legislation do not violate the (WTO) Agreement. This is especially the case in the European Union because the authorities there have greater discretionary powers than they do in the United States and it is still too early to tell whether past administrative practices will really be corrected[17].

On the whole, Japan's views seem to be shared by the 'Four Tigers' (Hong Kong, South Korea, Singapore and Taiwan) and other Asian exporting nations within the ASEAN group[18].

(b)   People's Republic of China

According to Chinese officials, the EU policy does not target China but it is based on wrong ideas about China – for example, the assumption of the EC Commission that China is not a market economy, which allegedly allows the Commission 'arbitrarily' to determine the value of the dumped product by reference to a third country. This practice is considered by the Chinese as unfair. Another practice with which the Chinese Government is not happy is the alleged indiscriminate imposition of antidumping duties on all imports of a certain Chinese product, even if the said duties are fixed only in relation to one particular Chinese company[19].

4   CONCLUSION

Following the enquiry made for the purpose of the present article, it appeared to the author that as the EU antidumping rules express a general protective policy, they are not aimed specifically at Asia: the EU rules conform to WTO criteria; they are not discriminatory as to the national origin of the product.

EU antidumping measures are generally taken following complaints from EU private industries (or groups of industries) which feel disadvantaged by foreign competitors. The reason why there are so many antidumping measures against Asian products seems to lie in the fact that there are more complaints against Asian products than against products from any other region of the World. Those complaints flow from EU industries' feeling that without protective measures they will lose out to their Asian competitors. In fact, when the danger comes from elsewhere in the world (e.g. Eastern Europe or Latin America), they react similarly. This can be illustrated by a recent written question addressed by an Italian member of the European Parliament to the EC Commission, in relation to Moroccan oranges, claiming antidumping measures to protect Sicilian oranges[20]:

> Under the recent agreement between the European Union and Morocco, approved by the Foreign Ministers, Morocco's quota for exports of oranges to the European Union is set at 300,000 tonnes at an entry price of ECU 275 in place of previous ECU 369. The resulting fall in the price from approximately Lit 765,000 to approximately Lit 580,000 will inevitably facilitate the entry into EU countries of Moroccan oranges, which will aggravate the crisis in the Italian citrus-fruit sector – particularly in Sicily, where production and marketing costs are extremely high.

This example shows that the high number of EU antidumping measures against Asian companies expresses the fear of EU industries faced with Asian competition (because of the particular dynamism currently shown by Asian businesses) rather than official targeting of that specific area of the world. The possibility is not to be overlooked, however, that the EC Commission, using its discretionary powers like any administrative body, might act arbitrarily in applying the general rules to particular cases, whether those cases relate to Asia or not.

In other words, whilst the EU antidumping rules are not expressly targeted at a given region of the world, the systematic application of these rules to particular countries may possibly have such effects in practice.

Notes

1. The author thanks Mr Gilbert Nyatanyi, the late Mr Li Ma and most particularly Mr Jeroen Smets (all of Claes & Partners) for helping gather materials for this article; he also thanks Ms Ninette Dodoo from Studio Légale Pappacardo (Brussels) for her valuable comments.
2. The most recent GATT/WTO antidumping Code was adopted on 15.04.1994 in Marrakech (Morocco); see *The Results of the Uruguay Round of Multilateral Trade Negotiations; the Legal Texts*, GATT, Geneva, June, 1994; Koulen, M., 'The New Antidumping Code through its negotiating history' in Bourgeois, Berrod and Fournier (eds) (1995), *The Uruguay Round Results*, European Interuniversity Press Brussels.
3. There are also some non-traditional new users like Mexico.

4. Van Bael, I., 'The 1994 Anti-dumping Code and the New EC Anti-dumping Regulation' in Bourgeois, Berrod and Fournier (eds) (1995) *The Uruguay Round Results*, European Interuniversity Press, Brussels, p 233.
5. See the The new GATT Agreements, leading to the birth of the World Trade Organization (WTO), which were formally adopted in Marrakech (Morocco) on 15.04.1994.
6. *O.J.*, No L 56/1 of 06.03.1996.
7. See Paragraph (4) of the Preamble of the Regulation of 22.12.1995.
8. This means that it is not sufficient that a product has been placed at the market at a lower price; moreover, dumping is not always illegal according to EU law.
9. See Vermulst, E. (1987) *Antidumping Law and Practice in the United States and the European Communities*, North-Holland, Amsterdam, p 194.
10. See EU Commission, *13th Annual Report to Parliament – 1994*, p 49.
11. Source: the EU Commission.
12. Source: the EU Commission.
13. Another region which was much affected by EU antidumping measures in the area covered by the Central and Eastern European Countries (CEEC's) with a total of 15 measures.
14. See the EU Commission, *Report to the Parliament – 1994*, p 5.
15. See the EU Commission, *Report to the Parliament – 1994*, p 21.
16. Hizon, E. M., 'Antidumping and the European Policy vis-à-vis the East Asian NICs', *World Competition*, 1994, p 118.
17. 1995 Japanese *Report on the WTO Consistency of Trade Policies by Major Trading Partners*, p 102.
18. Those countries are: Malaysia, the Philippines, Singapore, Thailand, Vietnam, Brunei and Indonesia.
19. This practice applies generally and not only in relation to China.
20. Written question E-3463/95 by Mr Sebastiano Musumeci (NI) to the EC Commission (18.12.1995; 96/C 109/79), *O.J.*, No C 109/44 of 15.04.1996.

Part II:
The Position of China

5 China and India: Economics and Performance

Indru T. Advani

China and India are aptly described as the Asian giants. According to census figures of the early 1990s, around 40% of the population of the world resides in these two countries. China, according to combined United Nations and World Bank statistics, has a population of 1.23 billion as against 0.93 billion in India. In the coming century, the demographic trends of the two countries will have a major impact on the overall balance of power in the world.

China and India are both ancient lands, in the sense that over several millennia the present has merged with the past – unlike certain civilizations in the Middle East and the Americas, where the past is now relegated to museums or protected reserves. At times, both China and India have tended to disparage their history, as was the case during the Great Cultural Revolution in China. The pendulum has swung back again and China continues to draw inspiration from its past. Ever since the death of Confucius, 25 centuries earlier, his descendants continued to live in the family property in the city of Qu Fu in Shandong Province until 1949, when they emigrated to Taiwan. There is no parallel of such continuity elsewhere in the world. The property has now been converted to a tourist centre and the city of Qu Fu has once again become a centre of Confucian learning. With the liberalization of China, the family is now claiming its rights to the property.

At the time of independence, an element of Indian youth attributed, albeit momentarily, the 'other-worldliness' of the Hindu religion to India's backwardness. These wayward thoughts are over and Indians now take great pride in their history. In 1992, a major civil commotion occurred with loss of life in connection with the ancient temple at Ayodhya named for the God-King Ram, of untraceable antiquity. It turned out to be a political gimmick, and by their own admission it boomeranged on its perpetrators.

The language and the written script are in each case major factors linking these countries to their past. China has not in essence modified Chinese script, however unwieldy it may be – although China's two immediate neighbours, Vietnam and Korea, have partly romanized their writing. In India, Hindi, the *lingua franca*, uses the Devanagiri script as for Sanskrit, the mother of Hindi. Sanskrit is now in disuse (except for ritual purposes) but

Hindi is being progressively Sankritized: broadcasts on the All-India Radio are barely intelligible to a substantial tranche of the population. Both China and India freed themselves from foreign domination in the late 1940s. India won its freedom in 1947, and China was liberated in 1949. The words *freedom* and *liberation* are not a pure exercise in semantics. 'Freedom', in this case, implies the rollback of the foreign ruler, whereas 'liberation' signifies the success of the revolution coupled to the rejection of the foreign presence. Both countries in the late 1940s had a built in suspicion of free enterprise and free trade and this was understandable. The Qing dynasty rulers were hesitant to have contact with Westerners whom they termed as *da pitze* or long nosed people individuals or worse still the term *gui lou* meaning foreign devils. Until the present day, this epithet has not lost its significance. Diplomats came first, merchants followed and priests came thereafter. The foreigner used superior arms to declare war and to dump opium and thereafter to secure humiliating concessions from a declining dynasty. He imposed his will in India to produce opium for sending it to China. Pious churchgoing buccaneers, in the garb of free traders, heaped these indignities on the country. The 19th century's morality was (at least in form) different from that of the 20th century. During Mao's time China traded most selectively on the basis of political alignment. On the banking side there was an outright ban on contracting loans from foreign countries. Mao considered foreign banking institutions to be an instrument of imperialism and the unfortunate managers of foreign banks who did not leave in time were detained in China. This has changed since the liberalization of the economy and the Chinese have become wise to finance, with the government constantly in the process of stream-lining and integrating the economy to the world outside. In the near future the currency *yuan* may become fully convertible. India also wants to make the Rupee convertible.

In India, right from the early 15th century, trade was indistinguishable from conquest. The Dutch came first and they were chased by the Portuguese; The French and the British came thereafter and they warred with each other until one of them gained supremacy. The traders built their own fully-fledged armies to fight each other The East India Company, a British based joint stock company, was the winner and they put their army to good use to progressively overthrow the Mogul dynasty which was already on its last legs. There was such a strong link between trade and conquest that when the company's own army revolted in 1857, the territory under the company's control was taken over by the British Crown and was called thereafter British India.

India firmly believed that the common heritage of both China and India at the hands of colonial powers would be a catalyst in forging an alliance of the two Asian neighbours. With the Himalayas as an impregnable barrier, there was no history of conflict between the two nations. Pilgrims and traders through the ages had crossed the mountain passes, travelled on the Silk Road from Jaisalmeer in India to Beijing in China (and, even further, across the seas) to carry their wares and their thoughts. These exchanges had been peaceful and friendly. The Buddhist religion had left India more than two millennia earlier and had found an abode in the East, China included.

At the time of independence, there were some festering border disputes, but they were the heritage of the colonial past. With patience and understanding, these questions could be resolved. India, in the hope of closer ties with China, became the sponsor of the conference of non-aligned counties, much to the annoyance of the United States which during the Cold War era, considered this to be an unwelcome intrusion in geopolitics from an emerging nation. Suddenly, in 1962, Chinese troops rushed through the ill-defended north-eastern frontier of India, dispersed the defenders and reached the Gangetic plain in a lightning thrust. They left as suddenly as they came, leaving India in a state of shock. Foreign policy was Prime Minister Nehru's personal pastime and preserve. He treated this conflict as a personal failure. It possibly shortened his life.

What was the real reason behind this conflict? History alone will tell. Philosophically speaking, it was the impact of the yang upon yang. Co-habitation of yin and yang is the order of the cosmos – but the yang with yang can be a source of conflict. Over the last thirty years, relations between the two countries have been strained, and it is only since the early 1990s that faint signs of détente have been visible. A lesson had to be learnt. Foreign relations are not sentimentality: they are *Realpolitik*

1 THE INDIAN EXPERIMENT

The struggle for independence had at its helm the urbanized intelligentsia. It was essentially a non-violent movement, idealistic and on occasions not devoid of a certain sense of humour. The end was much more sanguine. The country was split in two, this division bringing in its wake ethnic cleansing on a mammoth scale. (The terminology employed in the 1940s was 'transfer of population'.) Two unlike and uneven twins, India and Pakistan, were born with a visceral dislike for each other. Nehru was in charge in India. On 14 August 1947, at midnight, India became free and Nehru declared lyrically, 'While the world sleeps, India awakes'. Salman Rushdie has teasingly called Indians 'midnight's children'. Nehru was born and raised in a prosperous family and he benefited from the most elitist education available, public schooling and blue-ribbon university. He chose dissent and spent sixteen years in British jails. A personality as complex as Hamlet emerged from the crucible.

The Indian intelligentsia of the thirties was greatly influenced by the Fabian Society and the London School of Economics. To them, unbridled capitalism and free trade was at the root of India's subjugation at the hand of foreigners. Even up to the present date, nearly half a century after independence, India's colonial past continues to influence Indian psyche. India after independence was desperately searching for a model to follow. Sydney Webb of the Fabians called for common ownership of production distribution and exchange. The Soviet Union seemed at least partly to be the answer. The command economy had permitted a giant thrust forward, side stepping several stages of development. An agrarian society well behind other countries in the Western world in a span of two decades had developed with major mother industries and had attained the status of a world power confronting and thereafter overcoming Germany. The violence that accompanied the movement was of course unpalatable to Indian intellectuals, but they lived in the pious hope that the command economy with an Indian face was the path to follow.

On the political front, India opted for parliamentary democracy. Questions were raised, albeit in muted terms, suggesting that the tandem development of parliamentary democracy and the command economy might not be the optimum recipe for high growth. Such inconvenient doubts were quickly brushed aside. The Indian constitution was drafted as a replica of the conventions and covenants of Westminster. India should normally have become the darling of the Western democracies, but this was not to be. India was asserting its independence and its preference for the command economy. To the West this was insubordination, and very deftly they resorted to a policy of establishing a balance of power with India's neighbours. Nehru a romantic, was no Machiavelli.

On the economic front, Nehru and thereafter his daughter Indira translated the prevalent Indian thought to action. This was done in three distinct steps. Nehru commissioned Professor Mahalanobis, a left wing professor at one of the Indian universities to prepare the blue print for the future of India's economic system. The initial step was India's first five-year plan, a relatively innocuous document calling for state control of a limited tranche of industries, mainly capital goods. The balance of the industrial apparatus remained in the hands of private sector.

The second step took place five years later at India's second five-year plan incorporated a much greater dose of 'command capitalism'. It was a hybrid of several thoughts; Fabian socialism alongside with the ideals propounded by

Gandhi and Tolstoi, 'How much land does a man require'; Spartan living, self reliance and a disdain for a consumer society, similar at least in thought to the romanticists in France in 1968. India would become a self sustaining nation with reduced nexus to the world. Consumer goods would be in short supply and imports in this area would be banned. The basically agrarian society would transform itself into an industrial state. As in the USSR, there would be a high premium on industries involved in capital goods. Indians with their spiritual antecedents could do with a minimum of consumer goods. There were of course contradictions in the system; people disdaining consumerism, the lotus eaters would devote their time and attention to capital goods – the metal eaters. With reduced consumer spending, savings if any would be channelled to the manufacture of capital goods. It was the blue print for India to become a hermit state, with high moral content Imports were allowed for a limited number of infrastructure projects or industries producing capital goods. The ban on imports was so effective that several industries were constantly starved of imported spare parts inhibiting their growth.

India nationalized several big industries and controls were introduced for the private sector. India came to be known as the permit raj. Private industries were given directives on their location, their production and even the prices. In other words, it was the anti-thesis of Adam Smith and there were not only losers but there were winners also. Private companies authorized to produce were free of competition and in time they became one of the most pampered tranche of society. They were the first to decry any attempts at liberalization of the economy thirty years later.

In the early seventies, Nehru's daughter Indira Gandhi had taken her father's mantle and she tightened the system by a few more notches. Even imports of capital goods for infrastructure projects were discouraged. Indian banks were nationalized and they were directed to support areas designated by the state. The result was a spate of bad loans. The 1970s became a period of economic stagnation

In 1991, India was in the throes an economic convulsion. The foreign exchange reserves were at their very lowest, the potential investors were avoiding any commitments and inflation was on the rise; it was an economist's nightmare. It was evident that the path chosen by India, which was an article of faith which few dared contradict, was progressively leading the country to bankruptcy. It was even feared that, a major economic crisis could trigger a political implosion with the encouragement of some neighbours unfriendly to India.

To ward off the imminent threat of a moratorium on payments, India applied for a standby loan from the International Monetary Fund. The IMF was willing to oblige but India would have to follow the IMF's classical cure.

State intervention had to be reduced, the market forces be allowed to play; India would have to open its frontiers to foreign investment, devalue the rupee and to increase the prime lending rate to reduce inflation. It was the scrapping of the permit raj. State functionaries entrenched in their privileges of power and patronage chaffed and were outraged.

Yet the results of the reform have been encouraging. Although the budget deficit is worrisome, with heavy debt servicing, there is greater investor confidence. Nevertheless, a major change has been blocked due to uncertainty in the political arena. This is despite the fact that there is practically a unanimity amongst a vast majority of political parties to avoid returning to Nehru's pattern of economics.

2   THE CHINESE SYNDROME

Marco Polo was fascinated by the advance of the Chinese compared to his own people. The wheel turned and the Chinese civilization, which at the time of the Tang dynasty was at its zenith, went gradually through its declining phase. While the West grew rich, China was torn by warring factions. After the fall of the Qing dynasty in 1911, China had a long period of instability: Yuan Shi Kai usurped power, the warlords asserted their authority, the Japanese invaded China, and finally China had a civil war of major proportions. The battle lines were well arrayed between the communists and the rightists. The battle was long and bitter. The communists won and China appeared to have exorcized its history. China after liberation was on the upward path. After the fall of the Berlin wall, in the eternal quest of yin to have its yang, China stands poised to assume the mantle of a super power facing the United States. Mao, at liberation, expressed his unqualified commitment to Marxism. Even, when mortally stricken in the mid-1970s, he would refer to his impending meeting with Marx. Despite Mao's personal antipathy to the Soviet leaders – Stalin and his successors – the Soviet model was adopted for nation-building. It had the advantage of being readily available. Mao went on to conduct experiments on a national scale to radicalize further the soviet model. The Great Leap Forward brought untold misery. The great Cultural Revolution which was its consequence resulted in a lost decade.

It was in 1978, two years after the fall of the gang of four, that Deng Xiao Ping, the pragmatist, announced 'The cat may be black or white, as long as it catches the mice'. He wanted the state economy, which had been held in the Stalinist strait-jacket with state ownership and import substitution, to be replaced by opening to the outside world. The results have been spectacular;

the real GNP has grown by 8 to 9% per year and South China is very nearly matching the performance of the 'tigers' South Korea, Taiwan, Thailand and Malaysia. According to statisticians, if the present tempo of growth can be maintained, which is not certain, the real overall Chinese GNP may exceed that of the USA in 2010.

Deng's reforms initially directed his attention reforms in farming by dismantling the commune system; this gave an increase in food supply of the order of 7% per annum. The enhanced agricultural output generated the savings for financing the industrialization of China.

One of the major elements that has spurred China's growth has been the proliferation of industries in the countryside, which are neither owned by the state nor by individuals. They are called 'Township and Village Enterprises' or TVEs. They are controlled by the local governments of the counties. These units are much more resilient as compared to the state behemoths and they serve as the conduit for conveying surplus earnings from agriculture to industry. They are in the present form a half way house between capitalist and Marxist society.

Another element of Deng Xiao Ping's reform is 'The Open Door Policy' The special economic zones in the Guangdong and Fujian Provinces served as locomotives for the Chinese nexus to the outside world. Having achieved their object, these economic zones are now being reappraised so as not to create excessive disparities in growth in China. The direct result of the reforms and the success of TVEs has been the diminishing impact of the state controlled units on the national economy. According to the evaluation of the Chinese Ministry of Finance and the World Bank, the Government revenues as a percentage of the GNP have steadily been going down. The figure was 35% in 1978 and it stood in 1991 at 19%.

Notwithstanding the set-back suffered during the Tian An Men incidents in 1989, Deng despite his advanced age, urged the government in 1992 to put the economy in a higher gear. China has since been going through a phase of expansion with the annual rate of growth exceeding 12% sending alarm bells ringing in Government circles. Measures had to be taken to cool the economy. The vast majority of the state-owned industries have a social function, by providing avenues of employment, in addition to being an instrument of production. The state-owned companies to a large extent ignored market forces and were responding to centralized planning. There is the well known adage about the three irons in China: 'the Iron rice bowl' for feeding the workers, the 'iron salary' for management and the workers, and the 'iron chair' of the party cadres. Pragmatists have decried these three irons and have confronted them with the new irons: 'the iron face', the 'iron hand' and the 'iron heart'. Pure economics is certainly not for the faint hearted.

A large number of state-owned enterprises need state subsidies and are a drain on the exchequer, fuelling inflation. The Chinese Government issued directives in August 1995 whereby 99,000 state – owned enterprises amongst 100,000 will be called upon to generate profits, failing which they may be called upon to cut down employment, to merge with other firms or be shut down. This reform could generate redundancies unto thirty million employees in the coming five years. About twenty million workers were planned to be put to premature retirement between 50 to 55 years. About ten million workers were destined to seek alternate employment. These are drastic measures, constituting a major departure from earlier practices. Since the issue of the directives, their application have been somewhat moderated. These drastic reforms could have a tendency to loosen the control of the Party over the industrial apparatus, triggering a social upheaval

3   PERFORMANCE OF THE GIANTS

After the momentous changes in the late 1940s, both China and India had in essence the policies of self-reliance through import substitution and planned economy. The Chinese government was in a position, thanks to its political system, to have minimal inequalities – there were about ten scales of employees – to provide employment and to generate revenue which was invested in industry for the manufacture of capital goods. China lived in isolation with the country was cut off from the fountain head of technology. Moreover the large Government factories were and even now continue to be over staffed and are inefficient. For nearly thirty years after liberation, growth in agriculture stagnated. After scrapping of the commune system, it moved ahead at the rate of 8 to 9% per annum.

In India, with the heavy handed intervention of the state in industry, growth stagnated from 1960 to 1980. A greater private initiative was possible in agriculture and thanks to the Indian Green Revolution, agriculture gave a better performance. From 1980 until 1991, the Indian economy, as a result of some timid attempts at liberalization there was some improvement, but from 1991, when India decided to liberalize the structures, a marked improvement is discernible.

Exhibits derived from the *McKinsey Quarterly*, Number 2 of 1995, give the comparative figures of growth for China and for India.

Both countries, at present, are progressively liberalizing their economies and are discarding the strait-jacket of the command economy. China started opening in 1978, whilst India opened in 1991. China has at its helm, engineers who are not encumbered by the party system of Government. The implementation of decisions is fast and in certain cases, China is the envy of some Western countries. On the score of commercial practices, China has yet to get used to the rough and tumble of competition. India possesses a superior macro control of the financial system. The Indian stock market has much longer traditions as compared to that of China. India has a legal system for settlement of disputes with longer traditions. At a seminar held in Hong Kong in the summer of 1995, the comparative merits of Chinese and Indian liberalization were discussed. Experts favourable to China advanced the argument that the Chinese reform has a better chance of success thanks to the

(a)
Growth in India and China

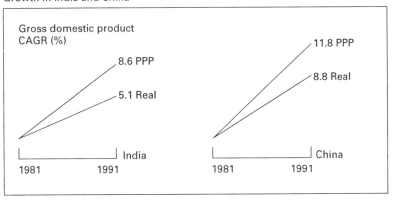

Gross domestic product
CAGR (%)

8.6 PPP

5.1 Real

India
1981   1991

11.8 PPP

8.8 Real

China
1981   1991

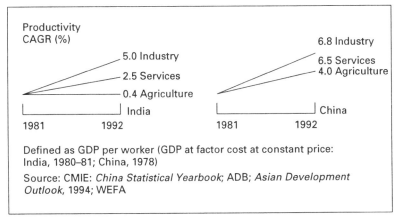

Productivity
CAGR (%)

5.0 Industry

2.5 Services

0.4 Agriculture

India
1981   1992

6.8 Industry

6.5 Services
4.0 Agriculture

China
1981   1992

Defined as GDP per worker (GDP at factor cost at constant price: India, 1980–81; China, 1978)

Source: CMIE: *China Statistical Yearbook*; ADB; *Asian Development Outlook*, 1994; WEFA

Figure 5.1

(b)
GDP growth differences, 1981–91

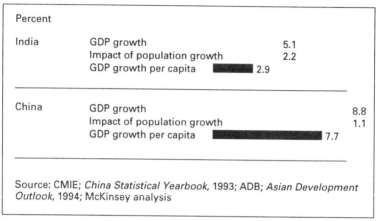

Percent

India   GDP growth   5.1
         Impact of population growth   2.2
         GDP growth per capita   ▰▰ 2.9

China   GDP growth   8.8
         Impact of population growth   1.1
         GDP growth per capita   ▰▰▰▰▰▰▰ 7.7

Source: CMIE; *China Statistical Yearbook*, 1993; ADB; *Asian Development Outlook*, 1994; McKinsey analysis

Figure 5.1 *continued*

existence of the TVEs. The implementation proceeds from bottom up, unlike the Indian liberalization which is top down and hence less effective. It was stated that the Indian legal system while theoretically protecting the investor is excruciatingly slow. It would take up to 325 years to clear up the pending cases.

India is conscious of the fact that further reform is necessary. Democracies are slow-acting: Athenian parliament was in debate while the enemy was at the city gates at Thermopyle. Under threat of economic dislocation in 1991 India was compelled to act. The benefits of economic reform will be blunted unless there is an adjustment of the political system – borrowed from Westminster – which in its integral form may be suited neither to the Indian psyche nor to its geography. Implementation of decisions, if and when taken is excruciatingly slow and too often is caught in a web of political shenanigans. Excessive political manoeuvre is a luxury which India can ill afford, when it is beset with demographic and ethnic issues of mammoth proportions.

India is a checkerboard of ethnic groups. If ethnic issues are not handled with care and compassion, the diversity which would normally enrich the body politic may degenerate into tribalism, particularly at times of economic distress. Differential treatment of ethnic groups incited by self-serving politicians for electoral ends, creates a cleavage in society. Economic crisis will continue to repeat itself unless India braces itself to effect a valid political reform.

4 INFRASTRUCTURE PROJECTS

Infrastructure services – electricity, telecommunications and transport – are the heartbeat of the nation, and in a developed economy they are taken for granted. Statisticians use them as the index of the country's well-being. The developing world and even some of the developed countries prefer to keep exclusive control of these services. Both China and India have therefore put a high premium on infrastructure projects, not only in terms of their construction and operation but also in terms of fostering industries for their construction.

The first incursion into this sacrosanct preserve of the state was in the Guangdong Province in China. This coastal zone situated next door to Hong Kong and Macao had development bursting at its seams. A Hong Kong developer operating in the Pearl Delta experienced severe difficulties in his projects owing to lack of electricity. A person who never took 'no' for an answer made a proposal to the Chinese Government to build and operate a major coal-fired power plant on a fast-track basis – within 30 months – a period considered to be unbelievably short. The *quid pro quo* was a high return on investment (exceeding 20% per annum) and a handsome bonus in case he completed the plant ahead of schedule. The developer succeeded: he collected his reward and became rich and famous.

This was the crack in the Chinese armour and the race is now on in Asia to complete projects on a 'Build-operate-transfer' (BOT) basis. The other side of the coin is the higher cost of production of electricity as compared to the conventional state projects. Furthermore, the capital, the operational fees and the profits have to be repatriated during the concessionary period. To some state officials it is tantamount to a steady haemorrhage of foreign exchange reserves. Although the Chinese authorities have signed several memoranda of understanding, there are afterthoughts. The Chinese want to impose a ceiling on return on investment: a figure of 15 to 16% has been suggested, which is considered to be inadequate by developers in view of the risks and effort involved. Furthermore, the Government insists on straight project financing, in the absence of any guarantees from the Chinese banks for repatriation of funds. These are possibly the maximal conditions proposed by the government and may be relaxed case by case. This has undoubtedly dampened, to some extent, the original enthusiasm.

India has been through a similar phase of development. It was initially believed that privatization would instantaneously and miraculously resolve India's chronic shortages in electricity, telecommunications and transport, but now a new wave of doubt has surfaced. India's difficulties are compounded by the fact that the utilities responsible for the production and distribution of electricity are suffering from a shortage of funds, stemming from the fact that electric power, in certain cases, is sold below cost to subsidize farmers, is stolen and at times is even used at no cost at the urging of politicians. The result is that the government-owned utilities are chronically short of capital for expansion.

Foreign investors have shown their willingness to invest in the production of power and be paid on the basis of generated power – but the distribution of power and the collection of dues from the consumer would continue to rest with the local utility. This could certainly give short-term relief for the availability of electric power, but if applied on a massive scale may lead to the steady depletion of state resources which have to make good the payment in the case of default by the utility. It is a 'no win' situation unless the utilities are fully empowered to secure the dues.

The aforesaid backdrop notwithstanding, several memoranda of understanding have been signed by state governments with private investors for the construction of power plants on a BOT basis. One major power station in the state of Maharashtra, which was approved and was under construction has run into a blazing controversy with allegations of a 'sweetheart deal'. The Department of Energy of the US Government tried to persuade the Indian authorities not to cancel the contract, but to no effect. In the meantime developers of other projects have unilaterally lowered their pretensions in the hope of salvaging their projects, giving credence to the contention that firmness pays.

In the field of telecommunications, India is planning to privatize developments and concessions for cellular telephones have already been granted. China on the other hand has no plan at present to go private in the telecommunication field.

5   CONCLUSIONS

What does the future hold for these two countries? Deng is old and infirm but he has put in place the structures to ensure a smooth succession. Over the last few years, he has held only the post of Honorary Chairman of the Chinese Bridge Association and he does not participate in the day-to-day running of China. Guessing what will happen in China is like divining the colour of a watermelon: either you have to be inside the melon or you have to wait until it is opened. The Chinese reform movement is in progress, with the Chinese economic accordion in play. The bellows open and close.

India is also in the mood for reform. Departure from reform seems improbable; the question is what will be the extent of the reform. Will it embrace the political reform, or will India follow the Athenian syndrome until the barbarians are at the gates?

India has embraced the democratic and pluralistic society; it has the sympathy of the Western democracies but certainly not their help. Unless India is economically strong, it is unlnerable to dangers inside and outside the country; it thus needs political firmness to give it greater economic strength.

REFERENCES

India: *The Economist*, 4 Nov., 1991 (Article by Clive Crook).
China: 'The Titan Stirs'. *The Economist* 28 Nov., 1992 (Article by Jim Rohwer).
'China and India: Asia's Non-Identical Twins'. The McKinsey Quarterly, 1995, Number 2.

6 China's Integration into the Regional Economy

Shaun Breslin

In July 1995, Li Boxi, a senior economic researcher for the State Council, announced her proposals for the development of China's Special Economic Zones (SEZs) (CNS 3/7/95). Amongst the proposals were the objectives of ensuring that the SEZs 'meet the needs of the international community' by keeping 'a close watch on structural adjustment in the international community and the international market' and an assertion that China should try to attract more investment from major transnational corporations (TNCs). Li's comments would not be out of place in Taiwan, South Korea, Singapore or in any number of the European regions competing for investment. Although it still sounds somewhat strange to hear the Chinese Communist Party (CCP) complaining that there are not enough TNCs in China, this approach to the international economy has been an important component of Chinese policy since the mid-1980s.

But when CCP leaders first spoke of expanding China's contacts with the international economy in the late 1970s, they did not talk in terms of integration (publicly, at least). On the contrary, the original opening to the West was designed to maintain China's sovereignty and independence from international economic forces by retaining strict control over foreign economic contacts. In identifying the causes and extent of this loss of sovereignty over international economic relations, this paper will focus on three key issues. The first relates to the imbalance between different types of foreign investment. The second concerns structural changes in the regional economy in the 1980s, and the pivotal role of Japanese investments in East Asia. The third concerns Chinese misunderstanding of the internal functioning of the Chinese party state during the reform process.

Economic reform in China has resulted in power flowing downwards from the central government to local authorities, and outwards to foreign economic actors. The combined result of these two challenges to central power is a situation where one of the key determinants of China's economic development is the interaction between the local and the international. This is not to say that the central government is irrelevant. On the contrary, the official move back to reform in 1992 and the 50% *de facto* devaluation of the

Renminbi in 1994[1] both had dramatic effects on the extent and type of foreign involvement in the Chinese economy. But it is clear that the local state is playing a much more active role in directly negotiating with foreign economic interests than at any other time since the establishment of the treaty ports in the nineteenth century, and this will continue to influence China's external economic policy and the trajectory of China's political economy *per se* for the foreseeable future.

1 PENETRATION, INTEGRATION, AND FOREIGN DIRECT INVESTMENT

The key to understanding China's growing economic linkages with her East Asian neighbours lies in an analysis of foreign direct investment (FDI) in China. FDI from country A to country B obviously creates an economic linkage between the two countries. However, FDI takes on an even greater importance in the Chinese case because of the significant contribution that foreign-funded enterprises have made to the growth in China's foreign trade. Indeed, the investment – export linkage is so strong in some parts of China that it now dominates the local economy.

1.1 Phases of Opening

There have been three overlapping phases in China's strategy for attracting FDI. The first was a process of expanding the geographical scope of areas that were open to foreign investors. The initial move was the establishment of the four Special Economic Zones in 1979. The relative success of this move led the central leadership to expand the open areas in 1984 after Deng Xiaoping's inspection tour to southern China gave the open policy the highest possible official seal of approval. Five cities were originally targeted as new centres of enhanced foreign investment and trade, but fierce lobbying from other local authorities resulted in the opening of fourteen coastal cities (Hamrin, 1990, p 83).

The growth rates in terms of foreign involvement in this early period were dramatic. Foreign capital inflow into China increased from around zero in 1979 to US$47 billion by 1984 (World Bank, 1990, p 63). This success in attracting much-needed foreign investments paved the way for the incremental extension of trade and investment rights to virtually the entire country by the end of the decade. Five or so years later, vast parts of China still remain relatively unaffected by foreign investment or trade. But although the geographic penetration of investment in China remains far from complete, foreign hesitation, rather than Chinese legal constraints, is the main consideration here.

The second stage accompanied the implementation of economic retrenchment in the autumn of 1988. During this period, the central leadership's enthusiasm for regional integration became somewhat muted in response to some of the 'negative' consequences of integration: the perceived foreign contribution to an overheated economy; the low quality and impact of foreign investment; and the growing quasi-autonomy of Guangdong and Fujian, the main recipients of foreign investment. In addition to the reinstitution of a number of central economic control mechanisms, the central authorities tried to encourage foreign investment to spread away from the 'Gold Coast'. A key element in this strategy was the opening of the Pudong development zone in 1990: partly to assuage the concerns of the Shanghai leadership[2]; partly to focus investment in a location that the central authorities thought they had more influence over; and partly to emphasize quality and technological upgrading by promoting capital-intensive higher quality investments.

The third phase, which started with Deng Xiaoping's momentous tour to southern China in 1992 (but in formal legal terms can be dated from 1994), has seen the rapid extension of investment opportunities into new economic sectors. The traditional focus on industrial developments remains the main source of investment, but developing the infrastructure through foreign investments is now one of the main and most visible targets for central and local government investment.

1.2 Types of Foreign Investment

Despite opening virtually every geographic region and economic sector to foreigners, the majority of FDI remains concentrated on the coast and in light industrial projects. Indeed, attracting more foreign capital into the interior and for infrastructure projects are two of the pillars of the Ninth Five-Year Plan. However, the success of these initiatives depends to a large extent on changing the structure and type of FDI in China.

At the risk of over-generalization, we can identify three (perhaps really two and a half) broad groups of foreign participation in the Chinese economic 'miracle': that investment, primarily originating in the West, which is mainly aimed at developing a presence in the domestic Chinese market; investment, primarily from East Asia, which uses China as a base to re-export to Western markets; and investment and other capital sources originating in Japan.

1.2.1 Market-based Investment

The majority of Western investments are concentrated in large projects in China's major cities or traditional industrial centres, which **primarily** aim to access domestic Chinese markets. These projects are likely to be joint ventures (JV) which bring new technologies and new skills into the Chinese economy. They also draw on Chinese raw materials and suppliers, and are increasingly forging forward and backward linkages through the Chinese economy. The creation of new foreign-funded industries in some ways replicates the classic import-substitution stage of the capitalist developmental state model – although in the Chinese case, there were few imports to substitute in the first place, particularly when it came to the consumer goods that the CCP has encouraged the Chinese people to aspire to own.

The quality of these investments is relatively high, and they also have collateral benefits in terms of developing service industries, training Chinese managers and workers, and so on. However, these market-based investments are dwarfed by export-based investments, largely from the rest of East Asia, which have played the leading role in integrating China into the regional economy.

1.2.2 Export-based Investment

The majority of foreign investment in China comes from the surrounding East Asian region. Whilst some of this investment is clearly intended to access domestic Chinese markets[3], the **primary** focus of this investment has been to use China as a production base to produce exports for the Asian, European and – most important – North American markets.

In theory, this type of investment should bring four major benefits for the Chinese. First, it earns foreign currency (which remains relatively scarce in China) through increased access to foreign markets. Second, it creates employment. Around seven and a half million Chinese were employed in JVs in 1993 (Lian Zhong Xu, 1994), and although this is only five per cent of China's total industrial workforce, the concentration of investment in the southeast means that JVs are major employers in Guangdong and Fujian. Third, it generates increased tax revenues for local and national coffers[4]. Finally, it should facilitate the upgrading of the domestic Chinese economy through technology transfers, increased and new labour skills, the development of new managerial skills required in a market economy and so on. It should also have a wide footprint on the local economy as local upstream and downstream industries and services are created in the wake of the original investment.

In broad terms, the Chinese experiment has been much more successful in attaining the first three of these benefits than the last. The export led foreign investment sector has not created the collateral development that was originally envisaged, not least because of the poor quality and unreliability of many Chinese components[5]. Hong Kong and Taiwanese investments tend simply to produce in China, and that is that. Even the technology that they bring with them is typically low-tech second-hand equipment that is no longer profitable (or too polluting) in Taiwan (Qi and Howe, 1995, p 101). In the case of Hong Kong investments, management functions can easily be carried out in and from Hong Kong. The now well-developed infrastructural links mean that raw materials can be easily moved in, and the finished products moved out, for re-export at ease, so that only the more mundane tasks are left to mainland staff.

As Qi and Howe (1995) have demonstrated, this situation is even more extreme with investment from Taiwan. Management, raw materials, components suppliers, financial service organizations and transport facilities are brought *en masse* from Taiwan. Even major chemicals multinationals such as Bayer and Du Pont have been moving across the Taiwan Straits to follow their major customers. Indeed, such is the isolation of these Taiwanese investments from their host economies that the trend is now to create special Taiwanese Development Zones, Singapore Development Zones and so on within investment, or Special Economic Technological Development zones – zones within zones. With the overwhelming majority of this investment going to Fujian and Guangdong, Taiwanese and Hong Kong FDI has had a remarkably small impact on China as a whole. For Bernard and Ravenhill (1995), this insulation of the foreign investment sector from the host economy is a characteristic of the East Asian integration/development process. For example, they suggest that 'foreign subsidiaries in Malaysia's export processing zones were more integrated with Singapore's free-trade industrial sector than with the "local" industry'. Qi and Howe's analysis of Taiwanese investment in Xiamen certainly seems to confirm this point, and Hong Kong investments in the Pearl River Delta have long since conformed to this principle.

Some technological advances, including managerial and labour skills, will trickle down to the local economy. There are more tangible benefits in terms of rent income, service charges, taxes on profits and so on. There is also the provision of employment to consider, which is at the top of the CCP's list of concerns at present, and from the multiplier affect, the knock-on impact on the local economy. Nevertheless, the extent of this type of investment, and more important, the acceleration of this type of FDI since 1992, may have significant long-term implications for China's development strategy.

1.3 The Role of Japan

Although FDI flows give some indication of the relative importance of various nations in China's external economic relations, they do not tell the full story. In particular, they under-represent Japan's role in the growth of China's external economic contacts. Indeed, Japan's role has been so influential that it should really be considered as a separate and special case. There are three key factors here: Japan's trade relations with China; Japan as a loan provider; and Japan as an indirect export-based investor.

1.3.1 Japan as a Trade Partner

Japan's importance as a trade partner for China should not be under-estimated. While Japan has long been the single most important partner for China, it is notable that China is becoming increasingly important for Japan as well[6]. Again, the trend has rapidly accelerated in the last three years. Bilateral trade increased by 30% in 1993 over 92, and then by a further 22% in 1994 to reach US$46.24 billion, with an US$8.8 billion surplus on the Chinese side. These figures mean that China has risen from Japan's fifth to second biggest trade partner in the space of three years (JEN 24/1/94, and Drifte, 1996). In 1993, China became Japan's second largest destination for exports, increasing by 45% over 1992.

This astonishing rise in Japanese exports has to be considered in light of the continuing rise of China as a product assembly site. Japan has been very successful in tying its foreign subsidiaries (and even independent producers) into a system of dependency on Japanese components and technology. As Japan develops new subsidiaries in China and existing subsidiaries in the rest of Asia move their operations to China, so the market for Japanese components also moves to China. Thus Japan is not only a major market for Chinese exports, but much of China's exports to other markets is also indirectly dependent on the importance of Japan as a trade partner.

1.3.2 Japan as a Loan Provider

Japan's role as China's leading trade partner is reinforced by its position as a major provider of foreign capital for the Chinese. China is the single biggest recipient of Japanese overseas development aid. Furthermore, China benefits from particularly favourable conditions in terms of interest rates and repayment schedules, as well as being the only country that receives multi-year aid rather than support for specific projects. From 1979 to 1994, China borrowed a total of $1.6 trillion in low-interest loans, and the latest package for 1996 to 1998 is for a further $580 billion ($5.8 billion). However, it is notable that this latest arrangement was not for the five years that the Chinese requested, and all the available signs suggest that the Japanese foreign ministry is keen to end multiyear aid to China as soon as possible.

Japan's role as a major external funder of Chinese development appears to be entering a new phase, with the Japanese becoming slowly and gradually more internalized within the Chinese economy. Two specific changes warrant attention here, both of which have only recently become possible thanks to changes in Chinese investment and financial laws. The first is the growing presence of leading Japanese financial institutions in China. The Bank of Tokyo formally opened its offices in August 1995, ironically, almost 50 years to the day since another type of Japanese presence in China came to an end. Furthermore, of the fourteen foreign banks that have now had their applications to open in China approved by the government, ten are independent Japanese banks.

The second major change was Isuzu Motors' and Itochu's joint purchase of a 25% stake in Beijing Light Bus Corporation. The Japanese side will provide components and technology (and access to Japanese R&D), and also want to put a Japanese general manager in place (CNS 16/8/95). Such buying into Chinese companies, particularly in the motor industry, provides the Chinese with many of the benefits that they have always wanted from foreign investment. It also gives the Japanese investors longer-term security and control than the original joint-venture format.

Chinese dependence on Japanese capital is further reinforced by the relative position of the two countries in international banking organizations. China is the main recipient of Asian Development Bank loans, which Japan now clearly dominates. China is also now the World Bank's biggest borrower, and the World Bank is the largest source of foreign capital in China, having lent a total of US$22 billion so far (and committed themselves to another US$9 billion over the next three years). Whilst America probably remains the dominant force in the World Bank, and even tried to cut off cheap loans to China in March 1995, Japan's presence is now (officially at least) on a par with America. The internal politics of the World Bank may actually aid China in the short run, as the extent of Japan's interaction with the Chinese economy means that it is in Japan's own interests to maintain the level of funding to China.

In comparison with other nations at similar stages of development, the level of Chinese dependence on external loans to fund the modernization drive remains relatively low. China's total foreign debt at the end of 1994 was US$92.806 billion. This gives China a debt service ratio of 9.12%, which is comfortably short of the 20% figure that is often taken as a warning bell by international economists (CNS 20/7/95). Furthermore, the proportion of short-term debt is eleven per cent, which is also comfortable[7]. Nevertheless, there is some concern here, as those responsible for the debts are not always the same people who are making the profits in China. Government revenue as a proportion of GNP fell from over a third in 1979 to just over a tenth in 1994. Furthermore, the massive decentralization of power in post-Mao China, both deliberate and unintentional, led to the central government's share of this revenue declining from 60 to 40%. Indeed, it is not stretching the point too far to say that there is local control over profits and central responsibility for losses.

The fiscal reforms of 1994 may redress the imbalance to some extent, but central coffers remain heavily stretched by the desire to maintain employment (particularly in the ailing state sector) and purchasing power in urban China as a means of 'buying' social and political stability. Increased military spending adds another burden on central finances, and an additional long-term problem lies in China's projected need to become a major food importer in the next century and all the implications that has for foreign currency earnings. Thus, while there is no immediate problem, there is some justification for those who are concerned that China's development is more dependent on Japanese funds than they would like – and the extent of this dependency becomes even more striking when considered in light of China's growing trade dependency.

1.3.4   Japan as an Asian Investor

A considerable amount of Japan's large-scale investment conforms to the market-based model of FDI. But Japan is also a major export-based type investor in China. On one level, we can see that Japanese companies are moving their overseas operations out of the increasingly expensive Taiwanese and Korean economies and into China and the ASEAN nations. The structure of Japanese FDI in China is thus taking on a more export-based agenda. More important for the wider question of regional economic integration are Japan's indirect economic relations with China. These indirect contacts can be further divided into two main categories.

The first is a relatively hands-on approach, where Japanese companies establish or ally with companies in third countries with the specific intent of dealing with the Chinese. The strength of Japanese investment in Hong Kong in recent years is the most obvious example here.

The second type of indirect contact is where the Japanese involvement is almost passive in nature, and the original Japanese interest is far removed from the final investment decisions. The transfer of production to lower-cost locations has been an important determinant of economic growth in the East

Asian regional economy for many years. Within this regional development process, both the Taiwanese and South Korean states have consciously and deliberately adopted strategies designed to attract foreign investment and production. But the timing of these development strategies was heavily influenced by the position of their development trajectories relative to that of Japan[8]. Indeed, for proponents of (variations of) product cycle and 'flying geese' models of development, economic linkages between the Japanese, South Korean and Taiwanese economies are so strong that:

> it is misleading to assess the industrialization pattern in any one of these countries: such an approach misses, through a fallacy of disaggregation, the fundamental unity and integrity of the regional effort in this century. (Cummings, 1987 p 46)

Bernard and Ravenhill (1995) note that when Japanese companies started to invest in East Asia, they did not simply move the entire production process to the new low-cost production sites (as British companies did when the textile industry was introduced to Japan). Instead, they retained firm control over key high-tech components. Perhaps more importantly, even if the recipient companies learn how to copy these high-tech inputs, the speed and quality of research and development in Japan means that the product cycle has been shortened, and technology rapidly gets out of date. What this means is that the Koreans and Taiwanese companies can easily trade in intermediate markets in slightly dated technological production, but remain dependent on Japanese technology, R&D, and brand names if they want to participate in the most important markets with the most up-to-date equipment.

For example, Bernard and Ravenhill (1995) note that while Taiwanese producers account for over a third of the global production of computer monitors, they are in a position of 'structural dependence on Japanese technology' for the cathode ray tubes which constitute around a third of the total production costs. Thus, the Japanese 'parent' company does not have to take a hands-on approach to investment and trade decisions, but Japanese interests will nevertheless be considered by the technology-dependent Taiwanese producers.

This analysis of East Asian economic integration provides crucial insights into Japan's pivotal role in China's regional economic integration. In the latter part of the 1980s, and particularly since 1992, the newly industrialized economies have transferred some productive capacity to even lower-cost production sites, including China. What this means is that the extent of Japan's Asian-style investment in China is hidden by the fact that it does not appear at first sight to have anything to do with Japan. In the case of that Taiwanese investment indirectly carried out through Hong Kong, it does not even appear to have any Japanese impact at second or third sight. Indeed, the investment decisions may well be taken entirely by the Taiwanese board without guidance from Japan. But we should not ignore the fact that through the structural linkages between these companies and their Japanese 'parents' Japan is indirectly a major cause of the growth of Asian investment into China.

2   THE EXTENT OF FOREIGN INVOLVEMENT

While there was an initial gold rush to China by Western companies in 1984, the majority of subsequent FDI into China has come from East Asia. According to a *Wall Street Journal* report of 10 December 1993, the West provided only around a third of the investment between 1985 and 92.

An enormous proportion of investment into China is, at some stage of the process or another, Chinese in origin. Perhaps as much as 80% of FDI comes from Hong Kong, Taiwan, Singapore, the Chinese diaspora, particularly in Malaysia, and overseas Chinese in North America. What is more, this dominance in Asian investment occurred whilst some significant political obstacles to trade remained in place. Although China's diplomatic normalization with South Korea followed the establishment of economic links, particularly through Liaoning Province, the lack of formal political relations remained an important obstacle to bilateral economic relations. Furthermore, Taiwanese government restrictions on contacts with the mainland did not exactly facilitate investment and trade flows. Of course, there are always ways and means of avoiding obstacles, and in China's case this has primarily resulted in indirect investment and trade through

Table 6.1

Country	US$ million	Country	US$ million
Hong Kong (and Macao)	21,367	Singapore	400
Japan	3,729	UK	293
USA	2,797	France	220
Taiwan	1,749	Italy	216
Germany	505	Canada	125

subsidiaries in Hong Kong. For example, Ash and Kueh (1995, p 66) calculate that in 1992 49% of shipments from Taiwan to Hong Kong ended up in the PRC. Conversely, 29.5% of PRC exports to Hong Kong eventually found their way to Taiwan.

China's recent history of external economic contacts reached something of a watershed in 1992. There had been a considerable slow-down in FDI in 1989. This was not so much a consequence of international condemnation of China's human rights policy and the Tiananmen Incident, but more a reflection of worrying *economic* signals from China and structural changes in the regional economy. In particular, the recession and the banking crisis in Japan hit hard in 1989, resulting in significant reductions in Japanese investments across the globe and a dip in confidence from major Asian investors.

Internally, the summer of 1988 had been marked by worrying shortages of raw material supplies, particularly energy. Coal for electricity generating, already in short supply, became steadily scarcer and scarcer on the coast as the year progressed. For example, in Jiangsu, the supply of coal for electricity generating was only 90.5% of demand in the first half of 1988, falling to 86.41% and 75.18% in July and August respectively. As a result, major power stations were forced to stop operating, and the provincial supply of electricity was cut by a third. The net result was that by the autumn of 1988, Jiangsu's electricity-generating capacity was only the same as in 1982 (RMRB, 21/8/88).

Ironically, foreign investors were almost as concerned by the solutions to the problems as they were by the problems themselves. The turning point was not so much the spring of 1989 as the autumn of 1988, when Li Peng defeated Zhao Ziyang in a struggle over how to deal with a rapidly overheating economy. Zhao's proposed further round of price reform (which many foreign investors desired) was postponed indefinitely and replaced by an ultimately futile attempt to recentralize economic control and strengthen planning mechanisms.

This is not to say that political issues are irrelevant. Political stability remains a crucial determinant of China's re-entry into the regional economy. Investors in the early 1980s feared that China might revert to its old Maoist past and so destroy the nascent market and ruin their investments. From the viewpoint of 1995, we can state with utmost confidence that this is no longer a concern. But the extent to which China opens up different economic sectors, the transparency of the Chinese decision-making machinery, and the potential for social instability obviously remain crucial determinants of China's attractiveness to potential foreign investors. In particular, there remains distinct unease in Hong Kong over the colony's future, notwithstanding the *de facto* integration of the Hong Kong and southern Guangdong economies. China may no longer be the political risk that it was, but why take any risk at all if one of the many other governments in the region can assure stability and comparable returns on investments?

In 1992, all the political signals pointed towards a return to reform and a further extension of privileges and open sectors for foreign investors. In particular, Deng Xiaoping's inspection tour to the South was taken as a firm endorsement of the open policy, and is destined to be remembered as the point when China crossed the rubicon from Li Peng/Chen Yun ascendancy to an unstoppable reform momentum. Total FDI in 1992 was double that of the 1991, but even this increase was dwarfed by what happened in 1993. According to the Minister of Foreign Trade, Wu Yi, the amount of contracted foreign investment in 1993 was roughly the same as for the entire previous fourteen years. There were 83,265 new foreign investments in 1993 (up by 70.7%) and the amount invested increased 134% to US$25.76 billion (JEN 28/1/94). By the end of 1993, FDI accounted for 12.3% of all investment in China, up from 7.7% in 1992 (and less than one per cent a decade earlier).

It would obviously have been difficult to maintain this type of increase year on year, and the growth in investment has unsurprisingly fallen back slightly over the last couple of years. The slowdown in foreign investments first emerged in April 1994, largely due to fears of inflation and credit tightening and uncertainty over the implications of the new taxation system introduced in 1994 (although the murder of 24 Taiwanese tourists on Lake Qiandao also caused a loss of confidence, and the re-imposition of trade restraints in Taibei). Furthermore, the big boom in 1993 had in large part been caused by massive real estate deals, which had accounted for 38% of total investment in 1993, and up to 50% in some areas (CND 14/6/94). The imposition of a 60% tax on profits gained from property development and transfer in 1994 did much to dampen this type of investment (SCMP 30/3/94) and helps explain why foreign investment fell by around 50% in the first quarter of 1994. In addition, the Chinese argued that investment in 1994 was often literally building on the boom of the previous year, and the quantity of investment in 93 was giving way to quality investment in 1994.

According to the Far Eastern Economic Review (12/10/95), China's major trading partners in 1994 had all invested more in that year than in the entire 1985–92 period:

Bearing in mind the indirect nature of trade and investment patterns in East Asia, it is perhaps worth nothing that Japan remains the biggest investor in China's other major Asian investors: Hong Kong ($1, 788 million), Taiwan ($391 million), Singapore ($9.59 million) and South Korea ($429 million).

It is also noteworthy that the structure of foreign investments has also changed markedly in the recent era. Whilst joint ventures are still the dominant form of foreign investment, internal changes in China[9] have

Table 6.2

Country	US$ million	Country	US$ million
Hong Kong (and Macao)	48,700	Britain	2,700
USA	6,000	South Korea	1,800
Taiwan	5,400	Germany	1,200
Japan	4,400	Canada	890
Singapore	3,800	France	250

Table 6.3

1986	4.2	1990	306.4
1987	100	1991	727.6
1988	102.1	1992	3,340
1989	351.1	1993	6,481

facilitated a dramatic growth in the wholly foreign-owned enterprise sector, from a negligible amount in 1986 to over a quarter of all direct foreign investment in 1993 (calculated in terms of utilized capital investments). Investment in wholly foreign-owned enterprises more than doubled in 1993, and taking 1987 as the base year, this type of investment has increased as follows:

Notwithstanding the downturn in investment in 1994, China is now in a position where foreign investment is even more dominated by export-based investment than before. In addition to the growth in Taiwanese investments (direct and indirect) I suggest that a growing number of Korean[10] and Japanese[11] new investments are also conforming to this generalized pattern. So why has China's investment become dominated by this Asian style of investment, and what are the implications for China's political economy?

3 EXPLAINING THE PATTERN OF INVESTMENT

3.1 Obstacles to Market-based Investment

While it is true that some Western investors jumped at the chance of getting into China in the early 1980s, many of them were somewhat disappointed.

Official Chinese policy was simply not conducive to market-based investment, and the lack of convertibility of the Renminbi was a particularly crucial problem here. What was the point of making profits in China if you could not convert the profits into yen, dollars or marks, and take it home?

Another very basic problem here is that even now (1995), the purchasing power of most Chinese is still too low. 75–80% of Chinese still live in rural areas and have an average income of RMB1,000 (roughly US$121) a year (Reuters, 21/9/95). Although this still leaves an urban population of 300 million, the urban markets are too dispersed and diverse and incomes still relatively low to be easily penetrated. China is not one market, but a number of markets. It is extremely difficult – if not impossible – to access urban markets in Chengdu, Guangzhou and Changchun from one location, and potential foreign investors must disaggregate China and decide which Chinese market they are aiming at before getting involved. The lack of development of the Chinese infrastructure is an important consideration here. Foreign producers are often unable to get hold of the raw materials and energy that they are promised; others find that the available raw materials are simply unusable. For example, coal remains the primary source of energy in China, yet some 80% of coal is unwashed, making it unsuitable for some production techniques (and highly polluting), which means that high-quality coal has to be imported from Australia.

In addition to these hard infrastructural constraints on investing in China, there have also been many problems in dealing with the mire of the Chinese bureaucracy. It is bad enough dealing with the rules and regulations, but it is even worse when no regulations exist. The Chinese bureaucracy remains dominated by a culture of personal relations and *ad hoc* (and frequently illegal) negotiations. Whilst new laws can be introduced overnight, old cultures and habits cannot be eradicated as quickly, and even when transparency has been formally increased, informal constraints and mechanisms often remain firmly in place[12].

A number of studies have expanded on these hard and soft constraints on dealing with China in some detail, and it is not my intention to repeat them here[13]. Suffice it to say that although there are profits to be made from China, an Andersen Consulting and *Economist* Intelligence Unit survey found that there is a long way to go before profit margins reach those in developed markets. Perhaps the most sensible strategy for Western investors is to let others create and then overcome the problems for the time being, and then invest once the main problems have been smoothed over. Another alternative that many American-based TNCs are now adopting is to leave their Chinese operations entirely for their Taiwanese subsidiaries to manage (Goldstein, 1992). So although the hand of multinationals may not appear to be particularly strong in China at present, their influence is often masked by indirect action through Taiwan, which is in itself often indirectly routed through Hong Kong.

There are, however, two other points relating to Western investment in China that are worth noting. First, after giving China a certain amount of leeway for many years, there is an increasing militancy in some companies opposed to the discrimination that they face from Chinese officialdom. For example, the extent of hostility to the proposed higher VAT rate for foreign firms ultimately led to the plans being shelved. And although the 1994 devaluation helped exporters, it created a *de facto* 50% price rise for services for Western companies in China. Over 1,000 foreign companies formally lodged complaints, and half of those refused to pay (DJ, 5/2/94). The biggest disinvestment in China to date came with Occidental's withdrawal from a joint-venture colliery in Shanxi Province. Occidental had been increasingly frustrated by the late arrival and non-arrival of trucks to transport the coal, and the disappearance of a number of full trucks in transit. They were also none too impressed by the local authorities' insistence that Occidental should tolerate the illegal coal mines that had sprung up mining their coal as a service to the local host economy. Although this type of actual disinvestment remains scarce, we will never know how much extra investment was foregone (or went elsewhere) as a result of these problems.

This brings us to the second and very much related point. Many of the problems that the Western investors face stem from local authorities, which frequently levy illegal fees, charges for services, and local taxes. Most, if not all, pay up, because they recognize that it is impossible to get hold of most things of importance – particularly energy, transport facilities, and credit – if you cross the local power holders. Managerial responsibility reforms notwithstanding, state control remains a crucial component in the Chinese economy. But as we shall see below, economic reform in post-Mao China has resulted in a situation where the local state is an increasingly influential player, a factor that has had (and will continue to have) a profound influence on China's integration into the regional economy.

3.2 External Factors

If the CCP overestimated the attraction of Chinese markets for Western investors, they underestimated the implications of becoming a low-cost production centre for Asian investors. A common linguistic and cultural heritage and notions of loyalty to one's 'home' may have had some influence here, but the structural changes in the East Asian regional economy are far more important. China entered the regional economy at a time when

Japanese capital was no longer generating sufficient profits from Taiwan and South Korea and was searching for new low-cost locations. In addition, Korean and Taiwanese capital (although the structural links between Japanese and Taiwanese companies remain very strong) is now also searching for low-cost production centres.

Throughout the 1980s, land and labour shortages resulted in steady increases in rents and wages in the newly industrialized economies. The two major advantages that China offered were cheap green field sites[14] and a cheap and well-disciplined labour force. This last factor has perhaps been under-emphasized by some analysts of comparative advantage in East Asia. The passivity of the labour force, either through 'social engineering by government and management' (Johnson, 1987, p 150), more overt authoritarianism, or through inclusionary incomes policies (Deyo, 1987, pp 196–7) has been an important determinant of growth in the capitalist developmental states. The labour movements in Taiwan and South Korea might not be particularly strong by Western standards, but they are in comparison to the recent past, and in comparison to China. For example, labour militancy in South Korea has played a particularly important role in influencing Japanese investment decisions. Whilst changes may be under way in the functioning of Chinese trade unions, they have to date been more a force for stability and the functioning of state power than representatives of workers' interests – so much so that some foreign investors actually want their workforce unionized because they know it will quell any militancy.

Another sometimes neglected factor is comparative environmental legislation in East Asia. The growth of environmentalism, particularly in Taiwan, is influencing industrial location policies. However, it is somewhat difficult to isolate environmental issues from other cost issues, because, as Thomas (1992 p 6) notes:

> Production has continually moved to parts of the world where the costs are lowest. These tend to be where labour is cheap, local expertise and finance for environmental clean-up lacking, and environmental legislation weak or absent.

Perhaps the most concrete example here is Taiwan Plastics' welcome from the Fujian authorities after their proposed naphtha plant in Taiwan became the subject of much opposition, although other cost imperatives were also important in this case.

In addition to rising production costs, the appreciation of the major East Asian currencies against the dollar reduced the competitiveness of Asian exports to the lucrative North American markets. And here we have an excellent example of how China's integration into the international economy was influenced by factors outside its own control. The Plaza agreement of 1985 resulted in an agreed appreciation of the Japanese yen against the dollar. As this made Japanese exports less competitive, many producers moved to Taiwan and South Korea, not only because of lower production costs but also to take advantage of their exchange rate relations with the US. However, these currencies in their turn have also appreciated against the dollar as a result of growing trade imbalances and American economic diplomacy[15]. Thus, these producers are now in their turn moving to China to take advantage of the low value of the renminbi against the dollar, and also to utilize Chinese quotas on American and European markets (although American concerns about cheap Chinese imports may have important consequences here soon).

Thus, although the Chinese wanted to control their integration into the regional economy, they were playing with factors that they could not control. Indeed, in many ways, the investment boom of 1993 shows China to be an unwitting third-hand recipient of a bilateral deal between America and Japan. This is not to say that all states are totally powerless to influence 'natural' economic forces. On the contrary, the Chinese state deliberately and consciously introduced rent reductions, tax holidays and other incentives to emphasize China's comparative advantages as a production centre. The maintenance of an unrealistic exchange rate with the USA – particularly in 1994 – has also enhanced the competitiveness of both exports and re-exports from China.

But the trick in playing the 'low cost' card is choosing (or being allowed to choose) the right moment to trade up to a new strategy. The big danger is that, rather than trade up, the state decides to compete (or is forced to compete) by going ever lower. In China's case, whatever the central state decides to do is now, in some ways, irrelevant. On one level, it is impotent because too much power has now been devolved to provincial and lower-level authorities – local authorities which are increasingly in competition with each other. On another level, the extent to which China's international trade is now heavily influenced by the foreign investment sector has also vastly reduced the national state's freedom of movement.

3.3   Internal Factors – The Growth of Local Autonomy

While foreign investment was limited to the SEZs, or through State Council approval of projects, the national government retained significant control over the pace and scope of China's entry into the regional economy. Once the geographic and sectoral expansion of investment and trade privileges was extended, particularly after 1984, this control became ever more tenuous.

From 1984 onwards, the CCP deliberately decentralized a considerable degree of economic power to the provinces. In addition, much of the power intended for enterprise managers became lodged in the hands of newly strong provincial authorities[16]. Whilst these provincial authorities formally accepted national criteria for regional integration, they frequently deployed different criteria in practice. Expanding investment links with regional entrepreneurs brought in local finances through taxes on profits and also earned valuable foreign currency, which – in the SEZs, at least – benefited the locality much more than the national government. By the end of the decade, Guangdong and Fujian in particular had used the development of the foreign sector in conjunction with a vibrant domestic sector and enormous central government privileges to develop their own quasi-autonomous economic strategies.

4   CHINA'S NEW ROLE IN THE REGIONAL ECONOMY

The CCP remains committed to expanding its regional economic integration. Indeed, central leaders seem to have decided that the only way that effective infrastructure development can occur is by letting the foreign devils do it for them. There are massive incentives for anybody who will take on the task of bringing the infrastructure into the twentieth century (before the twenty-first is too far gone). The central State Planning Commission has announced a fifteen per cent reduction in profits tax for infrastructure investments, and if you make a long-term commitment – for example, a fifteen-year contract to develop a harbour – you get a 50% rebate (CNS 8/7/95). These and other privileges are augmented by various local offers, such as the five-year rent holiday (followed by a 50% fee for the next five years) offered by the Dalian authorities (CNS, 14/8/95).

Despite the CCP's initial desires to limit and control the process of regional integration, it is clear that the central government is no longer able to dominate affairs without returning to a form of centralized control that would throw the whole of the country into chaos. Although the localities have a significant degree of control, the more successful an area is in attracting inward investment in the short run, the more it abandons significant degrees of autonomy to the vagaries of the regional economy in the long run. As Qi and Howe note (1995, p 106), the Xiamen authorities have been forced to totally rewrite their development plans so that they matched the reality of Taiwanese investment priorities rather than the aspirations of the local political leadership.

4.1   The Dangers of Downward Mobility

While China may not have the pattern of integration that the CCP wanted in the 1980s, or even the pattern that local leaders wanted in the early 1990s, does this really matter? The foreign investment sector has made a big contribution to China's rapid growth, and earned valuable foreign currency. Furthermore, although the Taiwanese investors in particular used to isolate themselves from the local economy, their investments are now beginning to have collateral impacts. For example, the Taiwanese authorities have now lifted regulations which forced Taiwanese textile factories in mainland China to import all of their bonded cotton from Taiwan (CNS, 10/8/95). Whether this will benefit Chinese cotton producers in the long run is an entirely different question. Furthermore, some of the suppliers that originally went to China solely to service their Taiwanese clients are now expanding their operations into the domestic sector[17].

One of the biggest problems is that the investments can dry up and disappear almost as soon as they arrive. Production in East Asia is now highly fragmented and internationalized. Rather than produce from start to finish on one site, companies spread small tranches of the production process around the region. As each individual investment is relatively small, this means that they can be transferred from one place to another at relatively little cost and at relatively short notice if there are political problems in any individual country or if production costs rise. The fewer the forward or backward linkages with the local economy, the easier it is to transfer production, and the less dependent the parent company is on political and economic change in any one country.

Let us take a recent example from China. In June 1994, TDK announced that as a result of rising labour costs in Taiwan, it was to move its magnetic head production units from Taiwan to China. The building costs of its new plant in Xiamen were US$14.3 million, but sales in the first year alone were expected to be around US$95 million – nearly seven times the original capital construction investment (AFP 9/6/94). Presumably TDK would rather not have to transfer its production again in the near future, but the impact on its profits would be minimal if it felt it had to. In a rapidly changing market where new-generation products are emerging ever more quickly, the Chinese subsidiaries also easily become dependent on Japanese technology and R&D. If TDK left, and the Chinese tried to copy their production techniques, they would all too soon be out of date and unmarketable.

Many investors have come to China to take advantage of generous tax breaks, rent reductions and other incentives. One problem here is that the portability of investment in East Asia means that the companies might simply move on once the incentives dry up and find another lower-cost cite elsewhere with its own start-up incentives. Indeed, a survey in Beijing found that investors promise to do whatever they need to do to qualify for benefits, but do not match their formal contracted investment with actual investment in the long run. Of the companies surveyed in Beijing, the average actual investment was as little as 29% of the contracted amount (CNS 17/7/95).

China is not the only nation in East Asia with low wage and rent costs, limited environmental regulations and artificially low exchange rates with America. Much of Southeast Asia is in the same game, and if China wants to keep these investments in the long run it may well be forced to extend privileges long beyond the expected end date. Indeed, Chinese economists are particularly concerned about the recent expansion of foreign investment in Vietnam and India. But even if the central government wants to change the position and trade up to a new strategy, the extent of local autonomy alluded to above provides an important constraint. China is not only in competition with other nations for investment, but it is also in competition with itself.

China has not added only one new rung to the bottom of the regional ladder of development, but three or four new rungs. Competition between different parts of China for investment is forcing costs downwards (and in some areas, labour control upwards) and, not surprisingly, some foreign investors are exploiting this. Vast areas of China remain relatively untouched by foreign investment. As land and labour prices rise on the coast, these areas may become more attractive to investors and lead to an internal transfer of investments. Indeed, it is the CCP's great hope (and a pillar of the increasingly inappropriately named Ninth Five Year 'Plan') that foreign investment will become more evenly spread across the country, and concrete steps have been made to attract more investment. These include tax breaks of up to 50%, the opening of extraction industries and infrastructural projects for foreign investment, and the establishment of Chengdu and Xi'an as financial centres for the southwest and northwest respectively.

Whilst there is an increasing amount of investment going to the interior, it remains relatively small in terms of total investment. In the long run, the interior may well provide competition to the coast as export-based production centres. But the chances that there will be a sizeable transfer of investment to the interior in the short run remain somewhat slim. If this is to happen, two things have to change. First, the hard and soft infrastructure in the interior must be developed along the same lines as the changes in the coastal region since 1984. Second, it requires a fundamental change in the approach of foreign investors from export-bed priorities to Chinese market-led concerns – in other words, a reorientation in the balance of Western and Asian investment.

Some investors are taking the plunge and moving into the interior to take advantage of these incentives – and particularly the very attractive incentives to invest in the infrastructure, which is another pillar of China's current development plan. The biggest name to move into the interior recently is Pepsi. They admit that cheap land and labour were important considerations, but their main priority was accessing the huge local market – Sichuan alone has a population of over 150 million (AP 13/2/94). But while 'Western' investors may move their activities inland, for the time being intra-provincial competition for export-based investment will remain within the coastal region itself. And although it is of course entirely possible – even desirable – to compete on quality rather than cost, the danger is that these pressures will force China in a downwardly mobile direction.

There are three main considerations here. The first is that although we are beginning to see rising labour costs in some coastal areas, there is still a sufficiently large supply of labour at the moment to keep costs relatively low. De-collectivisation of the countryside has created perhaps as many as 150 million rural unemployed, many of whom are desperate to move to the gold-paved streets of southern China. Indeed, as wage costs rose in parts of Shenzhen, young migrant female workers were brought in from surrounding areas to maintain stability and drive wages down. The fact that many of these women work illegal hours and live in illegal conditions[18] does not appear to concern too many of the interested parties. Who represents the workers in the workers' state when the state doesn't want to know?[19]

The second relates to the geographical spread of investment along the coast. For example, while land may be in short supply in Guangdong, it is not a problem in Guangxi. The province may not be part of the Gold Coast, but it has good access to Hong Kong and is relatively well endowed with natural resources. Foreign investment in the province increased by 23.9% in the first half of 1995 (in monetary terms), with over 80% of the funds coming from Hong Kong, Taiwan and Macao (CNS 11/8/95). Whilst comparative labour and land costs are clearly a feature here, provincial development zones in Guangxi have put together attractive inventive packages that effectively undercut provincial competitors. In Beihai, for example, there is a five-year income tax reduction from the first profitable year; a 50% reduction of tax on fixed assets investments; a stepped (and apparently negotiable) reimbursement of VAT and business taxes; and other various incentives relating to land use, residency, education for dependants and so on (CNS 24/8/95).

Investment from Taiwan and the rest of East Asia is also increasing further north on the eastern coast in Jiangsu, Shanghai, Shandong, Hebei and the Liaodong Peninsula[20]. In a recent interview, an investment manager working for a Chinese-Malaysian client said that the Gold Coast was now saturated, and they were looking to open new operations in the Nanjing area. Their main concern was neither land nor labour costs, but guarantees of raw material supplies and tax holidays and other incentives.

The third consideration relates to competition among existing investment centres. The early pattern of China's opening was that investment tended to move into areas that were closest to their host. Thus, Guangdong received the lion's share of its investment from Hong Kong, most Taiwanese money went into Fujian, nascent Korean investment into the Liaodong Peninsula and Japanese investment into the north and northeast. Of course, this is partly explained by the different priorities of respective donors, Japanese investments in the industries – and particularly the motor industry – of northern China being a case in point here. However, it is notable that there is increasing competition for new and existing investments between existing investment centres. For example, Guangdong is actively trying to lure Taiwanese investment away from Fujian. There are now over 7,000 Taiwan-invested firms, and Taiwan's total investment in the province is over US$4 billion[21].

4.2 Environmental Concerns

The dangers of downward mobility are usually referred to in terms of declining labour conditions, falling real income and other related economic-social indicators. Another danger that we have to consider seriously in the Chinese case is presented by the environmental implications of downward mobility. According to the Nash equilibrium theory, China should not be in a position to exploit its environmental comparative advantage because of the size of the Chinese economy. For example, Kanbur *et al* (1995, p 294) argue that it is not rational for large countries to undercut smaller neighbours environmentally 'since the number of firms that can be attracted by undercutting standards is relatively small'. Does this mean, therefore, that China will not aggressively undercut other countries in East Asia, or does it instead infer that the Nash equilibrium model is in some way flawed? The answer (as it so often is to these types of question) is a bit of both. The Nash model assumptions appear to lose validity when we move from a simple analysis of relations between two countries to a more realistic multilateral analysis. China may not be able to attract many firms from, for example, Taiwan alone by cutting its environmental legislation, but if you also consider production transfers from Japan, South Korea, Hong Kong, Europe and so on, the total impact may well be impressive.

But there are two more important issues in the Chinese case that run against the Nash equilibrium conclusions. The first is the intensity of the desire by Chinese elites to create employment, raise standards of living and so on. Rational choice assessments of comparative environmental legislation appear to neglect (or at the very least, underestimate) the importance of regime survival for policy makers, thus rendering notions of what is 'rational' more complex than some would have us believe. The second is, I think, the crucial element here. The Chinese national government may well have decided that it is not rational to keep lower environmental regulations than neighbouring countries. However, what the central government says and what local governments do are often two different things. The Nash equilibrium approach is more (only more) relevant to China when you disaggregate the national economy. Thus, while the number of Taiwanese producers attracted to China as a whole may be insignificant, if they are concentrated in one area – Fujian, for example – then this will have a profound significance for that province. It may therefore be rational for Fujian and others to lower their environmental enforcement (i.e. not regulation, over which it has only limited control) to compete for investment both with other countries and with other parts of China.

It is clear that despite an impressive array of environmental rules, many of these regulations are simply not being used at local level. If it comes to a trade-off between investment, jobs and taxes on profits on the one hand, and forcing an investor away by enforcing legislation on the other, then the former consideration wins out in many cases.

5　TRADE RELIANCE ON FOREIGN INVESTMENT: INTEGRATION OR DEPENDENCE?

The final area for consideration here is the way in which China's trade interests are becoming dependent on the foreign investment sector. Ash and Kueh (1995) and Qi and Howe (1995) have both demonstrated that the massive increase in Chinese trade – particularly to North America through Hong Kong – since 1978 has been considerably influenced by exports from Asian investments in China. Indeed, China's presence in American and European markets owes an enormous debt to Taiwanese, Japanese and Hong Kong (including third party) investment decisions.

The growth of China's trade dependency has been remarkable, with foreign trade rising from less than a tenth of GNP in 1978 to over a third in the 1990s. China's trade dependency in 1993 was 38%, compared to 14.2% in Japan (China's major trading partner) and 16.7% in America (Kenji Nogami and Zhu, 1994). These trade dependency disparities lend strength to the concern of some officials that China is becoming over-dependent on

Japanese and American markets for exports[22]. Whilst the Chinese authorities might like to change this structure to make them less vulnerable to bilateral economic and political conflicts (particularly with a post-Clinton Republican America) their room for manoeuvre is severely limited because of the growing importance of foreign investments in Chinese trade. Indeed, trade from China's main coastal areas is now dominated by imports of components and raw materials to, and exports of finished produce of, foreign producers. Again, the *de facto* renminbi devaluation of 1994 was a crucial watershed: after a trade deficit of $12.2 billion in 1993, China had a 100 million surplus in the first eight months of 94 after a 31.5% increase in exports and a 18.3% increase in imports (AFP 7/8/94). The same period in 1995 saw a further 37.2% increase in the value of exports, and a 26.3% increase in exports, with the trade surplus at $15.28 billion at the end of August (CNS 14/9/95).

Official Chinese customs sources show that the main explanation for this foreign trade increase was the expansion of import – export activities by foreign-funded enterprises. For example, bilateral trade with Taiwan through Hong Kong grew by more than 35% (CNS 3/10/95). This has helped create an amazing level of Chinese trade dependence on foreign investment. By the end of September 1995, foreign-funded enterprises accounted for some 38% of Chinese trade (CNS 13/10/95). Thus, around 15% of China's GNP is now generated by the import-export activities of foreign investments.

What is more, the geographically uneven spread of foreign investments in China means that this dependence is even more pronounced in some areas. The most obvious example here is Guangdong, which has received 40% of all foreign investment since 1979, and which now provides 41% of the entire country's exports (CNS, 27/9/95), of which 68% are re-exports (CNS, 11/8/95). But with the expansion of foreign investments further north in recent years, this heavy investment – trade linkage is increasingly noticeable in other areas of China as well. For example, the value of foreign-owned exports from Shandong increased by 90% per annum from 1990–95, compared to a 16% per annum increase in 'Chinese' exports (CNS 3/9/95). In Tianjin, foreign-owned enterprise trade now exceeds 'Chinese' trade, reaching 57.7% in the first half of 1995 (CNS 22/7/95).

A final example here[23] comes from Beijing, where Taiwan is now second only to Hong Kong as the capital's major investor of funds. The influx of Asian investment has totally restructured the nature of Beijing's foreign trade, pushing the value of exports of mechanical and electronic products up by 470% in the first seven months of 1995. Exports of these goods have risen from 14% of total exports (by value) to 41%. What is more, some 76% of these exports are produced by foreign-funded firms, which is also reflected by the growth in product assembly rather than manufacturing (up from 41% to 76%). To cut through all these figures, we can generalize and say that foreign-funded product assembly is now the major determinant of Beijing's international trade (CNS 16/9/95). If Mao were buried instead of embalmed in Tiananmen Square, the fact that China's capital is becoming an assembly point for Taiwanese capitalists would make him spin in his grave.

This dependence on foreign investments clearly has important implications, not only for China's ability to control its deepening integration into the regional economy but for economic development in general. If disinvestment sets in, China's trade surplus will soon disappear. And one of the major reasons why China is so keen on extending its global economic presence is China's long-term food requirements[24]. China is already a major player on the world grain markets. As the population increases, consumption per head rises, and grain production slows down as a consequence of urbanization and environmental degradation, China will become increasingly dependent on global grain markets[25].

6 CONCLUSIONS

Despite the best intentions (if that is the right phrase) of the CCP national leadership to ensure that national sovereignty and increased international economic contacts could go hand in hand, China has been steadily pulled into a regional pattern of interlocking investment, trade and production networks by external forces. And what was a relatively fast process from 1984 to 1992 has been rapidly accelerated in the last three years – indeed, perhaps the speed of the changes is more startling than the trajectory of the process itself.

From a position of relative international isolation and very strong domestic control of the economy at the end of the 1980s, China is now in a situation where foreign investment accounts for an eighth of total investment and over a third of all foreign trade. China is now also a major consumer of international loans and aid, has relatively high foreign trade dependency, and its major export markets remain relatively few in number. Whilst it is going too far to say that China is dependent on international investment and trade, it is somewhat vulnerable to fluctuations in the international economy, and much more vulnerable than its major investment and trade partners. Furthermore, the uneven spread of international economic contacts in China means that those areas that have done best from opening to the West are also the most vulnerable areas.

China's reform experiment is still far from over, and could yet follow new and unpredictable paths. Nevertheless, it seems clear that one of the major conclusions of reform to date is that the national government's economic control has been severely weakened. As such, our old paradigms for studying pre-reform China have lost much of their validity, and we must increasingly deploy comparative political economy approaches to best understand how the local state – perhaps the local competition state – is interacting with international economic forces to generate both economic dynamism and potential economic instability.

Notes

1. Caused by the abolition of foreign exchange certificates.
2. For details of Shanghai's concerns about Guangdong's preferential treatment, see Wang Huning (1988) and Zhang Zhongli (1988).
3. And some Western investments use China as an export base, often operating through third parties in Taiwan and Hong Kong.
4. An estimated RMB 10.7 billion in 1992.
5. NSK decided to import bearings from Britain rather than rely on Chinese producers.
6. Chinese and Japanese figures are relatively, but not totally, close. For example, while Japanese figures give 1993 trade as US$37.84 billion, the Chinese put it at US$39 billion.
7. Although informed Japanese observers are wary of the extent to which short-term debts are rolled over.
8. And also by changing American priorities.
9. Particularly the State Council '22 provisions' to encourage foreign investment in October 1986.
10. For example, Samsung's new semiconductor operation in Suzhou, and a camera factory in Tianjin.
11. For example, TDK's operations in Xiamen.
12. It is notable that in his study of management in China, Child (1994) notes that Japanese Joint Ventures find it much easier to adapt to Chinese practices than American projects.
13. For example, see Pearson (1991) Chin (1989) Pomfret (1991) and others.
14. This was not necessarily the formal legal position. New investors who dealt with the official central government agencies were expected to establish expensive and detailed social welfare in their factories along the traditional Chinese *danwei* style. Those who chose to take a short cut and establish relatively small operations by dealing directly with local leaders were often spared these expenses.
15. The Japanese yen appreciated by roughly 40% from 1985–87; the Taiwanese NT$ by about 28% from 85–87; and the Korean won by approximately 17% from 1986–88 (Bernard and Ravenhill, 1995, p 180).
16. For a detailed account of the development of local autonomy in the 1980s, see Breslin (1995).
17. For example, Eastman Chemicals (Reuters, 20/7/95).
18. There have been a number of horror stories recently about fires in factories which incinerated the sleeping workers illegally housed above or alongside the

factory. In one case, workers were even forced to continue producing as fire swept through the dormitory.

19. An added complication here is the ongoing transferral of political power to economic power amongst CCP officials. At the most basic level, this can involve simple corruption to ensure that safety regulations are not enforced. On a deeper level, the creation of interlocking economic elites which straddle the border with Hong Kong is also a significant factor.

20. Dalian has absorbed more foreign capital than any other Chinese city. Since the establishment of the Dalian Economic and Technological Development Zone in 1984, the municipal government has spent RMB 4 billion on developing the local infrastructure. The major investors are leading Japanese companies such as Mitsubishi, Canon, Fujitec, Konica, Toshiba and Sanyo, the majority of which have export-based operations (CNS 5/9/95).

21. The development of special Taiwan Development Zones is an important feature of this inter-regional competition. Although they are very attractive to Taiwanese investors, they only serve to further insulate the export-led investment sector from the Chinese host economy.

22. Although Hong Kong is second in the list of China's export markets, in excess of 80% of these exports are subsequently re-exported. The primary destination for these re-exports is America (36%) (AP-DJ 15/2/94).

23. This pattern has been replicated across the country, particularly the coastal region. The most dramatic rise came in Jinan City in Shandong, where there has been an amazing 575% increase in the export value of wholly foreign-owned companies in the first half of 1995 (CNS 24/8/95), but the low level of previous investment distorts the figures here.

24. Note also the marked rise in oil imports.

25. Hence the embargo on food exports in December 1994, and the almost obsessive desire to enter the World Trade Organisation and play the European Union off against the Americans.

REFERENCES

Abbreviations of News Services

AFP	Agence France Presse
AP	Associated Press
CND	China News Digest (Daily electronic newspaper from CND.ORG)
CNS	China News Service
DJ	Dow Jones
JEN	Japan Economic Newswire
RMRB	Renmin Ribao (People's Daily)
RMRB	HWB Renmin Ribao Hai Wai Ban (People's Daily Overseas Edition)
SCMP	South China Morning Post

Ash, R., and Kueh, Y. Y. (1995), 'Economic Integration within Greater China: Trade and Investment Flows Between China, Hong Kong and Taiwan' in David Shambaugh (ed.) *Greater China: The Next Superpower?* (Oxford: OUP) pp 59–93.

Bernard. M., and Ravenhill, J. (1995), 'Beyond Product Cycles and Flying Geese: Regionalization, Hierarchy, and the Industrialization of East Asia' in *World Politics* No 47, pp 171–209.

Breslin, S. (1995), *China in the 1980s: Centre-Province Relations in a Reforming Socialist State* (Basingstoke: Macmillan and New York: St Martins).

Child, J. (1994), *Management in China During the Age of Reform* (Cambridge: CUP).

Chin, K. (1989), *China's Open Door to Foreign Investments 1978–84* (PhD Thesis: Ann Arbor).

Cummings, B. (1987), 'The Origins and Development of the Northeast Asian Political Economy: Industrial Sectors, Product Cycles, and Political Consequences' in Deyo, F. C. (ed.) *The Political Economy of the New East Asian Industrialism* (New York: Cornell UP) pp 44–83.

Deyo, F. (1987), 'State and Labor: Modes of Political Exclusion in East Asian Development' in Deyo, F. (ed.) *The Political Economy of the New East Asian Industrialism* (New York: Cornell UP) pp 182–202.

Drifte, R. (1996), *Japan's Foreign Policy in the 1990s: From Economic Power to What Power?* (London: Macmillan).

Goldstein, C. (1992), 'Strait Talking' in *The Far Eastern Economic Review* 3 Dec, pp 44–48.

Hamrin, C. (1990), *China and the Challenge of the Future* (Westview: Boulder).

Johnson, C. (1987), 'Political Institutions and Economic Performance: The Government – Business Relationship in Japan, South Korea, and Taiwan' in Deyo, F. (ed.) *The Political Economy of the New East Asian Industrialism* (New York: Cornell UP) pp 136–164.

Kanbur, R., Keen, M. and van Wijnbergen, S. (1995), 'Industrial Competitiveness, Environmental Regulation and Direct Foreign Investment' in Goldin, I and Winters, L. (eds) *The Economics of Sustainable Development* (Cambridge: CUP) pp 289–302.

Kenji Nogami and Baoliang Zhu (1994), 'Quantitative Analysis of the Chinese Economy' in *East Asian Economic Perspectives*, Vol. 6 No. 4, Dec., pp 11–20.

Lian Zhong Xu (1994), 'The Impact of FDI in Energy and Transportation on China's Economy' in *East Asian Economic Perspective*, Vol. 6 No. 4, Dec., pp 2–7.

Pearson, M. (1991), *Joint Ventures in the People's Republic of China* (Princeton, New Jersey: PUP).

Pomfret, R. (1991), *Investing In China: Ten Years Of The Open Door Policy* (London: Harvester Wheatsheaf).

Qi Lou and Howe, C. (1995), 'Direct Investment and Economic Integration in the Asia Pacific: The Case of Taiwanese Investment in Xiamen' in David Shambaugh (ed.) *Greater China: The Next Superpower?* OUP, pp 94–117.

Thoburn, J. (1990), *Foreign Investment In China Under The Open Policy: The Experience Of Hong Kong Companies* (Aldershot: Avebury)

Thomas, C. (1992), *The Environment in International Relations* (London: RIIA).

Wang Huning (1988), '*Zhongguo Bianhuazhong De Zhongyang He Difang Zhengfu De Guanxi: Zhengzhi De Hanyi* (Ramifications of Changing Relationship Between Central and Local Government in China)' in *Fudan Xuebao (Fudan University Journal)* No. 5, pp 1–8 and p 30.

World Bank (1990), *China: Macroeconomic Instability and Industrial Growth Under Decentralized Socialism* (Washington DC: World Bank).

Zhang Zhongli (1988), '*Shanghai He Shanghai Jingjiqu Zai Zhongguo Jingji Xiandaihua Zhong De Diwei He Zuoyong* (The Position and Role of Shanghai and its Economic Zones in the Modernisation of China's Economy)' in *Shehui Kexue (Social Sciences)* No. 1, pp 18–22.

7 Foreign Direct Investment in China and the Economic Integration of East Asia

Yunnan Shi

1 INTRODUCTION

Resorting to external financing is part of the policy of opening-up which has been adopted since the end of the 1970s by the Chinese Government. They have been giving preference, on the one hand, to the assisted loans (long-term and low-interest rates) that some countries and, above all, international institutions (the International Monetary Fund and the World Bank) have granted China and, on the other hand, to foreign direct investments. If at the beginning of the 1990s, international loans were a major part of the foreign capital introduced into China, foreign direct investments supplanted loans for the first time in 1992 with more than eleven billion dollars against less than eight billion in loans[1].

Foreign direct investments (FDI) in China are presented in three main forms: joint ventures, contractual joint ventures[2] and entirely foreign firms. These foreign capital firms ('*sanzi qiyi*' in Chinese) have been rapidly developed in less than fifteen years. Thus, towards the end of 1993, there were about 168,000 firms, of which 65% were joint-ventures ('*hezi*'), 15% contractual joint-ventures ('*heyeng*') and 20% entirely foreign firms ('*duzi*')[3].

This article tries to bring to light the link between the strategy of direct investment in China by multinational firms and the economic integration of the region. First, we will examine the development of FDI in China since 1979, the year when the new Chinese Government started a policy of reforms and the opening-up of the Chinese economy. Secondly, the phenomenon will be explained from the point of view of 'supply' (multinational firms, the Chinese of the Diaspora) as well as 'demand' (the central power, the provincial governments). Thirdly, the impact of FDI on the integration of the Chinese economy into the regional and world economy and the speeding-up of the economic integration of the region will be examined.

2   THE HISTORY OF THE DEVELOPMENT OF FOREIGN DIRECT
INVESTMENTS IN CHINA

Before 1979, China was practically closed to FDI. In the 1950s, the only
partners of the scientific and technical co-operation were the then Soviet
Union and Eastern Europe. At the beginning of the 1960s, when the Soviet-
Union withdrew its aid, China turned towards Western countries. However,
the scale of the trade in technology was very limited, and the main means
were the purchase of equipment goods called 'complete' – that is to say, most
of time production lines with varying degrees of assistance in production on
the part of the transmitter. Up to the end of 1978, the total amount of
accumulated FDI was 6.4 billion dollars[4].

Since 1979, the year when the new Chinese Government started a policy
of reforms and the opening-up of the economy, FDI has rapidly developed as
one of the elements of the economic opening-up: the yearly amount of FDI
realized in China has passed from one billion dollars at the beginning of the
eighties to more than 27 billion in 1993, that is an average growth of 46% per
year (see Appendix 1). However, the amount of investments has much
fluctuated according to the different years (see Figure 7.1) both for political
and economical reasons, and those investments present specific characteristics as regards the identity of the investors, the regions and the receiving
sectors.

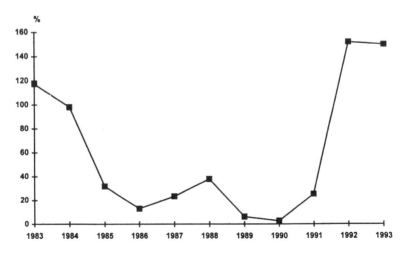

Figure 7.1 The yearly growth of foreign direct investments in China 1983–1993
(the realized amount)

We can split up this period of development of FDI and foreign capital firms into four main stages: the preparation and trial stage, the first development stage, the fluctuating development stage, and lastly, the very fast development stage.

2.1 Preparation and trial (1979–1982)

The Chinese economy was in reconstruction after ten years of 'cultural revolution'; the policy of opening-up had just started. This stage consisted in the preparation of the reception of FDI and the constitution of foreign capital firms: first, the mental preparation (propaganda showing the importance of the opening-up and the use of foreign capital) and then the legislative preparation (the promulgation of laws concerning foreign capital firms). At the same time, the Chinese Government had chosen to practise 'special and supple' policies in both coastal southern provinces, Guangdong and Fujian, and to create four Special Economic Zones (SEZ) open to foreign capital: Shenzhen, Zhuhai, Xiantou and Xiamen. The foreign capital firms were slowly developing and were mainly divided up into the four SEZ. At the end of 1982, there were more than 900 foreign capital firms with cumulative realized amount of 1.2 billion dollars. It can be emphasized that, within that period, the majority of the firms were contractual joint-ventures (see Appendix 2). This form does not necessarily call for a status of co-enterprise through shares. Thus, it has the advantage of being more supple, in comparison with the form of a joint-venture proper, notably during this trial period when both Chinese and foreign partners were extremely prudent; whereas among these more than 900 firms, only 83 joint-ventures could be counted, among which two-thirds came from Hong-Kong. However, it can be noted that the average amount of Western investment was much more important than Hong-Kong investment.

2.2 First development (1983–1985)

After some years of economic reform, the Chinese economy has undergone a rapid growth. The government actively tries to attract FDI through the simplification of administrative procedures, the decentralization of some powers of inspection and admission, and the opening-up of coastal towns with the attribution of privileges identical to those in the SEZ. These measures have indeed widely encouraged FDI: thus, more than 5,000 new foreign capital firms were created within this 1983–1985 period (more than 3,000 for the year 1985) absorbing almost 3.6 billion dollars. And if the contractual joint ventures have remained the most numerous, the number of joint ventures has grown in a significant way: they were in 1985 almost as numerous as contractual joint ventures. During this period, investors came from more than twenty countries. The investment sectors were firstly electronics and textiles, then, building construction and trade, and lastly communications, tourism and the primary sector. Regional investment has spread to all the provinces, townships and autonomous regions (except Tibet) but has focused mainly on the coastal province.

2.3   Fluctuating Development (1986–1990)

During this period, FDI underwent a fluctuating development. The economical problems (strong inflation being one among others) which sprang up in 1986 forced the government to practise a policy of rigour; FDI was affected by this policy. Projects in some sectors where FDI was concentrated, such as the construction of hotels, were practically stopped. But on the other hand, the government encouraged FDI in the manufacturing sector. Thus, if during this period the development of FDI was slowing down, generally speaking, that of the manufacturing sectors had, on the contrary, accelerated. In 1988, the economic reforms were accelerated and FDI found a new impetus after two years of slowing down. The government put the accent on the capacity of exploitation and administration of the concerned firms. The 1989–1990 period was marked by 'the events of the Tiananmen square' and by the economical sanctions placed by Western countries upon China. At the same time, the Chinese government readjusted in a more severe way the criteria of inspection and authorization of FDI. In total, within this period, more than 22,000 foreign capital firms were created, absorbing more than 13 billion dollars. Compared with the previous period, 1989–1990 presents some outstanding characteristics. First, joint ventures became the most current form of investment, representing 61% of the projects and 63% of the realized amount, against only 42% of projects and 26% of the realized amount for the previous period. Then, the number of entirely foreign firms was increasing, notably from 1988 onwards, as their numbers surpassed those of contractual joint ventures in 1990. Those characteristics show a passage from a pattern of short-term investment to that of long-term investment. Moreover, the number of countries from which the investors originated grew from twenty to fifty. More particularly, investors coming from Taiwan began to position themselves massively on the continent. For instance, they created in 1989 more than 500 firms (half of which were entirely Taiwanese firms), which represented in the same year around 30% of the entirely foreign firms which were created in China. Lastly, the distribution of investments among sectors was considerably modified: the proportion of productive investments grew every year, amounting to more than 90% in 1988, whereas on the other hand non-productive investments (such as the construction of hotels) were controlled[5].

2.4 Very Rapid Development (since 1991)

From 1991 on, diverse duty-free zones have been created; sectors not accessible to FDI up to then, such as finance, assurances, property, have opened up. FDI experienced an unprecedented development, reaching in 1993 an amount[6] of 27.5 billion dollars, that is to say almost the amount accumulated during the ten previous years. This rapid development of FDI was notably triggered off by Deng Xiaoping's journey to the southern province at the beginning of 1992, which was followed by political events going in the same direction – notably the improvement of working efficiency in the administration. All this contributed to an expansion of FDI in 1992, the year when the amount of the FDI realized exceeded for the first time that of international loans. This change in the structure of foreign investment shows that the main source of foreign investment (71% in 1993) is now direct investments: China has become the most important developing country receiving FDI. As regards regional distribution, if the coastal regions remain the privileged destination of investments (85% in 1993 for eleven coastal provinces[7] out of a total number of 30 provinces in China), statistics show here a very clear increase towards the North. Indeed, at the same time as the standard of living in the Southern coastal regions is increasing, these same coastal regions are slowly losing their superiority – whereas the North and the Centre are becoming more and more interesting for new investors: the drawbacks (geographically not so close, the absence of family ties) can be at least partially compensated by the advantages in regard to wage costs and other production factors such as the relative abundance of resources, the existence of a solid production base (heavy industries in the North, technology in Shanghai, textiles in the Jiangsu and the Shandong provinces). Thus, if the province of Guangdong (in the South) received in 1993 almost eight times as much FDI as in 1988, the provinces of Jiangsu (Centre) and Shandong (North) saw theirs respectively multiply by 30 and 43 during the same period. The coastal regions of the Centre and the North are now receiving as much FDI as those in the South, whereas they did not receive half as much five years ago.

In total, FDI in China has experienced an outstanding development, although it fluctuated notably in the second half of the 1980s. Its recent development will mark a turning point, insofar as not only has FDI in China leapt forward since the beginning of the 1990s, but this leap forward is coming more from a change of destination than from the speeding-up of the rhythm of investments – and this to the detriment of the ASEAN[8] countries, which absorbed the major part of the investments in the region during the 1980s (from Japan and from NIC[9]) and in which foreign investment was one of the keys to development. So, how can we explain this spectacular development, particularly in the most recent period? The second part of this article will try to give an answer to this question.

3   THE EXPLANATION OF THE DEVELOPMENT OF FOREIGN DIRECT INVESTMENTS IN CHINA

We can explain the phenomenon of spectacular development of FDI in China from the point of view of supply as well as of demand. From the supply point of view, FDI in China obeys both industrial logic (the international segmentation of the process of manufacture, the search of power production costs) and market logic (more than a billion consumers, strong needs for technologies). By reason of their dominating position in China, the Chinese of the Diaspora will form the subject of particular attention. On the demand side, China (the central power, the provincial governments) is integrating FDI in the process of development by adding to already naturally favourable surroundings numerous incitements in favour of foreign investors.

3.1   The Strategy of Investors: from Theory to Practice

The approach to corporate multinationalization which is most widely spread is probably Dunning's Eclectic Theory (1977 and 1988), which combines Hymer-Kindleberger's Theory of the Structural Market Imperfection, Buckley-Casson's Theory of the Internalization of Market and Hennart's Transaction Cost Theory, and proposes the OLI model (Ownership-Location-Internalization) to explain the existence of a multinational firm and the phenomenon of foreign direct investment. According to this eclectic theory, three series of advantages explain how a firm can engage in a strategy of direct investment abroad: a monopolistic or an ownership advantage, a location advantage and an internalization advantage.

The monopolistic advantage is composed of two parts: on the hand one, the exclusive possession of resource of raw material, of a process of production, of technology, and on the other hand management capacity for efficient administration, such as knowledge of the market. The advantage of location designates the difference of cost and the quality of production factors (labour force, energy, raw materials) and the infrastructure (communication, transports) of the different countries. For foreign investors, some countries have a relative advantage of location, for production and transport costs are lower in those countries than in others, enabling them to be efficiently competitive in a market of similar products. Thus, Dunning's concept of the location advantage gets its inspiration from the comparative advantage of Heckscher-Ohlin's international trade theory, whereas the concept of a monopolistic advantage comes from Hymer-Kindleberger's theory of the structural market imperfection.

The advantage of internalization is relatively more complicated than the two other advantages. In effect, according to Dunning's concept, those last two do not constitute necessary and sufficient conditions to make direct investment abroad. For a firm can very well benefit from these advantages through exports, transfer of technologies, hiring of material or exploitation concessions, while avoiding production directly on site. However, the existence and the increase of transaction costs of a product or of the cost of technology through the market can stimulate a firm to invest directly abroad and thus to internalize an imperfect market, so as to reduce the transaction cost.

The eclectic approach gives accounts of the implantation of firms abroad with the help of determinants. We will retain here some which seem to us the most important in the case of China: the supply of natural resources, the international disparity of salaries, the will to conquer or defend exterior markets. Moreover, the choice of the location lends an important role to the local environment (favourable measures, family ties).

China is a large country which disposes of abundant natural resources. However, the supply of raw materials has not been the dominant motive for foreign investments, for they have been mainly directed towards the tourist sector (in the first half of the 1980s) or towards an industrial sector (in the second half), and, in geographical terms, towards the southern coastal regions (notably the provinces of Guangdong and Fujian) where natural resources are not very abundant. However, the ascent in investment toward the north (always in the coastal provinces) shows the greater importance attached to the problem of supply.

China disposes of a huge pool of labour because of the importance of its population. The labour cost is not only inferior to that of the NIC in Asia but also lower than in most ASEAN countries (see Table 7.1). On examining the chart, it appears that the salary structure in industry almost perfectly follows the line of the slope of direct investments in the region. At its head, Japan has a position of a world-scale investor; then the NIC, after investment by Japanese multinational firms are showing themselves very active in the ASEAN and in China. Then the ASEAN countries which are under the

Table 7.1   Labour costs in Asian countries in 1990

Country	Average wage in industry ($ per month)
Japan	2,440
Taiwan	700
Korea	655
Hong Kong	590
Singapore	485
Malaysia	275
Thailand	120
Philippines	93
India	61
Indonesia	45
Sri Lanka	40
China	35

Source: Besson and Lanteri, p 46.

economic control of the Chinese of the Diaspora have recently been interested in China, the latter investing directly in the country. Thus, since the second half of the 1980s, the Japanese multinationals (and notably the Chinese of the Diaspora in the NIC and in the ASEAN) have managed to make the most of this advantage by setting up in China units of production destined to serve as a basis of re-export towards third markets, or even towards their country of origin.

The motive for the conquest of the market has not played a determining role in the process of industrial delocalization, at least up to the recent period. In effect, only Western and Japanese investors, far fewer, as far as levels of investment are concerned (compared to those from Hong-Kong or Taiwan) seem to be more attracted by the demand factor and the satisfaction of the Chinese home market. A firm can judge it as strategically important to take up a position in the most populated country in the world, which has recorded, during these last years, the strongest economic growth, whereas the developed industrial countries have experienced a profound recession and the NIC a slowing-down (see Table 7.2). The recent arrival of big investors (Philips, Hitachi, Siemens, Alcatel, Ford, Nestl!e, Danone.) in sectors such as household electrical appliances, telecommunications, transport and food-stuffs, reinforces the motive for the conquest of the Chinese market, because of the very nature of the products they make and by the fact that they have met more and more obstacles in their own countries through sheer industrial

Table 7.2 Growth rate of Japan, South Korea and China

In %	1991	1992	1993	1994*
Japan	4.3	1.4	0.1	0
Korea	9.1	5.1	5.6	8
China	8.0	13.2	13.8	11–12

Source: IMF, *International Financial Statistics*.
* Author's estimation.

delocalization (such as demonstrations and strikes by redundant or redundancy-vulnerable wage-earners, or the discouragement of the authorities).

Lastly, the local environment can also play an important role in the choice of the place of settlement. The creation of Special Economical Zones and the opening-up of coastal towns explain for a great part the geographical distribution of foreign investment in China. On the other hand, the main regions which receive investment coincide with those from which the Chinese Diaspora originated, dispersed throughout the whole world (notably in eastern Asia), for it is precisely the Chinese of the Diaspora who have massively invested in China – generally in their region of origin, for practical reasons (the knowledge of the place and of local dialects) but also on moral grounds and because of nostalgia.

3.2 The Investments of the Diaspora

The Diaspora is here used in its widest meaning, grouping together not only the populations who emigrated abroad and conserved their Chinese nationality ('*huaqiao*' in Chinese), but also the descendants of those emigrants who adopted local nationalities ('*Huayi*') as well as the populations of Chinese territories which are not at present administrated by Beijing, such as Hong Kong, Macao or Taiwan ('*Tongbao*'). Those Chinese of the Diaspora form a community of fifty million people which generates wealth that goes beyond the worth of the GNP of the People's Republic of China, although it is twenty-five times more populated[10].

The Diaspora is not homogeneous. Three components can be noticed: first, the Chinese from Hong Kong, from Macao and Taiwan who are presently living outside the control of Beijing, and who represent the near-total of the population in their territories; then, those in south-eastern Asia (ASEAN),

Table 7.3   The population of the Chinese Diaspora in 1990

Country or region	Part of Chinese (in %)	Chinese (in millions)
Taiwan, Hong Kong		**26.77**
and Macau*		
– Taiwan		20.75
– Hong Kong	97	5.64
– Macau		0.38
South-Eastern Asia	**7.4**	**19.73**
(ASEAN)		
– Thailand	10	5.58
– Malaysia	34	5.92
– Indonesia	2.8	4.98
– Singapore	76	2.28
– Philippines	1.5	0.92
– Brunei	20	0.05
Other regions		**3.70**
– United States		1.00
– Canada		0.45
– Europe		0.40
– Latin America		0.30
– Australia		0.30
– Others		1.25
Total		**50.2**

* in 1992.
Sources: For Taiwan, Hong Kong, Macau and ASEAN, estimations by the author from Xu, pp 196–214. For other regions, see Besson and Lanteri, p 156.

who constitute a minority of the population (except in Singapore) but who have done exceptionally well in business and often control the major part of the economy of the region[11]; then, the Diaspora Chinese residing in other regions (such as the United States or Europe) with an economic presence which is much smaller although also extremely dynamic.

Hong Kong is, by far, the first source of foreign investment in China: the city-state invested an accumulated amount of 38.6 billion United States dollars up to the end of 1993, which was 62.4% of the total amount invested by foreigners. However, according to the estimates[12], only half of this investment was realised by local companies. The explanation lies in the fact that Hong Kong plays the role of a window, both from foreign countries looking out towards China and from China upon the exterior. In the first case, non-Hong Kong foreign firms which bring technology and management are becoming partners with firms in Hong Kong, which contributes mainland relationships and knowledge of the Chinese environment[13]. Taiwanese firms have also used this method, notably for political reasons, for their government has forbidden them until recently to invest directly on the politically antagonistic continent. In the second case, Chinese mainland firms that have settled in Hong-Kong frequently return to China in order to benefit from the fiscal advantages granted to firms which have been created by foreign investment[14].

Since the beginning of the 1980s, Hong Kong has massively delocalized its industries in China, notably towards the coastal southern regions. Several factors explain this movement: increases in wage costs (doubling between 1986 and 1992) have meant that the manufacturing industries have lost their international competitiveness and have emphasized the attractiveness of low-cost sites and low labour costs on the other side of the frontier; the Sino-British agreement at the end of 1984 indeed deterred a number of shocked investors, but as the historic return date (1st July 1997) draw's near, a majority of the firms are launching out in search of opportunities helping to prepare for 'after 1997', and the earlier the better; the generalization of economic reforms in China has gained in credibility and at least partly removed uncertainties about the future of the colony. It is thus estimated that between two-thirds and 80% of Hong-Kong industry has been presently delocalized in China, among which is the near-entirety of the toy industry, and that around 50,000 Hong Kong managers are working in those delocalized firms[15].

Apart from delocalization operations there are also, to a lesser extent, investments in the services, infrastructure (electricity, roads, urban modernization). The latter investments, more recent, are the more important investment projects. Last, the creation of high-technology firms has attracted Chinese students who have studied abroad.

Taiwan is the second source of investment in China, although statistics from the 1979–1993 period show that its place is slightly behind that of Japan and the USA[16]. Indeed, before 1988, Taiwanese firms were investing directly in China, by-passing Hong-Kong, Singapore, the USA and the Philippines, who were playing an important role in the recycling of Taiwanese capital, and this essentially for political reasons: on the one hand, the Taiwanese government forbade all direct investment by its firms on the continent, and, on the other hand, the Chinese government did not recognize Taiwanese investment as eligible for the granting of advantages. In 1988, the Chinese government and the different local powers (notably in the coastal provinces and in the Special Economical Zones) granted privileged conditions to

Taiwanese investors; in 1989, the Taiwan public authorities recognized the equality of direct investment in China, authorizing at first investments for amounts less than one million American dollars. Since then, an investment boom has taken place from the island to the continent, and Taiwan became as early as 1990 the second investor in China, while remaining far behind Hong Kong[17]. This change of attitude from Taiwan is directly linked to the problem of the adjustment of the commercial world environment that the Taiwanese firms have had to face since 1988. In effect, the revaluation of the new Taiwanese dollar and the trade excess over the USA and Europe have exerted a pressure on Taiwan export products. In these conditions, the delocalization of production, notably in traditional sectors such as rubber and plastics, electronics and foodstuffs, has enabled Taiwan not only to reduce its commercial conflict with the USA and Europe but also to diversify outlets of Taiwanese products in order to reduce investment risk.

In much the same way as Hong Kong investors, those from Taiwan were first attracted by the low labour costs and the low prices of sites and raw materials in China, and industrial delocalization has often concerned labour-intensive production. Differences can be noticed, however, as far as recent investment strategy is concerned, which has had consequences for the characteristics of the investments (the sectors concerned and the receiving regions). Since 1992, China's great infrastructure projects have been the main subject of interest, and it is in that sector that the originality of the wave of foreign investment lies. Virtually all the infrastructure projects undertaken by Diaspora firms have been underwritten by investment from Hong Kong. Another privileged sector for Hong Kong investors is the real-estate business. Those two sectors absorbed 87% of Hong-Kong investments in China in 1992[18], whereas Taiwanese firms are significantly almost absent from infrastructure projects, as they do not have the same experience as their Hong Kong counterparts and remain rather prudent in regard to launching such projects without any juridical warrants from China. As far as the receiving regions are concerned, unlike Hong Kong investments – which are concentrated in the province of the Guangdong[19], notably in its three Special Economical Zones – those from Taiwan are far more dispersed[20]. This can be explained by the fact that Taiwan investors do not only aim (although it has been up to now their first motive) at securing advantageous conditions of production for export (the province of Guangdong is the most practical destination because of its proximity to the British Territories), but also wish to target the Chinese market, for which they must preferably settle in big industrial centres such as Shanghai and other inland towns[21].

The Diaspora of Southeast Asia has also been interested in China, but only more recently. Investment coming from these countries has also undergone a very strong increase, notably from 1992 on: in 1993, all those countries found themselves among the first twenty investors in China[22]. However, unlike Hong Kong and Taiwan, the Diaspora of southeast Asia does not consider China as the only privileged land for investment[23]. Apart from China and their own regions countries such as Vietnam and India are considered as interesting destinations. On the other hand, the main motive for investment is less industrial delocalization than economical and political considerations, for production and transportation costs, in Indonesia, in Thailand or even in Malaysia are comparable to those in southern China[24]. However, the latent hostility of governments (territorial conflicts) and populations (ethnic conflicts) of the adopted lands can lead the Diaspora to diversify its risks by investing abroad.

3.3 The Policies and Strategy of Investment Recipients

Analysis of corporate multinationalization has often stemmed from the country of origin of the firms in question. Such an approach remains incomplete when one becomes interested in such a huge country as China, with an economy long controlled by its authorities. In effect, the land has not remained passive in the face of the wave of investment. On the contrary, those waves have been triggered off by major elements in China (the creation of Special Economical Zones, the openings of coastal towns, the generalization of the economical reforms). The Chinese government has intervened not only to encourage foreign investment but also to orient and reorient it according to the priority which has been announced[25].

The privileged way of the Chinese government is legislative. At the end of 1979, the law on Sino-foreign co-enterprises was promulgated, which defined rules for the functioning of co-enterprises in China and the advantageous conditions granted to foreign capital. In 1985, the law on economic contracts was validated; this was to grant firms with foreign capital more complete juridical foundations for their development.

In October 1986, a communiqu!e on the encouragement of the use of foreign capital (the famous '22 Articles') was announced. It provided privileged conditions on salary, rent, the supply of water and electricity and the fixing of rates, and granted the greatest autonomy in fields such as hiring and dismissal of workers and the determination of salary levels. In 1992, the Chinese government modified the system of accountancy and the financial management of foreign capital firms. Thus, up to the end of 1993, the number of laws and rules elaborated concerning FDI and foreign capital firms had gone beyond 200.

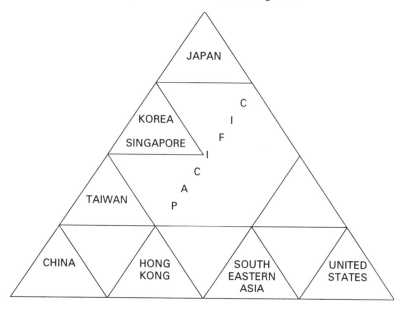

Figure 7.2   The three triangles of the Chinese strategy

Moreover, China has taken part in the Washington Convention and in organisations for multilateral investment, and has set up protection agreements on multilateral investments with around forty countries in order to reduce political risk and the commercial cost of foreign investment in China. In April 1993, the Chinese government decided to open up a part of the energy, transport and telecommunications markets, enabling foreign investors in those relatively backward but economically very important sectors. This measure means that the Chinese government is continuing its policy of opening up its economy.

If FDI in China is needed to speed up the economical development, its attraction is part and parcel of a global strategy in China. The Shanghai Evening Newspaper (*Xinmin Wanbao*) mentioned, at the end of 1993, 'the Chinese strategy of the 3 triangles' (see Fig. 7.2).

- the small triangle (Continental China, Hong-Kong, Taiwan)
- the middle triangle (Small triangle, other 'dragons', the rest of south-eastern Asia)
- the big triangle (middle triangle, Japan, USA)

The Chinese strategy would consist in making the small lower-left triangle (the 'big China') use the big one in order to dominate the smaller ones. The latter, sometimes called the CEA (Chinese Economic Area) constitute a Chinese network of economic influence which could, if things go on in the present way, be the third largest world trade zone, after North America and Europe, and well in front of Japan.

Of course, the economic integration of the various Asian states in the whole of the CEA has not yet been accomplished, and the economic co-operation of Asia – Pacific remains a more theoretical than real topic. However, the development of the FDI (notably on the part of the Diaspora) has led to one fact: the Chinese economy is now living within the international division of labour. FDI will constitute a key for economic development, and its speeding-up will reinforce the economic integration of the region.

4   FOREIGN DIRECT INVESTMENT AND THE INTEGRATION OF THE CHINESE ECONOMY INTO THE REGIONAL ECONOMY

The 1980s were marked by the general growth of FDI in the world, and the NIC of Asia have been supplanting Japan, from 1987 onwards, as the first investor in the Asia – Pacific region. In effect, from the middle of the 1980s, because of external factors (the rise of protectionist tensions from the USA, increases in exchange rates) and external constraints (the substantial rise of wage costs, the aggravation of environmental problems), the NIC of Asia have massively delocalized their industrial production towards the ASEAN and, to a lesser extent, towards China. Since the beginning of the 1990s, the latter has largely become the first destination for FDI in the region.

There is a close link between foreign direct investment and exterior trade in the case of China. On the one hand, the delocalization of plants (notably on the part of eastern Asia: Japan, Hong-Kong, Taiwan, South Korea) goes hand in hand with the export of machines, spare parts and some raw materials to China, leading thus to a surplus in the balance of trade of their countries (notably Taiwan, South Korea, Japan) over China. On the other hand, investment in manufacturing sectors oriented towards exporting has increased the export capacity of China (a third of the exports of the country are carried out by foreign capital firms).

The increase in investments from eastern Asia has stimulated Chinese foreign trade with those countries. For China, the involvement of eastern Asia in the foreign markets of the country has increased: between 1988 and

1993, bilateral trade was multiplied by 2.6. For eastern Asia the Chinese market is becoming more and more important. The case of Taiwan is the most outstanding: it has trebled its exports (including re-exports by Hong Kong) towards the continent between 1990 and 1993, the latter having actually become the second foreign market (behind the United States) for Taiwan. China is Hong Kong's major commercial partner (direct and indirect) as supplier and customer; China is so important for Hong Kong that without China, Hong Kong would not be able to be considered as an international commercial centre (or, at any rate, not without difficulty).

The growth in direct investment and the increase in foreign trade that it has generated will accelerate the economic integration of the region. The multinationals are undertaking transnational activities to make the most of the specializations of the different countries in the region and also of the economics of scale which can help them to gain a larger market share. The economic integration induced through direct investment is different from that which is initiated by government policy, characterized by the reduction or abolition of trade barriers between the countries involved and so, in fact, the creation of a free exchange zone. But in reality, the frontier between those two types of integration is not always clear. Integration by policy aims at developing the trade of the region. As this reaches a certain level, firms invest beyond the national frontier in order to adapt to a larger-scale market, thus bringing about a regional productive system[26].

The development of economic and commercial relations in the region of eastern Asia has created an international division of labour essentially based upon differences in productive endowment and technological levels. Japan, having massively delocalized its industries with labour intensity and standard technology towards the NIC and the ASEAN in the 1970s and 1980s, is specialized in the field of high technologies. The NIC dispose of standard technologies and are striving to develop high-technology industries, delocalizing their labour-intensive industries towards ASEAN in the second half of the 1980s and towards China more recently. Thus, the industrial division of labour which China was part of in the eighties is undeniably vertical. The vertical division of labour is described by the 'wild goose' model (Japan at its level, NIC in the middle, China and ASEAN behind), advocated by Japanese industrialists and some economists. The main advantage of this model is the complementarity of countries endowed with different wealth factors and different levels of technology. This model well characterizes Asian economic development in the 1970s and the 1980s.

Since the beginning of the 1990s, the massive arrival of large American and European firms has modified, to a certain extent, this mainly vertical labour division in the region. In effect, the non-Asian firms settled in China have a superior technological level to that of Asian firms. The average size of investment projects testifies to this[27]. This phenomenon is proof of the strategies of American and European firms aiming at the conquest of the Chinese market. Thus, just for one year (1993), the USA invested more than two billion dollars, largely exceeding Japanese investments. In the same way, European firms (notably the British and the French) have multiplied their investment projects. The multinational firms[28] are progressively integrating cheaper Chinese labour and qualified researchers into their own productive systems.

Competition and the challenge of the American and European multi-nationals have awakened the Japanese industrialists, who are progressively moving the centre of their investments from the traditional sectors (the textile industry and the food transformation industries) towards more modern sectors (the car industry, the machine industry, electronics, energy). Since 1993, the car industry has experienced the strongest increase in investment; big Japanese manufacturers such as Toyota, Mazeda, Honda and Nissan have all created joint ventures in China. In the same way, electronics groups such as Matsushita, Toshiba, Sony and Hitachi have been accelerating the rate of their investment.

The massive investment of the big multinationals is probably going to modify the technological content of 'made in China' products. The international vertical mode of the division of labour will be replaced by both a vertical and a horizontal mode.

5 CONCLUSION

In order to attract direct foreign investment, the Chinese government has striven to improve the investment environment since the end of the 1970s, granting considerable advantages to joint ventures (co-enterprises). But investment fluctuated in the 1980s because of interior political and economic factors. The beginning of the 1990s has been marked by an unprecedented speeding-up of investment development.

Generally speaking, direct foreign investment in China follows both an industrial logic and a market logic. If the American and European multinationals are more attracted by the potential of the Chinese market than by the low price of labour, the case of the Chinese of the Diaspora in eastern Asia (notably in Hong Kong, Macao and Taiwan) is different. They have almost solely been interested in low production costs (labour, sites, raw materials) at least up to the most recent period. The Chinese in southern Asia (ASEAN) are different yet again and above all very heterogeneous: some aim at a local market, others rather at advantageous production conditions; still others have fewer economic considerations than political or cultural ones. Faced with massive foreign investment, China has not been passive: actively attracting the investments and reorienting them, China includes them in its global strategy.

Direct foreign investment has conditioned the structure of foreign trade in China. It has favoured the integration of the Chinese economy within the international division of labour, notably in the eastern Asia region, and contributed to accelerating the economic integration of the region.

Notes

1. Source: *Almanac of China's Foreign Economic Relations and Trade, 1993/94*, p 720.
2. Also called firms in co-operation, the contractual joint-ventures are administered according to a well defined contract as regards the rights and obligations of the partners, but not according to the shares hold by both partners. For more details, see Gu and Xu, p 23–28.
3. Sources: *Almanac of China's Foreign Economic Relations and Trade, 1993/94*, p 56; *Statistical Yearbook of China, 1994*, p 528.
4. Source: Duan and Yang, p 101. This figure is the authorised or contractual amount, widely superior to the realised amount. Indeed, both amounts coexist in the official statistics in China.
5. The Chinese government, in order to stimulate foreign investments in the productive sectors, made a distinction in 1986 between the productive investments and the non-productive investments: only the former can benefit from bigger advantages.
6. Here and later on, the word 'amount' without other indications designates the realized amount.
7. The whole of the coastal regions includes 11 provinces and municipalities, among which four are in the South (Hainan, Guangxi, Guangdong, Fujian), three in the centre (Zhejiang, Shanghai, Jiangsu) and four in the North (Shandong, Tianjin, Hebei, Liaoning).
8. Association of South-Estern Asian Nations: Malaysia, Thailand, Indonesia, Philippines, Singapore, Brunei.
9. New Industrial Countries: Taiwan, South Korea, Hong-Kong and Singapore.
10. Bouteiller (1993) p 29.
11. For instance, in Indonesia, the Chinese represent less than 3% of the population but control at least 80% of the national wealth; in Thailand, the main banks (*Bangkok Bank, Bangkok Metropolitan Bank, Bank of Ayudhya*) belong to Chinese families. For more details, see Besson an Lanteri, p 156–160.
12. Carried out by *French Business Association*. Quoted by Bouteiller (1994), p 106.
13. For instance, for sometime, the Breton Group Le Duff (La Brioche Dorée, le Fournil de Pierre, Lucio, Bridor) has been intending to set up in Shanghai, by searching both for a Hong Kong partner and a Shanghai partner.

14. Still worse, the case of a Chinese living abroad or even in China and offering a share of capital under the form of currency, without intervening in the created firm is rather frequent.
15. Pei (1995).
16. According to the Chinese official statistics, the first four investors in China for the 1979–1993 period are: Hong-Kong (62.4%) Japan (8.5%) the United States (8.5%) and Taiwan (8.2%).
17. In 1993, the first four investors in China are: Hong-Kong (62.8%) Taiwan (11.3%), the United-States (7.5%) and Japan (4.9%).
18. The investments announced are here to be understood (not necessarily the realized investments), by the firms quoted on the Stock Exchange in Hong-Kong. See Bouteiller (1994) p 111.
19. 89.5% in 1992 according to *Hong-Kong Federation of Industries*. See Bouteiller (1994) p 111.
20. 33.9% in the province of Guangdong, 10.4% in the two main towns of Fujian (Xiamen and Fuzhou), 7% in Shanghai in 1992 according to *Taiwan Mainland Affairs Commission*. See Bouteiller (1994), p 113.
21. The cultural tradition also can explain the different behaviour of people of Hong Kong and Taiwan. If Taiwanese people speak the Fujian dialect well (the main origin of Taiwanese who left the continent before 1949), they also speak Mandarin (the standard language in popular China), unlike Hong Kong people who usually speak only Cantonese.
22. Singapore at the 6th rank ahead of South Korea, Thailand at the 8th rank ahead of the United Kingdom and France, the Philippines at the 12th rank ahead of Australia and Italy, Malaysia at the 15th rank ahead of Netherlands, and Indonesia at the 18th rank ahead of Germany.
23. Singapore realizes from twice to thrice as many investments in southeast Asia as in China.
24. It is to be noted that wage costs in the southern coastal regions are three times higher than those in inland China.
25. For instance, in 1986, the distinction between productive and no-productive investments has considerably modified the sector distribution of foreign investments.
26. The EEC has set a fine example.
27. The statistics show that the average size of the European and American projects is twice that of Japanese projects, six times that of Hong Kong projects and ten times that of Taiwanese projects
28. About a hundred of the five hundred bigger multinationals have already invested in China.

REFERENCES

Besson, D., and Lanter, M. (1994), *Ansea, la décennie prodigieuse: essai sur le développement en Asie du Sud-Est*, La documentation française, Paris.

Bouteiller, E. (1993), 'La Diaspora découvre Shanghai', *Asies Recherches*, N°10, November, Grenoble.

Bouteiller, E. (1994), 'Attirer un oiseau sur une branche: les investissements de la diaspora en Chine', *Economie Internationale*, N°57, Irst quarter, Paris.

Chesnais, F. (1994), *La mondialisation du capital*, Syros, Paris.

Duan, X. and Yang, Q. (1993), *Foreign direct investment* (in Chinese), Popular Editor, Shanghai.

Duanning, J. H. (1977), 'Trade Location of Economic Activity and the Multinational Enterprises: Search for an Eclectic Approach' in Ohlin *et al*, *The International Allocation of Economic Activity*, London.

Fouquin, M., Dourille-Feer, E. and Oliveira-Martins, J. (1991), *Pacifique: le recentrage asiatique*, Economica, Paris.

Gentelle, P. (1994), *Economie de la Chine*, Armand Colin Editeur, Paris.

Gu, G. and Xu, X. (1994), *Management of Co-enterprises* (in Chinese), Editions of Fudan University, Shanghai.

Lemoine, F., Saint Vaulry A. and Drame, M. (1994), 'Hong-Kong – Chine: un dragon a deux têtes. Comment se tisse leur intégration économique et commerciale', *Economie Internationale*, N°57, ler trimestre, Paris.

Lim, L. Y. C. and Pang, E. F. (1991), *L'investissement direct étranger et l'industrialisation: en Malaisie, á Singapour, á Taiwan et en Thaïlande*, OCDE, Paris.

Loeffler, C. (1993), 'L'essor des investissements directs étrangers des NPI dans la région Asie-Pacifique', *Asies Recherches*, N°10, novembre, IREPD, Grenoble.

OCDE (19991), *Le commerce international, l'investissement et la technologie dans les années 1990*, Paris.

Pei, C. (1995), 'Foreign Businessmen's Investment in Mainland China and Industrial Division of Labour in East Asia' (in Chinese), *Contemporary Asia-Pacific Studies*, N°2, Beijing.

Xu, T. (1994), *The economy of the Asia-Pacific towards the 21th century* (in Chinese), Planning Editions of China, Beijing.

APPENDIX 1: FOREIGN DIRECT INVESTMENT IN CHINA
1979–1993

Table 7.4

	Number of projects	In millions of dollars	
		Contractual amount	Realized amount
1979–1982	922	6,012	1,168
1983	470	1,731	635
1984	1,856	2,650	1,258
1985	3,073	5,931	1,658
1986	1,498	2,834	1,875
1987	2,233	3,709	2,314
1988	5,945	5,297	3,194
1989	5,779	5,600	3,393
1990	7,273	6,535	3,487
1991	12,978	11,980	4,370
1992	48,764	58,124	11,007
1993	83,437	111,436	27,515
Total	174,228	221,898	61,870

Sources: *Economical Yearbook of China 1992* for the data until 1991; *Statistical Yearbook of China 1994* for the data of 1992 and 1993.

APPENDIX 2:   THE FORMS OF FOREIGN DIRECT INVESTMENT (REALIZED) IN CHINA 1979–1993

Table 7.5

In millions of dollars

	Joint venture		Contractual Joint venture		Entirely foreign enterprise		Co-operative exploitation	
	Number	Amount	Number	Amount	Number	Amount	Number	Amount
1979–1982	83	99	793	532	33	40	13	496
1983	107	74	330	227	15	43	18	292
1984	741	255	1,089	465	26	15	-	523
1985	1,412	580	1,611	585	46	13	4	481
1986	892	804	582	794	18	16	6	260
1987	1,395	1,486	789	620	46	25	3	183
1988	3,909	1,975	1,621	779	410	226	5	213
1989	3,659	2,037	1,179	752	931	371	10	232
1990	4,091	1,790	1,317	645	1,860	751	5	214
1991	8,395	2,300	1,778	760	2,795	1,130	10	170
1992	34,354	6,210	5,711	2,060	8,692	2,460	7	277
1993	54,003	15,524*	10,445	5,151*	18,975	6,150*	14	693*
Total	113,041	33,134	27,245	13,471	33,847	11,240	95	4,033

* Estimation on the basis of the distribution of 1992.
Sources: Economical Yearbook of China 1992 for the data until 1991; *Statistical Yearbook of China 1994* for the data of 1992 and 1993.

APPENDIX 3:   THE 20 FIRST COUNTRIES INVESTING IN CHINA
IN 1993

Table 7.6

Countries	Realized amount (in millions of dollars)	In %
Hong Kong	17,445	62.82
Taiwan	3,139	11.30
United States	2,068	7.45
Japan	1,361	4.90
Macau	588	2.12
Singapore	492	1.77
South Korea	381	1.37
Thailand	234	0.84
United Kingdom	221	0.80
France	141	0.51
Canada	137	0.49
Philippines	123	0.44
Australia	110	0.40
Italy	100	0.36
Malaysia	91	0.33
Kuwait	84	0.30
Netherlands	84	0.30
Indonesia	66	0.24
Germany	62	0.22
Switzerland	47	0.17
Total of 20 countries	**26,974**	**97.13**
Total	**27,771**	**100**

Source: *Statistical Yearbook of China 1994.*

8 China: an Evaluation of Political Risk

Maria Weber

1 THE CONCEPT OF POLITICAL RISK

Before making any decision about investing in another country, business people have always questioned whether such an investment could be risky due to political factors, such as a sudden change in regime, a revolution or a coup. However, while economic and financial risk analysis has received much attention during the past thirty years, and many techniques have been developed for this analysis, this does not appear to be the case for political risk. But what is political risk? Some have defined it as the risk of a political change or political instability. Others have seen it as the result of a change in politics and the probability that certain events will occur and, therefore, change the prospective profits of an investment. Even today, there is no agreement upon the definition of 'political risk'. Political risk is sometimes considered as a particular aspect of the broader 'country risk' and sometimes as the 'probability that a political event will intervene and modify the economic situation' (which more correctly means an evaluation of an index of political stability). Other wise, it is thought of as the more general 'possible trends in the international credit market'. Obviously, as the definition changes, so do the variables considered in analysing political risk.

It was only from the mid-1970s, and thanks to the oil crisis, that the close link between economic conditions and political events became evident; therefore, since then, intellectual attention has been focused on the evaluation of political risk with the aim of establishing general guidelines and systematic theories on the subject. Major international banks, pushed by the growing indebtedness of developing countries, have been the promoters of much research into the analysis of 'country risk' in order to be able to forecast the risk of non-payment by countries applying for loans. In the following years many indexes used in the evaluation of country risk from a political viewpoint were created. Some of these indexes emphasize social rifts, such as ethnic or linguistic divisions, tribal wars and religious tensions, intended as variables of social fragmentation which are potentially conflictual in nature and which can give rise to guerrilla warfare, revolts,

144

etc. Other indexes try to focus on the potential impact of non-economic factors on investments, like government politics and the attitude of governments towards foreign investors. This would help in evaluating the risk of expropriation or nationalization, in addition to the risk of civil war and political instability. Moreover, these indexes are based on explicit causal relationships and supported by econometric analysis; this provides the obvious advantage of allowing comparison between different countries even if the rigidity of indicators often prevents us from adapting them to the individual countries in comparison.

Two indexes can be drawn out of the many country risk indexes and, in particular, political risk analysis: the BERI index and the WPRF index. The BERI (Business Environment Risk Index), one of the first of this kind, allows the enquirer to carry out an analysis founded on the classification of variables into four basic categories: political, management, financial and national factors. The index is created on the basis of expert opinion worldwide, which is then evaluated by other experts. Another assessment system is the Frost and Sullivan WPRF (World Political Risk Forecast), which is very similar to the previous index but allows users to weigh certain variables differently, depending on specific needs, or to include new information when this is considered as an improvement.

The PSSI (Political System Stability Index), devoted to the analysis of political risk, joined these two general indexes in 1979. Developed by Haendel in the same year, it measured the stability of a political system starting from fifteen socio-economic and political indicators which facilitate the construction of conflict and stability indexes. The concept of political stability deserves some thought: the instability of a political system does not, in itself, coincide with political risk. Moreover, it is only one of the factors to check when trying to carry out an analysis of political risk. The measure of political instability on the basis of empirical indicators, such as coups, does not necessarily contribute to the evaluation of risk. As effectively highlighted by Gori, 'there can be political risk both in a stable and in an unstable situation, just as political risk can be absent in situations which, from our point of view, we would define as far too unstable. In any case, what destabilizes one political structure may not have the same effect on another'. For example, if coups are only one manifestation of political instability, they certainly must not be assumed to represent a political risk. Indeed, in some contexts, the recourse to authoritarianism has fostered the emerging and strengthening of modernizing leadership, opening up the way to the economic development of the country.

Hence, political risk takes on different values depending on different viewpoints. In the eyes of foreign investors, political risk seems different than when seen by international concerns or banks. For this reason, political risk analysis must be as rich in information as possible and always with a view to comparison. Supplying a lot of information is a way to encourage the interpretation of data. For example, if some social disorder occurring in a country has caused a radical change in regime, this is registered as a politically seriously unstable country, but that does not necessarily mean that instability will continue in the future, nor that it involves political risk. We can therefore define 'political risk' as the product of the negative effects of political events on economic and financial decisions. Political risk is a sort of 'uncertain strategy' which can be quantitatively defined as 'the product of the probability for a political event to occur with an intensity determined over a precise period of time, based on the damage related to such event'.

2 ECONOMIC REFORMS AND POLITICAL AUTHORITARISM IN CHINA

China is the third largest country in the world: 1.2 billion people, over one-fifth of the world's population, live there. The labour force is over 565 million: 60% in agriculture and forestry, 25% in industry and commerce, 5% in social service, 5% in construction and mining and 5% in other sectors. Of the population over 15 years, 78% are literate and can read and write at least 1,500 Chinese characters.

China's economic development is guided by a twenty-year plan, including the ten-year plan (1991–2000) and the current five-year plan (1991–1995). Since the latter part of 1978 the Chinese leadership has been moving from the Soviet-style centrally planned economy to a more flexible and productive economy with market-driven elements. The 'open door policy' decided in 1978 opened as an export-oriented policy with many incentives to foreign investors.

There are several types of priority investment area. The first type are the SEZs (Special Economic Zones): Shantou, Shenzhen and Zhuhai in Guangdong province, Xiamen in Fujian province and Hainan Island. The second type are the open coastal cities (the 'Gold Coast'), including (from 1982): Quinhauangdao and Dalian in Liaoning Province; Yantai and Qingdao in Shandong Province; Tianjin and Shanghai; Lianyungang and Nantong in Jiangsu Province; Ningbo and Wenzhou in Zhejiang Province; Zuzhou in Fujian Province; Guangzhou and Zhanjiang in Guangdong Province; Beihai in Guanxi Province. From 1992 they also included: Heihe and Suifenhe in Heilongjiang Province; Hunchun in Jilin Province; Manzhouli in Inner Mongolia Autonomous Region. Some economic and technical development zones, such as Pudong District of Shanghai opened in

1990, are intended to become an integral part of the social and economic surroundings, unlike the SEZs which are fenced off and separated from the surrounding area.

In March 1993 the People's National Assembly approved the decisions made by the Communist Party Congress during October. Reform consolidation was institutionalised with the introduction of important changes to the Constitution and the amendment of eight of its 138 articles. The 'socialist market economy' was officially introduced into the Constitution and, from now on, the Government will abandon the planned-economy model in favour of the 'Socialist market economy' model; the definition of 'government-controlled companies' has also changed into 'state-owned companies'. The responsibility system, which started linking individual income to production some time ago in the agricultural field, was officially introduced in industry as well, by entrusting the management with the company's economic results.

The success of the 'open door policy' is shown by a few macroeconomic indicators. Today China boasts the highest GNP growth rate at a worldwide level, an import – export increase of US $195.8 billion, a steady growth trend of foreign investments totalling 174,000 projects approved for basic industry and facilities, equal to an amount of US $63.9 billion. The 'open door policy' produced also an economic overheating with a monetary overhang and high levels of inflation (+25% in 1993). The government's efforts to get the inflation rate down below 15% were successful. In September 1995, it was announced that the consumer price index was on line with the government's objectives, even if consumer price inflation, which includes services, remained higher (+19% in 1995). Part of the inflationary pressure continues to come from the expansion of the money supply, which is the result of the rising public sector deficit as well the continuing inflow of foreign exchange. Foreign trade continues to generate a surplus, but year on year GNP growth fell to 9.8% in the third quarter of 1995.

The strategic combination of economic growth and political control was facilitated by the strong psychological support provided by most of the population to the economic welfare produced by the consolidation of reforms. Jiang Zemin, Secretary General of the Communist Party and President of the Republic, summarized the reasons for political stability as economic growth and political control. These were the features of the 'political development with Chinese characters', as the Communist leadership emphasized also on the occasion of the fifth anniversary of the Tienanmen slaughter.

All observers agree that China will go on pursuing its economic reform policy, preserving the peculiarities of its political system. It is not mere chance that the Chinese leadership looks with sympathy at the model of Singapore, where economic growth was closely led by a firm one-party regime. However, some authors argue that Chinese authoritarianism is developing from the typical form of vertical authoritarianism to a new form of 'horizontal' or 'fragmented' authoritarianism. Horizontal authoritarianism is still an authoritative system, however less customized and more institutionalized, that is able to better respond to the challenges set by the social environment in a country moving towards quick economic renovation.

The distinction is a major one, since horizontal authoritarianism, according to some authors, is very likely to develop, in turn, into a more pluralistic system. The elements that participated in changing the decision-making process in China from vertical authoritarianism to horizontal, or fragmented, authoritarianism may be detected both in the effects produced by the economic reform process, that is in the progressive decision-making decentralization, and in the plan for the reorganization of the political and administrative system, implemented starting from 1982.

Deng Xiaoping was always a firm supporter of a more effective administration. To this end, he considerably streamlined the governmental system, trying to ensure greater decision-making autonomy to some organizations, such as the National Assembly, and giving start to the actual reorganization of the Government 'in the name of efficiency and of the specific skills of the administrative staff'. The plan for Government reorganization, approved in March 1982, gave start to a number of actions that enormously changed the complex bureaucratic system of the People's Republic of China. After abolishing the concept of appointment for life for political officials, a system for task assignment was introduced, based on professional and managing skills. The state system was renewed by encouraging senior cadres to resign and leave the floor to younger and better educated workers.

This action, aimed at improving the professional skills of the bureaucratic system, is even more important since in no other country in the world has the public administration set such deep roots as in China. Ever since the remotest times, the vastness of the territory has called for the development of a widely decentralized administration. Centralized administration is an institution dating back to the Empire's foundation (Ch'in dynasty, 221–206 b.C.). Bureaucracy turned China into a wide unified Empire, endowed with well-established administrative traditions that ensured its stability through the centuries. The power of the Empire's bureaucracy was undoubtedly great, as was the social status of bureaucrats. A famous saying, still widespread today, states that 'if you want to hoard riches, you must enter the public administration' and gain access to the highest offices of the State. As a matter of fact, studies focusing on the history of Chinese administration highlight how widespread was corruption, an aspect of daily life which was mostly accepted or tolerated. From the time of the Han dynasty to the abolition of the state examination in 1905, the framework of public administration was reformed several times with the introduction of new government bodies, but the original bureaucratic structure, inspired by Confucius, remained mostly unchanged in its principle and functions. When the People's Republic of China was established in 1949, many traditional elements were preserved, such as territory divisions and the unitary (non-federative) state model, with the decentralization of functions to peripheral institutions.

During these eighteen years of reform, the progressive improvement of professional skills within the bureaucratic system was combined with a widespread decline in recourse to ideology, meant as a tool to control the population through mass campaigns, as well as in the use of compulsion. Indeed, the reform policy contributed to a redistribution of information flows within the political system, and enormously limited the role of ideology as a form of policy implementation. However, the bureaucratic framework of the system, though professionally developed, renewed and considerably reduced in numbers, still influences the implementation of any political decision.

A recent analysis of decision-making processes in the Chinese political system highlights the fact that most of the bureaucratic frameworks of Mao's time have remained unchanged and still strongly influence political power. Economic reforms, in particular, strengthened the decentralization of the bureaucratic system, since a fragmented and deep-rooted bureaucratic framework still exists between central ministries and regional governments.

3   WHICH WAY WILL THE CHINESE POLITICAL SYSTEM DEVELOP?

At the not-too-far-away death of Deng Xiaoping, reformers and conservatives will resume their struggle within the party. Deng is well aware that, as long as he is alive, no other leader may stand out, but he is also aware of being old and seriously ill. His indirect power is enormous, but not absolute, since reforms still clash against the opposition of many within the party. Which way will the Chinese political leadership follow at the death of this great charismatic leader? Many observers agree that the political system after Deng may only go on along the same way and consolidate the horizontal, or fragmented, authoritative model with the gradual and progressive expansion of the decision-making base. Should the horizontal authoritative model be consolidated in the next few years, we may reasonably suppose that the field for political participation would be widened with the progressive opening of the 'control room' to emerging social forces. Within this context, the decision-making base is likely to spread to political groups, accepting the 'leadership of the CCP' and prepared to co-operate in view of economic reforms.

Besides the consolidation of the current horizontal authoritative model, other ways are still open, offered by regional division and based on an aggravation of the struggle between the centre and the periphery. The map of China shows the existence of at least three Chinas: a 'red' one, a 'pink' one and a 'white' one. The three Chinas are something more than a mere *divertissement*: they are three precise realities that clearly appear from the macroeconomic results of the last few years. From a geographical viewpoint, 'red' China is located in the north of the country, particularly in the region around Beijing, where the party's control is still very strong. In 'red' China, the power of bureaucracy and political control are clearly visible, finding expression in the huge number of bureaucratic shackles, in the lack of efficiency of big state-owned companies and even in people's conversation. However, the free-market wave has altered the streets of the capital and attracts something more every day, so much so that we may even wonder how long ideological loyalty may prevail over individual economic interests.

'Pink' China is located in the east-central area of the country, with Shanghai as potential capital, where ideological and market values have always co-existed. Since last century Shanghai has been the Chinese town most open to the outer world and to the values of Western culture, even though it always kept into account the dictates of political interests. Today Shanghai, with 14 million inhabitants and an urban area of 518 sq.m., is with good reason the leader of development in the central regions of the country, although it has never equalled the growth rate of coastal areas. So far Shanghai has just claimed greater political power in the decisions of the central government and an adequate number of ministerial appointments. But a feeling of revenge against Beijing's leadership is now growing in the town, and some observers claim that Shanghai is preparing to claim the right to the country's leadership, maybe heading a possible revolt of southern regions. These are just assumptions, for the time being, but they will show some grains of truth if 'white' China puts forward separationist claims.

'White' China, located in the south of the country, has its focus in the Guangdong province, where the economic success of SEZs (Special Economic Zones) contributed to the dissolution of the weak ideological links while bearing in triumph the free market values. The Guangdong province was favoured by foreign investments (+115%), both thanks to its closeness to Hong Kong and to the presence of Shenzhen (one of the first

SEZs), towns created from nothing at the onset of the 'open-door' policy, today counting over two and a half million inhabitants. While the growth rate is fastest in the Guangdong province, the whole coast of southern China has attained a development by far greater than the rest of the country, thanks to the presence of the SEZ's and the 14 coastal towns where the 'open-door' policy towards foreign investors has been implemented for fifteen years. The success of the 'Gold Coast' has produced many social problems: above all, social mobility from the rural areas and the inner regions, where rural unemployment drove more than 100 million illegal immigrants to the Gold Coast.

The enormous difference in economic development between north and south, the worsening of the current conflicts in the fiscal sector, the difficult relationships between the central government and the local governments of Southern regions are all likely to increase in the next few years. Hence it is appropriate to wonder what will happen at Deng's death or, perhaps more appropriately, some time after the fateful year 1997, when Hong Kong will be back under Chinese jurisdiction. 'White' China could take inspiration from Hong Kong's case to apply for a *de facto* separation from the rest of the country. The wish to imitate Hong Kong may already be detected in the political leadership of Guangdong province: as an example, let us just think about the recent trip to Germany made by the managing group of the Guangdong government, and about the agreements signed directly with Chancellor Kohl. These are autonomous deeds which the central government tolerates, but since the government in Beijing could hardly accept a shift from autonomy to separationism, what would happen should this be the case? Many variables should be considered in this respect, making the scenario even more complex.

We should understand whether the separationist pressures exerted by southern China may indirectly strengthen the conservative group within the party, always critical towards reform, and justify, as a reaction, an attempt to restore the party's absolute power in the country, with a revival of the vertical authoritative model. Should this attempt occur, the scenario would be considerably widened. In particular, we may wonder what the army would do. Facing the possible request from the government in Beijing to restore the socialist order in the southern rebel regions, how could the army respond?

4   AN ASSESSMENT OF POLITICAL RISK

Besides the consolidation of the current horizontal authoritative model, however, two more scenarios are possible: (a) the restoration of absolute power to the party, along with a revival of the vertical authoritative model, and some form of restriction or limitation to economic reforms; (b) the revival of a new form of the 'warlords' regime. Both hypotheses are founded on the crucial role played by the army in the outcome of the political crisis of June 1989. Before that, the last military intervention in politics dated back to the Cultural Revolution in 1967, when Mao asked the army to support him and to eliminate the Red Guards. It took fifteen years, from 1970 to 1985, to bring the armed forces back to their barracks and to limit their power. The armed forces' involvement in the 1989 crisis brought them back on the political scene, and their influence is demonstrated by the growing importance of the party's Commission for Military Affairs in political matters. Should the succession to Deng Xiaoping bring along a new crisis, the army's importance would be conclusive.

We have to consider also the fact that China is acutely sensitive to any real slight to international prestige. Such sensitivity is revealed by the fact that the unification of China is an important goal for the leadership. Unification means not only Hong Kong and Macao, soon coming back to China, but also Taiwan. The Sino-British Joint Declaration signed in December 1984 will allow Hong Kong to return to Chinese sovereignity on 1st July 1997. A similar joint declaration with Portugal was signed for the return of Macau in 1999. Even so, we have to consider another important variable: China's tension with Taiwan.

Since 1949, Taiwan has been seen from Beijing as one province of PRC. Relations with Taiwan have improved substantially, although both Beijing and Taipei still claim to be the sole legitimate government of China. So, even if it has reduced over the past decade as economic ties have increased, tension with Taiwan remains. There will be a risk that the Chinese Army will invade the island. International observers fear military confrontation: from the military point of view, Taiwan would win a direct confrontation with China, but according to many observers the risk remains. Once the ripples from the missiles which splashed down just off the Taiwan coast in the summer of 1995 had faded away, Jiang Zemin invited the Taiwanese President, Lee Teng-hui, to visit Beijing, looking for a diplomatic solution. Mr Lee didn't ask his government to consider the offer 'rationally'. The Communist Party, while reiterating its right to defend Taiwan by force, has decided to strengthen and raise the status of the Central Leading Group for Taiwan Affairs. According to a statement issued by Xinhua, a public relations job is to be done on world opinion by arguing that China's position on Taiwan is justified under international law.

While political integration may be as far away as ever, the economic integration of the two economies continues apace. Trade between the two, via Hong Kong, rose 35% in 1995. Taiwan's government has begun to face up to the implications of Hong Kong's return to China, and in a significant move has signed an agreement to allow Dragonair of Hong Kong and Air Macao to carry passengers from Taiwan to China: this is the first time since 1949 that direct flights have been allowed. Economic reunification is running ahead of political unification.

On the international field, there are also some border disputes: the current disputes include the boundaries with India, with Tajikistan, with Russia and with North Korea. A complex dispute is over the Spratly Islands with Malaysia, Philippines, Taiwan, Vietnam and Brunei. Another dispute is on Paracel Islands, occupied by China but claimed by Vietnam and Taiwan. Claims are also made to the Japanese administered Senkaku-shoto Islands. Relations with Vietnam have improved, even if claims remain on the maritime boundary in the Gulf of Tonkin.

The Chinese Red Army is not necessarily compact inside, and the division of China into 'red' and 'white' parts could be reflected by the military framework as well. In particular, the armed forces of the southern regions are enormously favoured by economic reforms, and personally manage companies and hotel chains. It is not easy to say how deep the rifts are within the Red Army, although military commanders have given evidence of regional rather than national loyalty on various occasions. China's history teaches us that the armed forces often played a decisive role in political balance, but the age of the warlords belongs to a feudal model, and feudalism may hardly be associated with a diffusion of economic welfare. Tensions with Taiwan might increase the Army's wish to control the situation and to maintain a strong power inside the political system.

In conclusion, an overall analysis of the political risk for foreign investors in China may be summarised as three possible scenarios. At present, the first scenario, involving the consolidation of economic reforms with a progressive structural diversification and a gradual functional specialization, is by far the most likely. In the next few months the main thing will be to see whether the present political leadership succeeds in stopping the circulating monetary mass and in blocking inflation, while remaining on the road to reform. The reallocation of resources and the considerable economic growth are undermined by unprecedented inflation rates. And inflation, besides frustrating the immediate effects of the great economic growth, also tends to widen the existing gap between towns and countryside and to increase the farmer's dissatisfaction. Welfare expectations, widespread among people, may undergo harsh repercussions in the next few months and the farmer's dissatisfaction has already emerged from several protests. However, these expectations seem to represent a powerful spur to social cohesion and, as long as economic growth brings along wealth distribution, town-countryside imbalances may only produce politically irrelevant tensions, at least from the viewpoint of the risk involved for foreign investors.

Should the management of inflation require the Chinese government to adopt a more moderate reform policy and detrimental political decisions for southern regions, the political risk would still be low, even though we should see whether the central government is able to avoid conflicts in its relationships with these regions. For example, we may assume that Beijing will grant a quiet and implied approval to a progressive increase of the decision-making autonomy of the southern regions, i.e. of the richest regions of the country, provided that these do not question the political legitimacy, and therefore the power, of the Communist Party, as well as its 'ideal' supremacy.

A higher political risk would certainly be involved if the country's southern regions required greater autonomy, arousing a strong reaction by the central government in the long run. If the southern regions, possibly establishing an alliance with Shanghai, wanted to achieve actual secession from the rest of the country, Beijing would call in the armed forces, and the burst of a civil war could not be excluded. A situation similar to that of the age of the warlords would be established, when each country fought against all the others, and China was dragged to the verge of total fragmentation. Actually I consider this scenario, feared by some Western Sinologists, as basically unlikely, at least as long as this strong economic growth goes on. Even if tensions with Taiwan might increase the Army's wish to control the situation inside the political system.

REFERENCES (SELECT BIBLIOGRAPHY)

Banerjee, D., 'China's policies in the 1990s', in *Strategic Analysis*, 14 (1), Apr. 91, pp 3–16.

Baum, R., 'Political stability in post-Deng China: problems and prospects', in *Asian Survey*, 32 (6), June 92, pp 491–505.

Bell, M. W., Khor H. E., and Kockhar K., *China at the Threshold of a Market Economy*, International Monetary Fund, occasional paper 107, september 1993.

Boddewyn, J., and Cracco, E. F. 'The political Game in World Business', in *Columbia Journal of World Business*, January 1972.

Bunn, D. W., and Mustafaglu, M. M. *'Forecasting Political Risk'*, in *Management Science*, 24 November, 1978.

Garnaut R., and Guoguang L. (eds, *Economic Reform and Internationalisation: China and the Pacific Region*, Sydney, Allen & Unwin, 1992.

Gibelli, M. C., and Weber, M. (eds), *Una modernizzazione difficile: economia e sociéà in Cina dopo Mao*, Milano, Angeli, 1983.

Gori, U. '*Analisi critica dei metodi di valutazione del rischio politico*', in *Guida all'esportazione dei beni industriali*', Roma, Efibanca, 1985.

Gori, U. '*Rischio politico e politica estera*', in *Affari Esteri*, 71, 1986.

Green, R. T. '*Political Structures as a Predictor of Radical Political Change*', in *Columbia Journal of World Business*', Spring 1974.

Howell, Jude *China Opens Its Doors, The Politics of Economic Transition*, Harvester Wheatsheaf, Lynne Rienner Publ., 1993.

Lieberthal, K. G., and Lampton, D. M. (eds), *Bureaucracy, Politics, and Decision Making in Post-Mao China*, Berkeley, University of California Press, 1992.

Segal, G. 'Opening and dividing China', in *The World Today*, May 1992, pp 77–80.

Shapiro, J. A., Behrman, J. N., Fischer, W. A., and Powell, S. G. *Direct Investment and Joint Ventures in China*, New York, Quorum Books, 1991.

Simon, J. D. *Political Risk Assessment: Past Trends and Future Prospects*, in 'Columbia Journal of World Business', Fall 1982.

Solomon, R. H. *Mao's Revolution and the Chinese Political Culture*, University of California press, Berkeley, 1971.

Stobaugh, B. B. *How to Analyze Foreing Investments Climates*, in 'Harvard Business Review', September 1969.

'Studies in Comparative Communism', special number on China, n. 2–3 (1989).

'The Annals of Americam Academy', special number on China, n. 519 (1992).

Tisdell, C. *Economic Development in the Context of China*, New York, St. Martin's Press, 1993.

Van Agtmael, A. W. '*How Business Has Dealt with Political Risk*', in '*Financial Executive*', January 1976,

Weber, M. '*La valutazione del rischio politico*', in Peviani, L. and Weber, M. *Le economie emergenti del Sud Est Asiatico*, Torino, Fondazione Agnelli, 1990, pp 3–33.

Weber, M. *China: from a quasi-free market economy to a more democratic system?*, paper presented at INSEAD International Meeting on 'The Future of China', Paris, 4–5 February 1994.

Weber, M. *Rapporto Cina*, Torino, Edizioni della Fondazione Agnelli, 1995

Xiao Zhi Yue, *The EC and China*, Current EC Legal Developments, Butterworths, London, 1993.

Zhao Quansheng, 'Domestic Factors of Chinese Foreign Policy: from Vertical to Horizontal Authoritarianism', in *The Annals of the American Academy*, n. 519 (1992).

APPENDIX

Figure 8.1   The Phases of Chinese Political Development

1949–1969
TRANSFORMATION PHASE:
STATE FORMATION
NATION FORMATION
PREVALENCE OF IDEOLOGY

1970–1978
CONSOLIDATION PHASE:
INSTITUTIONALIZATION AND
BUREAUCRATIZATION OF THE POLITICAL SYSTEM

1979–1991
ADAPTATION PHASE:
ECONOMIC REFORMS, PRAGMATISM AND
PROGRESSIVE STRUCTURAL DIVERSIFICATION

1992–
RESOURCE REALLOCATION PHASE:
LESS CENTRAL CONTROL OVER THE PERIPHERY
POTENTIAL INCREASE OF PARTICIPATION

Figure 8.2   Possible medium-term political scenarios

1. CONSOLIDATION OF REFORMS:

CONTINUING ECONOMIC REFORM POLICY IN THE
WHOLE COUNTRY
STRUCTURAL DIFFERENTIATION AND GRADUAL
FUNCTIONAL SPECIALIZATION
GRADUAL EXPANSION OF POLITICAL PARTICIPATION

2. RETURN TO ECONOMIC CONTROL:

ECONOMIC REFORM POLICY LIMITED TO SPECIAL
ECONOMIC AREAS
ABSOLUTE POWER TO THE PARTY
GRADUAL SEPARATION OF SOUTHERN REGIONS

3. SECESSION OF THE SOUTHERN PART OF THE COUNTRY:
SEPARATIONIST DEMAND BY SOUTHERN REGIONS
MILITARY STATE CONTROL
REFORM POLITICAL BLOCK
RISK OF CIVIL WAR

9 Chinese Macroeconomic Reforms and the Japanese Model: Implications for Japanese Companies

Robert Taylor

1 INTRODUCTION: MACROECONOMIC REFORMS

In 1992 China's macroeconomic reforms, initiated in 1978, were intensified. Such reforms have been designed to hasten the transition to a market economy and provide an attractive environment for foreign investment. China is the world's fastest-growing economy and that rapid growth is often attributed to an authoritarian political tradition and a social cohesion born of Confucianism which China shares with such successful modernizers as the so-called 'four dragons' or 'tigers' of Taiwan, Hong Kong, Singapore and South Korea as well as, more importantly, Japan. Given richer natural resource endowments and a larger population, China will pursue a developmental path necessarily different, even though the Chinese leaders are targeting elements of Japan's economic experience as worthy of emulation.

It is in the area of macroeconomic reform that the Chinese leaders see the Japanese model as most appropriate, such measures being viewed as indispensable for the further development of market forces. Since the initation of the open door policy in 1978, central planning has been reduced and the concept of the socialist market economy gradually introduced. Lest they lose their own legitimacy, the Chinese Communist Party (CCP) leaders cannot afford to be seen as abandoning socialist principles and so China's market economy is said to differ from the capitalist one, even though certain characteristics are shared, the main divergence deriving from disparate social systems. In fact, Chinese sources repeatedly emphasize that the old administrative measures characteristic of the pre-1978 command economy are by themselves no longer effective in the context of a free market, whether

157

for commodities or, increasingly since 1992, the factors of production like money, land and labour. To address this need for indirect control of the market, Chinese economic journals have discussed such measures as the changing role of the banks, interest rate adjustment, varying the money supply, refining the taxation system and liberalizing pricing[1]. In addition, action is being taken to ameliorate the undesirable consequences of the market: a social security system is in the making to confront the problems of unemployment induced in part at least by the abolition of the 'iron rice bowl' or permanent tenure for employees in state enterprises and, more particularly, in foreign-invested companies. In a climate, too, where the creation of wealth is seen as honourable, welfare measures must ensure social stability by preventing too wide a gap emerging between rich and poor[2]. For their implementation, these measures in turn require the creation of new governmental institutions to replace the old central planning mechanisms.

Japan is ostensibly a free enterprise economy and yet ever since the Meiji Restoration of 1868, which brought to power an oligarchy of dedicated modernizers, the state has always played a major role in directing economic development. There is strong evidence that the Chinese seek to introduce institutional mechanisms of control similar to those of Japan. The Office of Trade and Economics, for instance, recently established by Zhu Rongji, Vice-Premier and China's economic overlord, has been modelled on Japan's Ministry of International Trade and Industry (MITI). Likewise, the State Planning Commission, again engaged in the direction of the economy, is currently being given a role more akin to Japan's Economic Planning Agency. These parallels suggest that Chinese policy makers are looking to post-war Japan, where planning and guidance on the part of the government and a market run by business have created a partnership to achieve high growth. China's leaders, however, do not seek to produce a replica; Japan's market economy is *sui generis*, even if similar to the one envisaged. China's system is socialism with Chinese characteristics; Japan is a capitalist country with Japanese features. The difference is in degree rather than in kind.

Among Western observers much attention has been focused on foreign-invested enterprises in China, which are seen by the Chinese leadership as pace-setters for reform in China's state sector, mainly centred on heavy industry. In this context areas of special focus are technology and employment. While undoubtedly backward in terms of means of production and saddled with overmanning, the state industrial enterprises, which provide housing and welfare as well as salaries, still account for slightly less than 50% of industry's contribution to gross national product. In the context of output they are losing ground to private and foreign-invested enterprises but their health is still crucial to China's economic future. Reform of such state enterprises began in the early 1980s when greater initiative was given to individual directors and managers in the plants themselves, the policy being to separate ownership from management. Such managers were forced to engage in strategic thinking for the first time, since they had to adjust to a socialist market economy, as reforms in areas like pricing, taxation and subsidies were instituted. The main objective was to provide incentives for both management and workforce, the enterprises thereby being revitalized and made profitable, with further reforms scheduled for 1995. Meanwhile, to further institutional reform, the State Commission for Restructuring the Economy is selecting, in the course of 1994, 3,800 medium and large state-owned enterprises as experimental sites for creating a modern enterprise system in a corporation form through joint stock arrangements, with investment input from both government and private sources[3].

In China, as elsewhere, privatization is in vogue – but there are as yet a number of obstacles to successful implementation. In the Chinese case, for instance, there is some contention as to whether the state or managers should enjoy the property rights of state enterprises; the joint stock method may be the solution. Most fundamental, perhaps, is the difficulty in attempting to change the complacent attitude of both managers and workforce in state enterprises, engendered by the seller's market of the old command economy. In addition, welfare provision by enterprises is still proving a barrier to labour mobility and the creation of factor markets. At the same time, however, given that welfare provision at the national level is rudimentary though being rapidly developed, the Chinese central leadership is fearful of social unrest occasioned by unemployment and economic disadvantage. Clearly, then, there is a need for partnership between government and enterprises, both state-run and private, in the funding of a new social security system; this, as discussed in a later section, is already underway, and as it becomes comprehensive, enterprise reform will be facilitated. In summary of the above, it is suggested that throughout the world state investment will still play a substantial role in some major industries, public utilities and infrastructure, since these may require financial input beyond the capacity of private interests alone. In fact, the Japanese case, to which we now turn, amply demonstrates this.

In Meiji Japan the state, because of the scarcity of investment capital, played a major role in economic enterprise, even though in later decades it sold off industrial concerns to private interests, and this close relationship between business and government has persisted during the post-war period, the famous system of administrative guidance through the bureaucracy being the hallmark of such co-operation. The Chinese leaders seek to effect Japanese-style government intervention whenever private commercial activity shows signs of threatening the overall national interest. In a more positive sense, Chinese policy-makers are attracted to the Japanese practice whereby government planning and guidance and a market run by business have in the past joined together to achieve high growth. The objective of the Chinese leadership is to release the full potential of the industrial and commercial sectors through unleashing market forces, while maintaining overall direction of economic activity via such instruments as taxation and pricing. Reforms in these areas will be considered in turn and in parallel with the Japanese experience, where appropriate.

2 TAXATION REFORM

Taxation is a key instrument of macroeconomic management and by 1994 China's new system, tentatively developed in 1984, was ripe for reform. In the days of the command economy, prior to 1978, personal income and company taxation in the conventional Western sense did not exist in China. Moreover, in the context of the command economy, the Chinese state allocated resources and distributed revenues by administrative fiat without reference to the profit motive. But as moves were made to separate ownership and management in the early 1980s, profit sharing between industrial enterprises and the state was replaced by taxation and these reforms remained in force until 1994. In a sense the 1984 system had been a compromise designed to meet the needs of the transition to a market economy, and as such still bore vestiges of central planning and state management by administrative fiat. By the early 1990s, however, the encouragement of market forces had meant that more and more spheres of economic activity were outside the range of central control. Accordingly, based on the decisions taken at the Third Plenary Session of the Fourteenth Congress of the Chinese Communist Party, in effect China's top national decision-making body, the State Council, the equivalent of a Western cabinet, moved to implement major structural reforms of the tax system, complementing the earlier measures of the open door policy in the fields of finance, investment and foreign exchange. The tax reforms are intended to increase national wealth through market forces and foreign investment while at the same time preventing social instability. To this end, the objective is to strengthen national macroeconomic controls and achieve a proper balance of revenue and expenditure between central and local governments. In the 1980s regional inequalities and disparities of wealth between individuals increased. The absence of an equitable taxation system only exacerbated this tendency. Prior to the 1990s central and local governments in China divided fiscal revenues as fixed sums rather than percentages. Thus revenue-rich provinces like Guangdong, which have received much of the country's foreign investment, grow wealthier but the funds the government draws from the provinces have not increased correspondingly. In addition, the gap between rich and poor among the population at large has been growing. To remedy this, the Chinese central government is now devising a tax system which will ensure a more equitable distribution of income and thus resources. The tax structure is to be readjusted, and tax rates and categories rationalized. Most importantly, a proper division of tax authority as well as more equitable distribution of revenue between the central and local governments are to be effected. In sum, progressive rates for income and company tax are being introduced to reduce excessive disparities in individual wealth; similarly, distribution of revenue is being adjusted to ensure more balanced development among the country's regions. Discernible here are echoes of China's Communist egalitarian past; yet the spirit of the tax reforms is undoubtedly one of equity rather than equality.

The revenue yielded by the new taxation system is divided between the central and local governments. Different taxes are allocated on the basis of administrative authority. For example, the central government receives fixed revenues like most income taxes, customs duties, general consumption taxes and profits of nationally controlled enterprises; local governments enjoy the income taxes of some local enterprises as well as a number of agricultural and livestock taxes. Some revenues, such as the value-added taxes on commodities, are shared, 75% being given to the central government and 25% to local governments. Finally, the central government uses some of its tax revenues to allocate monies to the localities. As in most developed countries, expenditures follow the division of responsibilities as between the centre and the regions. The national government incurs expenditure for such concerns as defence, foreign relations, state enterprises and central government organisations, while regional government spending is related to the local education and health systems, price subsidies as well as the encouragement of local business through technical renovation and new product development.

Traditionally in China there has always been at best a delicate balance, and at worst tension, between central and local authorities. Given the centre's desire to promote market forces, some coastal regions, for instance, have grown richer than the hinterland. Thus the central government is using revenue from richer localities to redistribute wealth to the less endowed regions. There is nevertheless a risk in such a policy. Some local governments may resent the concessions they have had to make. In purely economic terms, too, there could be disadvantages; in the 1980s richer local governments were able to invest heavily in infrastructure to promote economic development; this may in future be precluded if the centre makes further demands on local revenue[4]. The above measures have much in common with Western taxation systems but also draw heavily on the Japanese allocation system which is now being examined by the Chinese Academy of Social Sciences; one of the major features of that system is the apportionment of financial authority between central and local governments. In Japan, as in China, main initiatives lie with the centre which has the power to draft, approve and revise local tax laws. The government in Tokyo also largely controls financing. This has meant that while the localities have carried major burdens in implementing national policy within their jurisdiction, the central government initially takes most of the revenue. Thus to ensure equity, financial resources are redistributed through such means as remission of certain centrally collected revenues and subsidies to local governments. That the Chinese leaders are attempting to increase local accountability to the centre is reflected in the tentative steps taken in 1993 to tighten the collection of taxes by such means as preventing regional governments from granting unauthorized exemptions to individuals and enterprises as well as increasing the role of banks in the remission of revenue to the state treasury. For these reasons it is the Japanese system of taxation that is being given most attention in Chinese official sources[5].

3   REFORM OF THE PRICING SYSTEM

A realistic pricing system, like equitable taxation, is seen as indispensable for the proper operation of market forces, based on the laws of supply and demand. In the days of the command economy prices were controlled by the central government and inflation disguised – but reliance on market forces requires more sophisticated controls. Thus Chinese sources stress the need to replace administrative fiat with economic control. These two regulators are not, however, mutually exclusive, and in all systems governments play a direct part in the regulation of prices to a greater or lesser extent. Once again the Chinese view the state's role in economic enterprise in Japan as an object lesson. Since 1978 the Chinese leaders have sought to increase private regulation through the market, although aware that neither capitalism nor socialism can dispense with either the plan or the market. In Japan there are three price categories: the first, subject to direct control, relates to public utilities like electricity and transport, including, for example rail and air travel, in addition to the telephone and postal services. These together represent about 18% of consumer prices. The remaining two categories account for about 82% of the total; under the second fall prices of agricultural products and other commodities which seriously affect foreign trade, and these are allowed to move within certain bands. They are thus subject to indirect control, as is the third category which encompasses most industrial and consumer goods, whether subject to monopoly or free competition. But while the prices of Japan's retail commodities move freely, the Japanese government controls wholesale prices to guarantee what is called free trade and a stable consumer market. Significantly, 80% of fresh food and consumer goods prices are influenced in this way. Chinese sources have also remarked favourably on Japanese laws against monopolies and profiteering, and credible legislation would no doubt prove a crucial adjunct to the macroeconomic controls now under consideration[6].

Under the Chinese command economy the state controlled distribution, but now that the latter is being deregulated, nationwide wholesale markets are in the process of creation[7]. This, however, is seen to necessitate supervision by national commodity price departments, for which the Japanese system has been cited as a possible model. Nevertheless, while such indirect Japanese-style control over prices is likely to be retained, deregulation is proceeding apace. By early 1993, for instance, most agricultural and sideline products had ceased to be produced according to mandatory plans and their prices had been decontrolled. The prices of only six products – grain, cotton, tobacco, raw silk, tea and timber – were still set by the state, even though these closely followed the dictates of the market. There have been similar trends in the deregulation of prices of industrial products, of which the proportion subject to mandatory planning fell from 97% to 11.6% during the years from 1978 to 1993. By 1991 the proportion of consumer goods sold at state set prices had fallen to 21% and that of capital goods to 36%. Recent official sources suggest that the impetus for price reform will maintain momentum in coming months as deregulated commodity market networks are further developed[8]. Such trends towards a free market do not, however, preclude government intervention. In late 1993, for example, in the wake of the danger of social unrest and the rapidly deteriorating terms of trade for those in agriculture, the state administratively raised the price of grain. In future so much will depend on how rapidly and effectively macroeconomic controls are put in place.

4   HUMAN RESOURCE MANAGEMENT: THE JAPANESE EXPERIENCE

The Chinese leaders believe that the key to international competitiveness lies in the creation of a market economy, albeit one under socialist leadership. In turn, market forces can only operate effectively if factors of production, including labour, may move freely. To date a major barrier impeding labour mobility has been lifetime tenure of employment in China's state enterprises, which provide not only remuneration but housing, welfare and other benefits. This is why 1980s legislation regarding bankruptcy and merges of state enterprises (where appropriate) has been implemented only slowly. Given that welfare provision, like unemployment benefit, at national level is still in its infancy, the Chinese central leadership is alert to the danger of social disadvantage. Enterprise reform as a whole, then, must proceed gradually as a nationwide social security system is put in place. In November 1993 an official at China's Ministry of Labour stated the objective of having a comprehensive social security system in place by the turn of the century. Meanwhile, for example, the state is in the process of perfecting a comprehensive unemployment insurance system, funded by the government and the enterprises, a scheme applying to public as well as private and foreign invested companies. More than one million unemployed, earlier discharged from state-owned enterprises, are said to have benefited from the state unemployment insurance system since its inception in the late 1980s[9].

Such measures have facilitated the introduction of a contract system of employment. Beginning with the recruitment of new workers in some areas in 1986, it has become operational on a trial basis nationwide since 1987. Thus while contract and 'iron rice bowl' systems coexist in state enterprises, most new workers are hired under contract. Some well-developed coastal areas like the Special Economic Zones of Shenzhen and Zhuhai have been pioneers in labour recruitment reform, and most of their workers are already employed under the contract system. Joint ventures and other foreign invested companies are in any case seen as the pace-setters in the reform of employment practices, industrial relations and technological transformation. But even in the state sector 30% of employees now work under contracts which stipulate duties, obligations and rights of both sides of industry, with the objective of inducing competitiveness through worker motivation. By March 1994, according to Labour Ministry statistics, of the 80 million workers in state enterprises 23.3 million were covered by contracts[10]. The reforms appear to be especially advanced in Shanghai where, as of March 1994, 1.6 million employees in state enterprises, accounting for 97.53% of the total, were working under various categories of labour contracts[11].

In addition to unemployment benefit provision and labour contracts, employment agencies and recruitment fairs are fostering labour mobility. As of 1993, 9,700 job introduction agencies, 2,200 re-employment training centres and 200,000 labour service companies for redundant personnel had been established under state auspices over the preceding six years[12]. A notable feature is the careers fair, an example being that held in Beijing in September 1992. More than 550 enterprises and work units were in search of professional personnel: 180 were state-owned companies, 60 Sino-foreign joint ventures, 130 collective enterprises (which come under local governments) and the remainder private and shareholding firms. This was the first fair at which state enterprises had been represented, although significantly most job seekers were in search of positions with Sino-foreign joint ventures which, as stated above, are seen as pioneers in the creation of new employment conditions and management practices[13].

Labour flexibility is being achieved through an active competitive personnel exchange market, with extensive job transfer effected via means ranging across government-sponsored agencies mentioned above to private employment systems, careers fairs and media advertising.

A number of those changing employment have moved to positions in foreign-funded enterprises because of better remuneration, welfare and opportunities for promotion[14]. In fact, the Chinese authorities have encouraged foreign-funded enterprises to recruit widely in China and hire managers from abroad; in this way it is hoped that state enterprises will emulate the human resource and other management practices of, especially, Sino-Japanese joint ventures.

The reputed strengths of Japanese companies have been given much weight in Chinese official literature. For instance, there are two areas of practice in which the Japanese may be said to excel: training and consultation. These were the foci of a report written by a Chinese manager on his secondment to a Japanese company and published in the journal *Labour Economics and Human Resource Management*. The writer noted emphasis on continuous training, both on the job and by job rotation, even though this is supplemented by more formal instruction outside the company. This applies to managers and workforce alike and is a prerequisite for promotion; appropriate qualifications must be gained, whether through the company's own research centres or outside institutions. An integral part of such training is job rotation, whereby workers and managers are seconded periodically, especially during their first years of employment, to various departments both to impart their own expertise to younger colleagues and to acquire all-round knowledge of the company's activities. Such multiskilling also helps to instil commitment to the company and conformity, although in addition the above source reports a trend towards encouraging creativity as a crucial part of training, given the greater need for innovation in high-technology industries.

Traditionally, Japanese companies have been market-driven: that is, customer needs and specifications are seen as paramount, and this is where the Japanese stress on manager-worker consultation comes into focus, particularly in the context of total quality control, a practice developed to imbue both sides with the customer's standpoint. Thus those responsible for each stage of the production process view colleagues further down the line as their customers; quality is everyone's concern, not merely that of inspectors. Finally, Japanese companies in the past have put a heavy premium on seniority in the award of promotion and salary increases; both the latter are now increasingly determined by qualifications and performance[15].

While it is not possible nor necessarily desirable for Japanese management practices as a whole to be introduced in China, training and consultation have been very much on the agenda where Japanese companies have been involved in China. Senior staff have been sent down to the front line of production and new managers selected for their entrepreneurial skills. On-the-job training has also been augmented by sending senior managers to Japan for training. As a result, quality control and international competitiveness have been enhanced. Through consultation joint-venture managers from Japan are persuading Chinese staff of the virtues of closer relationships with the workforce. But in recognizing the importance of 'face' in instituting limited forms of consultation with Chinese workers, Japanese joint venture partners have taken care to build rapport with the venture's Chinese managers lest the latter feel threatened. One major barrier to the institution of such reforms is the legacy of the command economy, where there was no necessity to be market-driven, and middle and even higher-level managers did not need to undertake strategic decision-making, which was the responsibility of the state ministries. But in time, with a new generation of Chinese managers, such problems may be resolved.

Joint ventures with foreign partners are considered pace-setters for management reform in state enterprises. We now turn to a success story; an example of Sino-Japanese co-operation. The enterprise chosen is Kanebo, which set up a joint venture, the Shanghai Huazhong Stocking Company in 1987. Kanebo, however, was no stronger to China, having made massive investments in China before the Second World War. Significantly, it had reinvested two-thirds of its profits in China. Moreover, post-1987 experience indicates that good public relations and labour relations are crucial determinants of success. First of all, the company's basic stance has been commitment to the modernization of China through the transfer of technology and business management skills. Learning, however, is a two-way process; consultation with Chinese managers and the workforce is designed to unleash the latter's creative potential. In this connection it was an advantage that managers and workers transferred to the venture by the Chinese partner were of high calibre. In addition, given the freer conditions under which joint ventures operate in terms of recruitment and remuneration in comparison to the state enterprises, motivation of Kanebo's Chinese workers has been high, with performance reflected in salary. A strong sense of identity with the company has been thereby fostered, as has dedication to quality control. Products are allegedly superior to those made by Kanebo in Japan. The joint venture, with an equity equally divided between Kanebo and the Shanghai No. 19 Cotton Fabric Factory, and now employing 500 workers, itself decides when to sell its products; currently 25% of production is taken by Japan, 45% by Hong Kong, and 5% goes to other countries. Importantly, the remainder is sold domestically in China. In fact, the huge Chinese market would seem to offer enormous potential to Sino-foreign joint ventures. Even more lucrative possibilities may open up as China's domestic markets are further liberalised; restrictions on foreign investment in retail outlets are already being lifted. To succeed, however, it is crucial that joint ventures and foreign enterprises manufacture high-quality products acceptable internationally and source their raw material in China itself, given that sales will be in foreign currency but costs in renminbi. They may thus reap exchange rate advantages. In turn, the benefits to China offered by such companies as the Kanebo joint venture are up-to-date technology transfer, high-quality goods and thus competitiveness on world markets. Such are examples to be followed by China's state enterprises.

The success of joint ventures and wholly foreign-owned companies in China has led to labour shortages, particularly of highly qualified managers. This has put upward pressure on salary levels, particularly in metropolitan areas like Shanghai. Moreover, young workers and middle-level managers are becoming increasingly difficult to recruit precisely because of economic expansion. There could, however, be downward pressure on labour costs and greater availability of labour as overmanned state enterprises lay off redundant workers. There is nevertheless no exact comparability between state enterprises and foreign ventures, as the former are generally concentrated in heavy industry while the latter are mainly engaged in textiles, electronics and high technology industries.

In 1992 the share of state enterprises in contribution to GNP finally fell below the 50% mark. Thus the remainder, the private and foreign sectors of the economy, could become a critical mass, setting the tone for reform of the state enterprises in areas like human resource management which necessarily have a bearing on other production factors like technology transfer[16].

5   CONCLUSIONS: TRADE AND INVESTMENT OPPORTUNITIES FOR JAPANESE COMPANIES

China's policy of utilising foreign investment for economic development differs from the approach adopted by other Asian countries – notably Japan, South Korea and Indonesia, which restricted and excluded investors from overseas in order to protect native industries. China's economic strategy, however, does share certain features with that of Japan. The Japanese, for example, gave priority to heavy and chemical industries, and Chinese policy has recently been moving in the same direction. In addition, in the initial period of take-off, Japan's economic growth relied more on a competitive domestic market than on exports, in contrast, for instance, with the so-called Asian dragons which have depended on a predominantly export-centred industrial structure. The Chinese, like the Japanese, have a huge domestic market which, given an increase in the number of consumers with discretionary income, provides opportunities for both foreign and Chinese manufacturers, even though initially, in the 1980s, China's leaders insisted on the export of goods produced by joint ventures. In the 1990s, however, such policy has been adjusted.

The Japanese are now set to play a major role in the development of China's heavy industries, in view of the growing interest of Japan's multinationals in the Chinese consumer market. In China, as elsewhere, there are two categories of foreign investment, direct and indirect: the former entailing foreign partners in manufacturing and service industries, the latter involving capital borrowing through government channels for large-scale projects, say in the field of infrastructure and energy, where application is likely to be nationwide. The Japanese have been active in both categories. As to the former, low-interest loans from the Overseas Economic Co-operation Fund (OECF) have increased year after year, for example from 97.2 billion yen in 1989 to 137.3 billion yen in 1992, making China Japan's second largest partner in economic co-operation. Projects constructed through such low-interest loans include the Beijing Ninth Waterworks supply project and the Baoshan Steel Company self-generating power station[17]. Improved infrastructure does itself, of course, help create the conditions for direct investment. There is growing interest by major Japanese companies in manufacturing in China. Sony Corporation, for instance, has announced its first direct investment in China with the establishment of a joint venture to manufacture video cameras. Significantly, Sony seeks to source as many key parts as possible locally. While 40% of its annual production is earmarked for export, Sony has undoubtedly been attracted by the lure of the Chinese domestic market[18]. There has certainly been a consumer goods boom in China during the late 1980s and early 1990s, especially in urban centres, but consumption is now also turning to housing, cars and other similar goods.

Production of these, however, requires the establishment of a heavy industrial base which in turn demands sustained accumulation of funds. Importantly, whereas much foreign investment in light industrial sectors has taken place on the south-eastern seaboard, heavy industry prevails in the Northeast and around the Gulf of Bohai. Domestic demand will thus increasingly favour the latter regions[19]. Significantly, a number of Japanese companies have been co-operating in the creation of the Dalian Industrial Park, construction of which began in October 1992. This is a thirty-year project and part of a Special Economic Zone. The park is the first Japanese government investment in a Sino-Japanese joint venture and has a high financial contribution from Japan's OECF, in addition to monies from the Dalian local government and Japanese companies like Marubeni and Mitsubishi. The Northeast will undoubtedly become a major focus of Japanese investment in coming decades[20].

Such a trend in borne out by Chinese statistics. As of the end of 1992, there were 394 ventures in Dalian worth in total US $1186 million, 339 in Shanghai worth US $810 million, 340 in Beijing worth US $121 million, 262 in Tianjin worth US $367 million and 183 in Shenzhen worth US $555 million. Japanese investment is being concentrated in the North. While, generally speaking, much Japanese investment is in textiles and other labour-intensive sectors, financial input is now moving into electrical equipment, electronics and transportation machinery. Household electrical appliance makers as well as motorcycle and automobile manufacturers are also moving into China. A buoyant Chinese market and the rising yen are the main incentives for such moves[21].

Foreign ventures in China are boosting China's exports. One source estimated that China was only able to increase exports of purely domestic products by US $140 million in 1993; foreign ventures, however, accounted for 27.5% or US $25.2 billion of China's total exports. Thus it is mainly the foreign ventures which give China its potential for export growth[22].

Japanese investment in China has itself contributed greatly to growth in Sino-Japanese trade which in 1993 was worth US $30 billion and in China's favour. In two-way trade China moved ahead of Germany, Taiwan and the Republic of Korea, to rise from fifth to second place among Japan's trading partners. Japan is China's second trading partner after Hong Kong and may well soon surpass the latter. Chinese exports to Japan in 1993 were stimulated by a number of factors, notably sales by Japanese manufacturers operating in China. At the same time, companies in Japan are exporting machinery and equipment needed by Japanese firms based in China and simultaneously providing the wherewithal to equip the transportation systems and infrastructure being partially financed by yen loans. China's current Eighth Five-year Plan as a whole also has an important bearing on Sino-Japanese trade, especially industrial plant exports to China.

The foregoing is not to suggest that the Japanese are the only beneficiaries of China's development programme. Western companies can also profit from China's fast-growing economy and buoyant consumer market. Europeans and Americans may assist in the training of Chinese managers, creating corporate cultures responsive to co-operation with Western countries. The Japanese do, however, have the advantage of a shared Confucian cultural heritage, geographical closeness and knowledge of the Chinese economic terrain born of wartime occupation, particularly of Northeast China. Chinese emulation of certain Japanese economic strategies is also conducive to co-operation. Thus, in spite of historical animosities and potential for conflict over influence in the Asia–Pacific region, Japanese investment in China seems set to accelerate in coming decades.

Notes

1. A number of Chinese sources discuss these measures. For advocacy of economic rather than administrative means, see 'For the Needs of the Socialist Market Economy, Create a System of Broad Control,' Jingji Guanli (Economic Management), No. 2, 1994, pp 19–20. The changing role of the banks is examined in 'Firmly Institute Money Supply Policies', Qiushi (Seeking Truth), No. 4, 1994, pp 28–30. Japanese macroeconomic controls in financial and banking areas are analysed in Zhang Shutian and Hong Feng 'Report on Japanese Price Controls', Shangye Jingji Shangye Jeye Guanli (The Commercial Economy and Company Management), No. 5, 1992, pp 135–144.
2. References to distribution of income and the social security system appear in 'Market Economy Reaching Critical Mass', JETRO China Newsletter, No. 109, March–April 1994, pp 10–14.
3. Asset ownership in state enterprises is discussed in Katsuji Nakakane, 'Whither the Economy', China Newsletter, No. 110, May–June 1994, pp 3–4. See also Yang Jishen, 'Next Years' Reform Will Bring Overall Impetus and Key Breakthroughs', Jingji Cankao, 30 November 1993 as translated in Joint Publications Research Service (hereafter JPRS), 21 January 1994.
4. Because of the constraints of space, it is not possible to give full details concerning the wide range of taxes recently introduced in China. These are, however, discussed at length in Ma Junlei and Luo Liqin, 'Important Reforms in China's Tax System, China Newsletter, No. 110, May–June 1994, pp 12–17. The issue of revenue sharing is covered in 'Market Economy Reaching Critical Mass', China Newsletter, No 109, March–April 1994, pp 10–14.
5. These measures to increase local accountability come into focus in a number of sources. For a discussion of China's taxation system against the general economic background, see Kazuhiko Mitsumori, 'China's Economy after the National People's Congress, China Newsletter, No. 105, July–August 1993, pp 7–10. Details of revenue sharing are examined by Zhang Shujing, 'Division of Authority', Shijie Zhishi (World Affairs), No. 15, 1 August 1992, p 15, as reproduced in JPRS, 30 October 1992. Defaulting by local governments is

reported by the New China News Agency, as reproduced in Summary of World Broadcasts (hereafter SWB) FE/1765, 12 August 1993.

6. For categories of direct and indirect price control in Japan, details concerning Japanese wholesale markets and Japanese laws against monopolies and profiteering, see Zhang Shutian and Hong Feng, opcit.. See also an article entitled 'Japan's Price Control Policies', Shangye Jingji Shangye Jeye Guanli, No. 12, 1992, pp 126–7.

7. The development of wholesale markets in China is examined by Zhang Shutian and Hong Feng, Opcit.

8. Chinese measures deregulating prices are covered in Geng Yuxin, 'China Turns to Market Economy', Beijing Review, 9–15 November, 1992, p 4.

9. See, for example, a report by the Xinhua news agency on 11 August 1993. A comprehensive range of such reforms is discussed in 'Social Security Reforms on Target for Completion by the End of the Century', Xinhua news agency broadcast on 22 November 1992, as reported in SWB FE/1860, 1 December 1993.

10. China Daily, 2 March 1994, as reproduced in Foreign Broadcasts Information Service, (hereafter FBIS) CHI/94/042, 3 March 1994.

11. 'Shanghai Reforms Labour Employment System', Xinhua news agency, 7 March 1994, as reproduced in FBIS, CHI/94/046, 9 March 1994.

12. See a Xinhua news agency report, 11 August 1993.

13. Xinhua news agency, 14 September 1992, as reproduced in SWB FE/WO249, 23 September 1994.

14. Huang Wei, 'Market Activates China's Talent Pool, Beijing Review, 1–7 February, 1993, pp 12–15.

15. Much of the foregoing is drawn from an investigation by a Mr Wang, an expert seconded to a Japanese company. His report 'A Japanese Company's Search for Talent' appears in Laodong Jingji yu Renshi Guanli, No. 11, 1992, pp 86–88.

16. The above details are drawn from Tsuneo Kobayashi, 'Kanebo's Joint Venture in China', China Newsletter, No 109, March–April 1994, pp 2–9.

17. For details of such funding, see a Xinhua news agency report on 22 December 1992, carried by SWB FE/WO 264, 13 January 1993.

18. The Sony venture was reported by the Kyodo news agency, Tokyo, on 30 August 1993 and reproduced in SWB FE W/0298, 8 September 1993.

19. Jian Wang, 'Some Issues of China's Long Term Economic Development', China Newsletter, No. 110, May–June 1994, pp 7–11.

20. The general development of Dalian is discussed in a report entitled 'Dalian Expands Ties with Japan', Beijing Review, 1–7 October 1990, pp 29–30. For details of funding, see ibid, 18–24 May, 1992, p 29.

21. These issues are discussed in JETRO, 'Investment Roundup, 1992–93', China Newsletter, No. 109, March–April 1994, pp 15–18. For attitudes of major Japanese companies regarding investment in China, see a report by a member of the Liaoning Province Social Science Institute, 'Japanese Conglomerates' Strategy for the 1990s', Shangye Guanli Shangye Jeye Guanli, No. 10, 1992, pp 137–141.

22. 'Foreign Ventures Drive China's Trade', China Newsletter, No. 109, March–April 1994, p 1.

10 Industrial Procurement Practices of Taiwanese Firms in the Chinese Market

Sam Dzever*

1 INTRODUCTION

This paper analyses the industrial procurement practices of Taiwanese firms in the Chinese market. It is based on data collected during the months of September through December 1995 and covers 95 firms currently doing business in this market. Industrial procurement practices of these firms were studied in *New Task* buying situations (Robinson, Faris, and Wind, 1967) and relate specifically to the following factors: (a) the role of purchasing managers in the purchase decision process for equipment and component parts, (b) the importance of different functional departments in the decision process, (c) the importance of technical, commercial, and social factors in the choice of a supplier, and (d) the impact of environmental factors such as market structure, economic, technology, and culture on the purchase decision process of buyers.

2 BACKGROUND

The policy of reform initiated by the central government in the late 1970s has largely been responsible for the rapid economic transformation now taking place in the People's Republic of China (PRC). And the pace of this transformation has been particularly rapid in the last few years. This has led some analysts to conclude that the PRC is fast becoming a major economic power (Davies, H. *et al*, 1995). Much has been written about the PRC's political evolution as well as its economic transformation in recent years. However, as far as analysis of its market (and particularly its industrial market) is concerned, it appears that research has not kept pace with these developments. This fact becomes even more evident as one searches through available literature on the subject. In its current five-year development plan, the government is seeking to modernize a number of state-owned enterprises. The modernization of these enterprises would require, in most cases, the complete restructuring of them, giving rise to an increased demand for various types of industrial products, most of which could only be obtained from foreign sources. In addition, the complete or partial privatization of some of these enterprises will, in turn, provide them with the much-needed autonomy in purchase decision making, particularly as it relates to the international sourcing of industrial products.

With the opening-up of the market (and the active encouragement of foreign investment on the part of the government), there are today quite a number of foreign firms successfully established in the PRC market. A government source that compiled a list of foreign countries with the highest investment in the PRC in 1993 placed Hong Kong on top of the list (with a total of US $17445 million invested). This was followed by Taiwan (US $3139million), the USA (US $2068million), and Japan (US $1361 million). The number one European Union (EU) country on the list was the UK (US $221million), followed by France (US $141million), The Netherlands (US $84 million), and Germany (US$62 million). The EU countries occupied 9th, 10th, 17th, and 19th positions respectively. (Statistical Yearbook of China, 1994).

Taiwan's second position on the list (and the fact that a significant number of its firms currently in business in the PRC market are known to source internationally for industrial products) makes it an interesting case for this study.

As noted in the introduction, four factors constitute the units of analysis in the study. These are:

(1) The role of purchasing managers at the different stages of the purchase decision process for equipment and component parts from foreign suppliers.
(2) The importance of various functional departments in the decision process.
(3) The importance of technical, commercial, and social factors in the decision process.
(4) The effects of environmental factors such as market structure, economic, technology, and culture on the purchase decision process of buyers.

3   LITERATURE REVIEW AND THEORETICAL FRAME OF THE PAPER

Three bodies of literature have been reviewed, each of which contributes some useful insight into the present study. These are:

(1) General models of organizational buying behaviour: Robinson, Faris, and Wind (1967), Webster and Wind (1972), Sheth (1973), Bonoma, Zaltman and Johnston (1977).
(2) Recent studies of organizational purchasing behaviour and supplier selection criteria: Campbell (1985), Anderson, E. *et al.* (1987), Carter and Narasimban (1990), Quells and Rosa (1995), Johnston and Lewin (1996), Deng and Wortzel (1995).
(3) Studies analysing different aspects of the PRC market: Kwan, P. *et al.* (1994), Chang and Ding (1995), Davies, H. *et al.* (1995), Walters and Mingxia (1995), Yadong Luo (1995)).

The basic theoretical frame of the study is an integrated conceptual model of organizational buyer behaviour analysis (Dzever, 1993a). The principal thesis advanced in this model is that organizational purchasing and buyer behaviour of firms is a multidimensional activity involving a complex combination of factors, a significant number of which cannot be sufficiently studied in isolation. These factors are firm-specific as well as environmentally determined. The firm-specific factors relate to the nature of the purchase decision process of buyer organizations, the nature of buyer-seller interaction and the relationships they are willing to develop with suppliers, the role played by intermediaries in the interaction and relationship development process, etc. The environmentally determined factors include the impact of market structure, economic issues, technology, and culture on the purchase decision process of organizational buyers. Both categories of factors play an important role in the decision process of purchasing firms, particularly as it relates to international sourcing of new and replacement industrial products.

The above theoretical model was the basis for the development of an integrated empirical model of industrial buying behaviour (Dzever, 1993b, 1994, 1996) on which the present study is based. Four measurable parameters were identified in the model as: (a) the nature of the purchase decision process of buyers in a given industrial market, (b) the role played by intermediaries, such as: trading companies, marketing agents, manufacturer's representatives, consultants, etc., in the decision process, (c) the patterns of buyer-seller interaction and relationships in a given industrial market, and (d) the effects of environmental factors such as: market structure, economic, technology, and culture on the purchase decision process of buyers. As can be observed, these factors correspond approximately to those with which the present study is concerned. A sufficient understanding of them has important implications for industrial marketing strategy of foreign firms in the PRC market.

4 METHODOLOGY

The source of the sample for this study is the directory of the Investment Commission (IC) of the Taiwanese Ministry of Economic Affairs. The IC is the state organ charged with the responsibility of monitoring and approving all inward and outward direct investments in Taiwan. It maintains a directory of all Taiwanese firms currently doing business in the PRC which is updated on a regular basis. The sample used in this study was drawn from this directory. We designed a structured mail questionnaire which was pretested on a small sample of Taiwanese firms in France, Belgium, and Norway (20 firms in all), the majority of which have branch offices or production facilities in the PRC. Based on the responses received from these firms, the instrument was refined and translated into Chinese. From the directory, we selected, at random, some 300 firms registered with the IC as among the 'top 1000' investors in the PRC market. The criterion for selection was the firm's total capital commitment in that market in fiscal 1994 (as registered with the IC). All 300 firms indicated that they source internationally for industrial products. In most cases we were able to identify from the directory the most appropriate persons in the organization to whom the questionnaire could be addressed. In cases where this was not possible, a telephone call was placed to the organization's headquarters in Taipei explaining the nature of our research and requesting information regarding the most appropriate persons to contact. In most cases we found that respondent firms expressed no particular hesitation in providing the requested information. Except for a few cases, the questionnaire was addressed to the purchasing managers of the respective organizations.

The questionnaire itself was divided into three sections. The first section dealt with personal and organizational characteristics. Questions relating to personal characteristics of the respondents concerned issues such as age, sex, field of education, specific function in the organization, and the functional department (or division) to which they were attached. Organizational characteristics focused on the size of the firm and its sector of activity. The Criterion for determining firm size was the total number of employees the organization had in 1995. Thus, firms that employed less than 500 people in

1995 were said to be small-sized, those with 500–1000 employees were classified as medium-sized, and over 1000 employees were placed in the large-sized category. We found that using employee size as a criterion for dividing the respondent organizations was appropriate since the latest data relating to, for example, total capital commitment in the PRC market were not immediately available.

The second part of the questionnaire dealt specifically with four groups of factors affecting the purchasing decisions of the respondent organizations. Respondents were asked to indicate on a five-point scale the importance of each factor ranging from 'completely unimportant' (1) to 'very important' (5). These groups of factors were identified as:

(1) The role of purchasing managers at different stages of the decision process to purchase an equipment or component part from a foreign supplier. These stages related specifically to *New Task* purchasing situations. There were, in all, nine such stages identified in the questionnaire (these stages were in accordance with the postulations of our empirical model) as: need recognition (for a new or replacement product), specification development, awareness of a product/supply source, generating the organization's interest in the product, evaluation of product/potential supplier, selection of product/supplier, negotiating with the supplier, contracting/acquisition of the product, post-acquisitional evaluation of the product.

(2) The importance of various functional departments at the different stages of the decision process. The following departments were indicated in the questionnaire as a guide to the respondents: engineering, production, purchasing, finance, department utilizing the product (respondents were asked to specify), other (respondents were asked to specify). In addition to these departments, respondents were asked to indicate the importance of intermediaries, such as trading companies, distributors, manufacturer's representatives, and consultants in the decision process.

(3) The third group of factors related to the importance of technical, commercial, and social factors in the purchase decision process of the respondent organizations. These were identified as: technical information (about the product provided by the supplier), product's technical advantages, the nature of training provided by the supplier, product's ease of operation/maintenance (technical factors); price, short delivery schedules, supplier's extended credit, pre- and postsale services offered by the supplier (commercial factors); and buyer-seller interaction and relationships, supplier's prestige in the market-place, and supplier's international reputation (social factors).

(4) Finally, respondents were asked to indicate the impact of the following environmental factors on their purchasing decisions: market structure, technology, economic, and culture.

The third and final part of the questionnaire was intended to measure perceived quality as seen in relation to country-of-origin (COO, i.e. country of conception, design, and engineering of the product) as against country-of-assembly (COA) for both equipment and component parts. Respondents were asked to indicate their preferences on a five-point scale ranging from 'strongly disagree' (1) to 'strongly agree' (5) relative to seventeen countries identified in the questionnaire as: Japan, France, USA, Sweden, Germany, UK, Norway, South Korea, Singapore, Taiwan, Hong Kong, Brazil, Mexico, India, Russia, Thailand, and the Philippines. In order to reduce bias, these countries were not ranked on the questionnaire in order of the level of their economic development. Respondents were asked to consider quality in relation to the technical and commercial attributes of the products/supplier identified in the second part of the questionnaire. (For reasons of space, data related to this part of the questionnaire have not been included in the present paper).

Usable responses were received from 95 firms, representing 31 per cent of the sample. Respondents displayed the following personal and organizational characteristics:

A considerable number of the respondents (51 in all) were aged between the mid-30s and the mid-40s.

In terms of sectoral distribution, the respondent organizations could be divided into the following industries: chemical, electrical and electronic, paper and pulp, textile, food processing, transportation, and construction.

Table 10.1   Personal and organizational characteristics of respondents

Sex	Frequency	Percentage
Male	79	83.2
Female	16	16.8
Age	Youngest	Oldest
	26	66

Table 10.2   Classification of respondents

Education	Frequency	Percentage
Engineering	50	52.6
Commercial	38	40.8
Other	7	7.4

Function	Frequency	Percentage
Managerial	58	62.1
Buyer	31	32.6
Other	4	4.2

Org. Size	Frequency	Percentage
Small	58	61.1
Medium	16	16.8
Large	21	22.1

5   RESULTS

The basic statistical tool used in analyzing the raw data was SPSS 6.1. The results of each of the four factors studied are outlined in Tables 10.3 to 10.6.

Table 10.3 shows the mean scoles of the role of purchasing managers (or executives with other titles who played active roles in the purchase decision process of the respondent organizations) in the purchase decision process. The different stages of the purchase decision process, as we indicated earlier, ranged from Need Recognition through Post Acquisitional Evaluation. What we want to measure is the importance of the role these managers played at the different stages of the decision process.

Table 10.3 is, in essence, a summary of the purchase decision determinants relative to the first factor to be analysed – the importance of the role of purchasing managers at the different stages of the decision process. The mean averages of the importance of this role are calculated along with their standard deviation. These can largely be grouped into three categories. The first category comprises negotiating with potential suppliers, selection of a supplier,

Table 10.3   Mean scores and standard deviation of the importance of the role of purchasing managers at the different stages of the purchase decision process for equipment and component parts in the PRC market

Variable	Mean Score	Std. Dev.
Negotiation	4.32	0.7
Selection	4.29	0.7
Evaluation	4.27	0.72
Post Acq. Eval.	4.23	0.75
Contracting	4.19	0.78
Awareness	4.15	0.82
Need Recog.	3.94	1.07
Spec. Develop.	3.86	0.92
Interest	3.66	0.88

and evaluation of the selected supplier. The second category relates to post-acquisitional evaluation of the selected product/supplier, contracting with the supplier, and awareness of the need for which the organization has for a new or replacement product. The role of purchasing managers in this category was important but not nearly as important as the first category of factors. In the second category, the role of purchasing managers was at its strongest with respect to contracting with suppliers. The last group of factors within this category relates to need recognition (for a new or replacement product), specification development, and generating the organization's interest in the short list of potential suppliers. This finding is perhaps not very surprising, since it is generally recognized that the role of purchasing managers is at its strongest with respect to the commercial and social aspects of the decision process, and less so with regard to the technical aspects. Need recognition, specification development, and generating the organization's interest in a short list of potential suppliers all relate to technical evaluative criteria in the *New Task* buy class. Table 10.3 indicates therefore that the role of purchasing managers was at its strongest with regard to an overall evaluation of prospective suppliers, negotiating with the prospective suppliers, selection of suppliers, and contracting with the selected suppliers. All of these roles are in relation to the more commercial aspects of the decision process. This finding is in conformity with the hypothesis that the role of purchasing managers would generally be at its strongest with respect to the more commercial aspects of the purchase decision process of industrial buyers.

The next factor we wish to measure relates to the importance of different functional departments in the purchase decision process. Table 10.4 is a

Table 10.4   Mean scores and standard deviation of the importance of various functional departments in the purchase decision process for equipment and component parts in the PRC market

Department	Mean Score	Std. Dev.
Engineering	4.38	0.76
Dept. utilizing product	4.35	0.86
Production	4.23	0.81
Purchasing	4.05	0.88
Intermediary	3.3	1.17
Finance	3.06	1.09

summary of the findings showing the means and standard deviation of the different departments indicated.

Table 10.4 shows that the role of three departments was particularly important in the purchase decision process of buyer organizations. These are: engineering, the department utilizing the product purchased (if this is different from those indicated in the table), and production. The roles of purchasing and finance departments, as well as those of intermediaries (identified in the questionnaire as a trading company, a distributor, a manufacturer's representative, a consultant) was not as important. This finding confirms the hypothesis that in general, the role of the more technical departments of industrial buyers would most likely be at its strongest relative to *New Task* buying situations. These findings suggest that in their activities in the PRC market, Taiwanese firms do not appear to deviate significantly from the established norms observable in other industrial markets.

The third factor we wish to measure is the importance of technical, commercial, and social factors in the purchase decision process of the respondent organizations. These factors were identified in the questionnaire in the following manner:

Technical Factors

- technical information
- product's technical advantages (relative to competing brands)
- nature of training provided by the supplier
- ease of operation/maintenance
- better utilization of space

Table 10.5 Mean scores and standard deviation of technical, commercial, and social factors in the purchase decision process of respondent organizations for equipment and component parts in the PRC market

Variable	Mean Score	Std. Dev.
Services	4.48	0.77
Price	4.47	0.86
Tech. info.	4.38	0.75
Tech. advant.	4.37	0.68
Operation/maintenance	4.3	0.79
Short delivery sched.	4.15	0.77
Training	4.08	0.82
Interaction	4.06	0.86
Better util. space	3.98	0.87
International Rep.	3.78	0.81
Supplier's prestige	3.54	0.81
Extended credit	3.18	1.15

Commercial Factors

- price
- short delivery schedules
- supplier extended credit
- pre- and postsale services offered by the supplier

Social Factors

- buyer-seller interaction and relationships.
- supplier's prestige in the market-place.
- supplier's international stature/reputation.

As can be observed in Table 10.5, the importance of technical, commercial, and social factors in the purchase decision process of the respondents can be grouped into three main categories. The first category relates to the nature of pre-and post-sale services offered by the supplier, the price offered by the supplier (relative to competing brands); the nature of technical information about the products provided by the supplier, the nature of technical advantages of the product as compared to competing brands in the market-place, and the ease of operation/maintenance of the product (relative to competing brands). Let us consider each of these factors briefly.

As Table 10.5 shows, services recorded a mean score of 4.48 and a standard deviation of 0.77, confirming once again the importance industrial buyers generally place on services when evaluating products from new and established suppliers. The next factor in this category relates to price, which recorded a mean score of 4.47 and a standard deviation of 0.86. This finding suggests that, contrary to established opinion in the literature, price does play an important role in the decision process of industrial buyers, even in *New Task* buying situations. In their international search for new/replacement equipment and component parts, Taiwanese firms in the PRC market clearly considered 'price competitiveness' as one of the most important determinant factors in their choice of a supplier.

Whereas both factors reviewed up to now are commercial in nature, the next four factors are primarily technical in character. These factors are: technical information, technical advantages, ease of operation/maintenance, and better utilization of space. The factors, as Table 10.5 indicates, had mean scores and standard deviation of 4.38 and 0.75, 4.37 and 0.68, 4.3 and 0.79, and 3,98 and 0.87 respectively. The findings suggest that Taiwanese firms in the PRC market appear to place just as important an emphasis on the more technical aspects of the decision process as they do on commercial ones in evaluating new suppliers of equipment and component parts.

The next group of factors that appear to assume some importance in the selection criteria are: short delivery schedules, the nature of training provided by the supplier to the purchasing organization, the extent to which the supplier is willing to develop close buyer-seller interaction and relationship with the purchasing firm. These factors constitute a cluster which is significantly different from the first group of factors. They display very little differences in their mean scores, and are primarily of a commercial and social character. It appears then that although purchasing organizations considered these factors to be important, they were by no means nearly as important as the first group in making the final selection for suppliers. After these factors, there appears to be less consistency in buyers' evaluative criteria. As Table 10.5 shows, there are significant variations in mean scores of the remaining three factors, ranging from 3.79 for supplier's international reputation, 3.54 for supplier's prestige, to 3.18 for supplier's extended credit.

The overall picture that appears to emerge from an assessment of the technical, commercial, and social factors is that in presenting new industrial products to Taiwanese firms in the PRC market, foreign suppliers need to concentrate their efforts primarily on the first five factors in this category in structuring their marketing strategy. The remaining factors do not appear to hold equal importance to buyers when making the final selection of suppliers.

Table 10.6 Mean scores and standard deviation of the importance of environmental factors in the purchase decision process of respondent organizations in the PRC market

Variable	Mean Score	Std. Dev.
Market structure	3.97	0.89
Technology	3.95	0.8
Economic	3.71	0.92
Culture	3.02	0.66

Table 10.6 shows the mean scores and standard deviation of the importance of environmental factors on buyers' decision process to purchase equipment and component parts. It is clear from this table that the importance of these factors are primarily in relation to market structure, technology, and economic factors. The findings suggest that Taiwanese firms do not consider cultural factors to be of particular significance when evaluating products from various suppliers. These findings seem to be at variance with those of Chang and Ding (1995), and Davies *et al.* (1995), who found significant influences of culture on industrial buyer selection criteria and business conduct in Taiwan and the PRC.

6 DISCUSSION

This study has found the following factors to be important to Taiwanese firms in the PRC market when selecting suppliers for equipment and component parts:

The Role of Purchasing Managers in the Decision Process

This is important primarily in relation to the 'commercial' aspects of the decision process such as: negotiating with potential suppliers, selection of suppliers, contracting, and overall evaluation of the suppliers. The findings are in conformity with the postulations in the literature which suggest that the role of purchasing managers would, in general, be at its strongest relative to the more commercial aspects of the purchase decision process for new/ replacement industrial products.

The Importance of Functional Departments in the Decision Process

As far as the importance of functional departments in the purchase decision process is concerned, the study has found that Taiwanese firms in the PRC market do tend to assign central decision roles to the more 'technical' departments such as engineering, production, etc. The study has found that the role of 'commercial' departments such as finance, purchasing, etc. in the decision process is rather weak relative to the technical departments. Moreover, Taiwanese firms in this market do not appear to utilize intermediaries to a significant extent in their dealings with foreign suppliers. These findings suggest that in approaching the PRC market, foreign suppliers of industrial products would be better off contacting potential buyers directly rather than going through intermediaries. The findings are also in conformity with the suggestion in the literature that organizational buyers generally prefer to be in direct contact with prospective suppliers rather than through intermediaries.

The Importance of Technical, Commercial, and Social Factors in the Decision Process

The study's findings are that the importance of these factors relates primarily to: pre- and post-sale services, price, the nature of technical information provided by the supplier, demonstrated technical advantages of the product (relative to competing brands), ease of operation and maintenance of the product, short delivery schedules, and the nature of training provided by the supplier. The overall picture that emerges from these findings is that in presenting new/replacement industrial products to Taiwanese firms in this market, foreign suppliers would be better off concentrating their marketing effort on these factors rather than the remainder indicated in table 10.5.

The Importance of Environmental Factors in the Decision Process

The importance of these factors in buyers' selection criteria relates primarily to market structure, economic, and technology. The study found that cultural factors did not play an important role in buyers' decision processes relative to foreign suppliers. These findings contrast rather sharply with those of other researchers (Chang and Ding (1995), Davies *et al.* (1995)) who found significant influences of culture on industrial buyer selection criteria of Taiwanese firms in Taiwan and the PRC.

7 IMPLICATIONS

The implications of these findings for the industrial marketing strategy of foreign firms in the PRC market are clear: concentrate your marketing effort on purchasing managers only in regard to the more 'commercial' aspects of the purchase decision process, such as price negotiation, contract arrangements, etc. Include in your sales team persons with a high level of technical competency relative to each product to be presented to the prospective buyers. This will facilitate 'technical' communication between the sales team and the buying centres of prospective clients. In approaching potential clients, emphasize the nature of pre- and post-sale services you are prepared to offer them, as well as the nature of the price-competitiveness of your products. You should furthermore provide as much technical information as possible about the product, and do not forget to explain as much as you can about the technical advantages of your product relative to competing brands. These are the factors on which Taiwanese firms generally place a high premium in evaluating products from foreign suppliers.

8 LIMITATIONS OF THE STUDY

The study relates primarily to Taiwanese firms and as such it does not constitute a basis for generalizing on industrial purchasing and buyer behaviour of firms in the PRC market. In order to have a broader perspective of organizational purchasing and buyer behaviour of firms in this market, further research is needed, preferably with a larger sample of respondents. The sample should include local, joint venture, and other kinds of firms operating in this market. They must also be firms that are known to regularly purchase industrial products from various sources (both locally and internationally). A study of this nature would be useful in enhancing our understanding of these problems.

REFERENCES

Anderson, P. F., *et al.*, 'Industrial Purchasing: An Empirical Exploration of the Buyclass Framework.' *Journal of Marketing* 51 (1987).

Bonoma, T. V., Zaltman, G. and Johnston, W. J., *Industrial Buying Behaviour*, monograph report nr. 77–117. Marketing Science Institute, Cambridge, MA. 1977.

Campbell, N., 'An Interaction Approach to Organizational Buying Behavior'. *Journal of Business Research* (1985).

Chang, K., and Ding, C. G., 'The Influence of Culture on Industrial Buying Selection Criteria in Taiwan and Mainland China'. *Industrial Marketing Management* 24, 277–284 (1995).

Carter, J. R., and Narasimban, R., 'Purchasing in International Market-place: Implications for Operations'. *Journal of Purchasing and Materials Management* (1990).

Davies, H. *et al.*, 'The benefits of «Guanxi»: The Value of Relationships in Developing the Chinese Market'. *Industrial Marketing Management* 24, 207–214 (1995).

Deng, S., and Wortzel, L. H., 'Importer Purchase Behavior: Guidlines for Asian Exporters'. *Journal of Business Research* 32, 41–47 (1995).

Dzever, S., 'Towards an Integrated Conceptual Model of Organizational Buyer Behaviour Analysis'. *ENBS Academic Review* 2 (1993a).

Dzever, S., 'An Empirical Study of Industrial Purchasing Practices in Japan'. *Les Cahiers de Recherche du CREA* 22 (1993b).

Dzever, S., 'Un Modele Empirique du Comportement D'Achat Industriel (An empirical model of industrial buying behaviour)'. *Le Cahiers de Recherche du CREA* 41 (1994).

Dzever, S., *Le Comportement D'achat Industriel* (Industrial Buying Behaviour). Economica, Paris, 1996.

Johnston, W. J., and Lewin, J. E., 'Organizational Buying Behavior: Toward an Integrative Framework'. *Journal of Business Research* 35, 1–15 (1996).

Quells, W. J., and Rosa, J. A., 'Assessing Industrial Buyers' Perceptions of Quality and Their Effects on Satisfaction.' *Industrial Marketing Management* 24, 358–368 (1995).

Robinson, P. J., Faris, C. W. and Wind, Y., *Industrial Buying and Creative Marketing*, Allyn & Bacon, Boston, 1967.

Sheth, J. N., 'A Model of Industrial Buyer Behaviour', *Journal of Marketing* 37 (1973).

Walter, P. G. P., and Mingxia Zhu, 'International Marketing in Chinese Enterprises: Some Evidence from the PRC', *Management International Review* 35, (1995/3).

Webster, F. E., Jr., and Wind, Y., 'A General Model for Understanding Organizational Buying Behavior'. *Journal of Marketing* 36 (1972).

Yadong, Luo, 'Business Strategy, Market Structure, and Performance of International Joint Ventures: The Case of Joint Ventures in China.' *Management International Review* 35 (1995/3).

Notes

*   The author is most grateful to Dr Wen-Jeng Kuo of Chung-Hua Institution For Economic Research, Taipei, for his assistance in collecting material for this paper.

Part III
Business Strategy in Selected Countries

11 Asian Economic Integration and the Role of the Japanese Corporate Networks: the Case of the Electronics Industry

Christian Milelli

1   ECONOMIC INTEGRATION

Asian economic integration is characterized by the revival and the relevance of regionalization. Regionalization as a supranational issue has become an object of discussion in economics relative to the international trading system.

During the 1980s commercial regional groupings grew worldwide, particularly in the free trade zone areas[1]. Nonetheless, this trend appears to be unevenly distributed on a spatial level. This development reveals a different pattern, however, for Asia compared with other regions. Accordingly, Europe is deeply involved in a politically driven process, the European Union, through the implementation of common rules and institutions, and the Americans have experienced various trade agreements leading to an extended free trade zone (NAFTA). In this respect, the singularity that characterizes Asia needs to stress regional evidence on another ground as many convergent clues signal the emergence of an economic integration process[2].

In addition, the spreading of preferential commercial zones is not interpreted quietly by economists. The debate is hot and reveals the encounter of the strong and irreversible tendency of economic globalization on one hand, and the past of stumbling trade blocs on the other.

The geographical scope of our analysis includes the Newly Industrializing Economies (NIEs), Association of South East Asian Nations (ASEAN) and mainland China. According to the Nomura Research Institute, the intra-regional share of Asian exports compared to Asian overall exports has increased steadily from 30% in 1980 to 50% in 1994. During the same period, Asian exports to the United States, its main market, decreased from 35% to 25%. There is evidence that a regional trade integration is going on. This conspicuous feature cannot be theoretically grounded on the classical approach of Jacob Viner, as it explicitly requires a prerequisite political agreement. However, we cannot acknowledge an explanation solely based on geographic and cultural propinquity, as trade flows require discrepancies *ex ante* in terms of product, factor or industrial structures.

Moreover, economic integration is not only limited to products flows (be they raw materials, intermediate or semi-finished or final goods); increasingly it embraces exchanges of technology, embodied in capital equipment, or through specific channels, information at large, and financial resources.

Over the 1980s, foreign direct investment inflows and outflows grew very steadily within Asia and other regions. Asian inward investment increased from $17 billion in 1989 to as much as $32 billion in 1992 [UNCTAD 1994]. Simultaneously, cross-investments are spreading throughout Asia through overseas Chinese networks. In this respect, foreign direct investments from Hong Kong and Taiwan are a major source of inward investment in Southern China[3].

But Asian trends are not unique in this respect, since European firms invest primarily in their home base as well, as do American firms in the United States (UNCTAD 1993). The role of Japanese firms as driving forces in the Asia investment scheme needs to be underlined. Outward foreign direct investment from Japan to Asia grew steadily from $2.3 billion in 1986 to $9.3 billion in 1994. Much of the increase was in relation to production facilities, since Japanese firms secured a regional base in production which in 1994 was nearly twice that of the American firms. The figure was equal during the early 1980s[4].

In short, without trade zone establishment the conjunction of this latter trend with the former (i.e. rapid growth of intra-regional trade) gives support to the role of multinational firms (be they insiders or outsiders) as main actors of the economic integration now prevailing within Asia. Economic integration in Europe, and to a lesser extent in North America, was preceded by an adaptation of the rules through political agreements which, in turn, largely determined the further pattern of economic regionalisation. Asia did not experience such a prerequisite settlement.

2 THE GROWING ROLE OF CORPORATE NETWORKS IN GLOBALIZATION

In term of strategies, organization, and spatial outlines, analysis and understanding in a growing number of industrial sectors from now on is focused on corporate networks. This form embraces a large range of functions, from R&D to production and sales. Over the 1980–89 period, evidence of such a trend was established by many researchers through the strong increase of international co-operative agreements which were at the core of corporate networks [Delapierre 1991, Mytelka 1991, Hagedoorn and Schakenraad 1993]. This tendency was particularly evident in the early 1990s. Equity acquisition is not the aim of these structures, as stress is put on the coordination of tasks between two firms or more. Recent trends give support to the fact that today's corporate competitiveness is increasingly based not only on proper organisation but more heavily on a firm's close co-operation with its suppliers, customers or even competitors. Corporate networks and intra-companies are becoming the standard of production in globalization. The new factors of industrial competitiveness as a whole are thus determined by this pervading framework. Obviously this trend has an important impact on the emerging regional groupings.

It is too early to assess whether corporate networks are a substitute for foreign direct investment, but anecdotal evidence suggests that initial agreements are often followed by the implementation of new production facilities.

3 JAPANESE CORPORATE NETWORKS: A PERVADING FEATURE

Contrary to American and European practice, corporate networks are not a new phenomenon for Japanese firms, at least on a national basis. Their origin is related to the emergence of modern Japan where economic co-ordination was, to large extent, based on market and hierarchical schemes through a thick texture of relatively stable networks. For the vast majority these networks were production-centred and based on a dualistic economic structure combining large, modern factories paying relatively high wages and small, low-skill and low-wage businesses (Minami 1986). In this respect, current Japanese networks exhibit two conspicuous patterns. First, they are characterized by horizontal structures which enhance extensive intra-group co-operation – illustrated, for example, by the linkages of chemical, mechanical and electronics firms within, typically, the Mitsubishi conglomerate [Figuière, 1995]. Second, they are represented by vertical structures according to a decomposition of the whole production process between a large assembling company and its suppliers, the most notable example being the Hitachi group. But reality is by itself complex. Even if vertical structures are prevalent in the Japanese electronics industry (as in assembling and processing industries in general), they cross the horizontal structures of large-sized enterprises owing to the diversity of their portfolios – contrary to American firms, which are more specialized[5]. Furthermore, Japanese networks are relatively closed and structured around a centre where control and co-ordination of the whole group is managed. During the late 1980s and to a lesser extent afterwards[6], the Japanese networks were boosted abroad by a massive outflow of foreign direct investment from Japan. Contrary to American and European practice, the Asian units were in the vast majority dedicated to production.

In implementing production facilities in Asia, Japanese networks had early backing by public and professional bodies in Japan. The role of the Ministry of International Trade and Industry is widely recognized, but the role of the Ministry of Foreign Affairs was also significant, through the Japan International Cooperation Agency which provided subsidies and technical support. In parallel, the Ministry of Finance, through the Overseas Economic Cooperation Fund, delivered concessional lending for infrastructures such as roads, harbours, airports and power plants[7]. The Japan External Trade Organization and professional associations such as Keidanren were also influential (see Box 11.1). These different actors have a common mission to foster a favourable business environment in which Japanese private business would be able to operate efficiently. Public aid resources – from 1988 to 1993 60 percent of Japanese official development assistance was targeted to Asian countries[8] – extensive technical training and political advice are the main instruments. They add fuel to the existing incentives aimed specifically at foreign investors by Asian host countries.

Box 11.1: Overseas-Aid Scheme Taps Corporate Execs

The plan is to match corporate executives from the Keidanren's huge membership with salaried jobs in international organizations or with private companies in developing countries. To help the right slots, Keidanren is linking up with the Japanese Foreign Ministry and the Finance Ministry. Keidanren argues that by 'lending' managers to other countries, it will establish human networks between Japanese and other countries. Basic training for the recruits will be offered by the

Japan International Cooperation Agency. Keidanren will encourage Japanese companies to pay their executives while on assignment. Officials point out that Japanese companies will save on salaries under the program because compensation packages will reflect local living standards.

Source: The *Nikkei Weekly*, 19 June 1995, p 21

At this stage we would allude to some remarks which will be addressed later. What kind of impact could Japanese networks have on Asian economic integration, inasmuch as these different enterprises are linked units based on a particular corporate rationality? Next, how suitable are these structures for a new context, as the characteristics are quite different from the original frame – and, conversely, what would be the impact at the regional level?

4   THE ELECTRONICS INDUSTRY: A STRATEGIC SECTOR

We will focus our analysis of the spread of Japanese production networks in Asia on the electronics industry. It is important to note that conditions for network strategies are particularly favourable here as regards high international standardization and prospects for splitting up production processes. In order to test our initial topic (i.e. the driving forces behind the Asian economic integration), we believe this choice is appropriate.

First, this industry covers a large spectrum of activities which constitutes a variety of industrial capabilities. It features broad diffusion of know-how, processes and products (with an important share of intermediate goods) toward numerous industrial sectors. Thus, the electronics industry becomes a good reflection of manufacturing activities and their pattern of evolution in general.

With technology and labour-intensive processes which are increasingly interlinked, it is a complex industry. In this respect, it combines on the one hand Taylor manufacturing schemes, grounded on a simple technical division, and on the other processes based on the absorption of sophisticated knowledge. The coexistence of this dual production rationality is due to the industry itself, which is built on a constant breaking-down and reconstruction of several tasks, thus allowing inside fusion strategies and/or specialization ones.

Furthermore, the electronics industry is driven by many interlinkages on a vertical and horizontal level. This feature is particularly crucial for national development policies. It is also at the heart of the regional integration process as multinational firms which established quite long ago production facilities in different countries now face reorganization requirements in favour of regional production bases in ongoing globalization [UNCTAD 1992].

Furthermore, the electronics industry has played a strategic role in national development in most Asian countries. For Asian NIEs this choice was made long ago, whereas this feature is relatively recent in other countries of the region. In the latter, industrial policies have generally been implemented to channel national and international investment flows toward specific sectors. The investments secured by multinational firms are largely regarded as a crucial vector of transfer (i.e. be they technology, industrial know-how or management capabilities) but governments are still dominant actors by their numerous mandates: infrastructure in general, public research programs disseminated to local firms, extensive educational and professional training, etc. (World Bank 1993). Macroeconomic instruments like monetary policy were combined with more specific measures, such as fiscal incentives, to reach a critical amount of financial resources. These mechanisms were periodically reviewed and adapted to upgrade the capabilities or to catch up as, for example, in the late 1980s with the implementation of a technology policy in semiconductors field by the Taiwan authorities.

For statistical reasons we have chosen the Electronics Industry Association of Japan (EIAJ) which is composed of three broad domains: consumer electronics products (colour TVs, VCRs and sound equipment); industrial electronics equipments (telecom equipment, computers and office equipment); and electronics components and devices (passive and connecting components, electron tubes).

5   A LONG ESTABLISHED PRESENCE IN ASIA FOR THE JAPANESE ELECTRONICS FIRMS

5.1   A Characterized Geographical Trend

The establishment of majority-owned subsidiaries by Japanese parent companies in Asia took place during the second half of the 1960s (see Table 11.1). Over this decade Taiwan accounted for the vast majority of investment flows, with local units exclusively dedicated to final assembly for export. During the late 1960s components plants were implemented in Taiwan. The main factor behind this phenomenon was the removal in 1958 of import-substitution policies and the adoption of export and investment promotion measures such as the phasing out of custom duties and import regulations, and the lending at low interest rates for export

Table 11.1 Japanese controlled production plants by year and country of installation in Asia (plant closures are not recorded)

					Country					
	A	B	C	D	E	F	G	H	I	All
Year										
to 1959								2		2
1960 to 1964		2		1				4	2	9
1965 to 1969		1		1	2	1	24	2		32
1970 to 1974		4	2	30	15	1	16	30	2	101
1975 to 1979	7	1	1	6	4	2	27	10	2	50
1980 to 1984	20	1	1	5	7	2	3	13	5	43
1985 to 1989	3	11	2	19	64	8	19	16	38	201
1990 to 1992	29	2	11	2	37	4	3	4	13	112

A = China   B = Hong Kong C = Indonesia D = South Korea   E = Malaysia
F = Philippines G = Singapore   H = Taiwan   I = Thailand   All = Asia
Source: Electronics Industry Association of Japan 1994

firms (Wade, 1990). The rate of increase in exports, which was less than 12% per year over the 1953–62 period, reached 28% from 1963 to 1972 (World Bank 1993). Malaysia, Thailand and Philippines were ranked next. As a policy mix was achieved through import-substitution measures and incentives aimed at enhancing domestic demand, Japanese firms were concerned with securing a national market share through direct investments. They tied with local partners through joint-ventures by assuming majority control.

A first boom of investments took place during the 1970–74 period (101 establishments). Taiwan and South Korea were the main recipients, Singapore and Malaysia were ranked the next highest. In the latter country a New Economic Policy was launched in 1971 with export promotion measures devoted to specific areas, the export-free trade zones. The favourable treatment was enlarged in 1975 to the industrial bonded warehouses. Over the following years, from 1975 to 1979, Singapore became the largest recipient.

As the engine of Asian economic growth, driven by export and foreign direct investment flows, Japanese transplants became export platforms for the markets of advanced industrial countries.

A second surge of investments took place from 1985 to 1989. It was a direct outcome of the *endaka* (dramatic appreciation of the yen) and hence of the rise of Japanese production costs after the Plaza Accord in September 1985. But the features of this wave were different from the previous one. First, there was a scale change from 101 to 201 establishments; second, the new investments were located in more countries and more evenly distributed. Nevertheless, Malaysia and Thailand emerged as relatively more attractive places. The specialization was the same, i.e. supplying American and European large markets even if some standardized goods were oriented toward domestic markets and in some cases toward an emerging regional market.

In the early 1990s mainland China ranked next highest behind Malaysia which has been the leading host country for Japanese Production Facilities Since the 1960s.

5.2   Asia as a Japanese production base

In 1993 Asia was the leading place for Japanese electronics plants with a 60% of the total of offshore Japanese units. North America (with 20%) and Europe (with 15%) were outstripped[9]. This feature was more or less the same for all EIAJ broad product categories: 65% of electronics components and systems units, 55% of consumer electronics and 45% of industrial electronics plants were located in Asian countries.

5.3   A Regional Specialization in Electronic Components

The decomposition of Japanese production in Asia gives evidence of the specialization of electronic components noted previously. With a rate of 60%, this category ranked first before consumer electronics units (25%) and industrial electronics ones (14%). Such a specialization has to be related at the regional level to the importance of Japanese consumer electronics establishments and to a lesser extent to that of industrial ones. Malaysia, Taiwan followed by South Korea, Singapore, Thailand and mainland China were the main sources for components activities production such as transformers, capacitors, connectors and mechanical micro-components. The establishment and the extension of consumer electronics-assembling plants in Malaysia and Taiwan in the first stage, and in Thailand and Singapore afterwards, in relation to electronic components units contributed to the build-up of Japanese production networks. The relationship between suppliers and assembly units could be held at the intra-enterprise level (for example, inside Matsushita Electric Industrial or Sony) or at the inter-enterprise level (between Sony, for example, and delocalized Japanese autonomous suppliers such as Alps Electric, Hosiden or SMK).

6 THE STRATEGIES OF JAPANESE ELECTRONICS PRODUCTION NETWORKS IN ASIA

6.1 A Path Dependency Type Constraint

The foundations and the trajectories of Japanese production networks in the electronics industry were in place at the beginning of outward investments from Japan to Asia, over the 1960s and the early 1970s. At this stage they were only assembly activities characterized by low technical evolution and weak local autonomy. In addition, investments were made essentially by large-scale companies such as Matsushita Electric Industrial or Mitsubishi Electric. This feature further determined the locational choice of Japanese small and medium-sized enterprises over the 1980s. In this respect they located around the assembly units controlled by Japanese large firms and hence initiated close co-operation. More generally, the strategies followed in Asia by these production networks were part of an oligopolistic competition behaviour between Japanese groups which had already been established at home. There were in some cases adventurous strategies, but the general trend here was a cautious and conservative behaviour of 'follow the leader'.

Furthermore, the importance of protected markets explained the necessity to be insiders. The first strategy followed by these networks was to establish production facilities to serve closed national markets. It was a reproduction of the Japanese system with the exception that it supplied the domestic market and overseas markets through exports. The result was the spreading of numerous units in different countries without integration on a regional level. This strategy was labelled multi-domestic, inasmuch as the investments were duplicated in neighbouring countries without exchange, rationalization of tasks or even integration of some functions[10]. The dual international division of labour was a salient feature. Despite a relative autonomy in their day-to-day management, the Asian units were closely linked to their parent companies for their capital goods and key components supplies.

6.2 Extension and Deepening of the Production Logic

Generally, from mid-1970 to mid-1980, the strategy followed by the Japanese electronics industry was largely constrained by economic frictions between Japan and the United States and Western Europe. The main complaint was the strain put on these markets by concentration, and dramatically rising exports by Japanese firms. Simultaneously, with the establishment of assembling units in Europe and the United-States, the assembly of some products – small and medium-sized colour TVs, VCRs – was transferred to Asian units for export to North American and European markets. During the 1980s and early 1990s mounting political tensions with trade partners and financial constraints compelled the Japanese networks to develop in two directions:

1   First, to stress the dualism between the parent company and their Asian affiliates. In this respect capabilities and knowledge were kept in Japan; the strategic aim was to preserve leadership in the technology field through production at home, based on sophisticated processes of technology-intensive products and systems to supply mature markets in developed countries. In an unstable industry such as the electronics industry, with incessant new products and processes emerging, it is quite difficult, *a priori*, to preserve such a dualism. Thus, the Japanese networks dynamized this relation through the product cycle: to a certain extent the evolution of innovation and markets triggered the transfer of production lines to Asian affiliates. Empirical evidence suggests that the Japanese electronics firms increased their dual production structure, at least until 1993. On the one hand, the control of main decisions and the supply of key components still come from Japan (in the case of microprocessors, the parent company supplies the video monitors, memories, some microprocessors, drives, mechanical and electrical components and even plastic and boxes to their Asian plants to be assembled locally [Borrus 1994]); on the other, low-grade production – such as TV sets of less than 20 inches, some VCRs, cameras, calculators and microwave ovens – has been shifted to Asia for assembly. If the local content increased to reach 60%, a lot of it is provided by Japanese affiliates which have been delocalized.

2   Second, the development of production network was based on sequential migration patterns (see Table 11.1). The new investments are thus moving from one country to another according to the evolution of the comparative advantages of host countries (labour costs, exchange rate, preferential trade access to advanced industrial markets). In addition, host country policies could be crucial for this phenomenon such as, for example, the measures implemented on 27 June 1995 by the Chinese central authorities to channel foreign investment toward more technology-intensive activities[11]. In short, as table 11.2 reveals, the labour cost gap between Asian countries is always the main engine of this dynamism, at least for labour-intensive operations. In the early 1990s Japanese affiliates began to introduce automatic production lines in existing facilities in ASEAN

Table 11.2 Asian labour costs in the manufacturing sector for 1993

Countries	US dollars per hour
Japan	16.91
Taiwan	5.46
Singapore	5.12
South Korea	4.93
Hong Kong	4.21
Malaysia	1.80
Thailand	0.71
Philippines	0.68
China	0.57

Source: Morgan Stanley Bank, September 1993

countries, particularly Thailand and Malaysia, because of rising wages [Eximbank 1994]. Table 11.2 identifies the path of this migration: except Japan which is no more in the same division, the road is from NEIs to ASEAN countries and mainland China.

So what is happening to the existing units – are they progressively getting obsolete or, on the contrary, upgraded for new functions through modern-ization, rationalization or reorganization? To this question, empirical evidence suggests three answers. First, the Japanese affiliates installed in South Korea for simple assembly activities, during the early 1970s, were not upgraded, with a few exceptions. This decision was taken by Japanese parent companies not willing to agree with local authorities' requests[12] aiming at the enlargement of technology transfers and the amount of local value-added. Second, Taiwanese affiliates were progressively upgraded toward more sophisticated production in reaction to the currency appreciation of the Taiwanese dollar, beginning in 1987, which contributed to an acceleration of the rise in production costs[13]. Third, the Asian activities were redistributed between units located in different countries according to labour costs which were still crucial for some process stages such as assembling, testing and packaging. In 1995, for example, the establishment by NEC of a microchip assembly plant in Indonesia was in fact the transfer of low-grade chips line production from a Malaysian subsidiary replaced by a more advanced chips line[14].

7   JAPANESE PRODUCTION NETWORKS' ROLE IN ASIAN REGIONALIZATION

Table 11.3 outlines the main factors which characterize the current structural impact of the Japanese production networks within the Asian area.

7.1   ASEAN Seems to be the Core of the Current Integration

This feature is grounded on empirical evidence. First, the Asian outcome of the majority-owned subsidiaries of Japanese parent companies located within ASEAN shows tremendous increase in the latest Eximbank surveys, from 33% in 1991 to an estimated 85% for the 1994–1996 period [Eximbank 1993]. Second, recent Asian trade data confirms that evolution. Furthermore, Singapore appears to play a pivotal role in this evolution by the establishment of operational headquarters or integration centres involved in the tasks of international procurement offices or central distribution centres as well as capital procurement and exchange risk management functions[15] [Tokunaga 1992].

Box 11.2: Sony International of Singapore

Sony International of Singapore is Sony's general headquarters for the Southeast Asian region, and Sony's Southeast Asian factories and affiliated companies are connected by a communications network. The distribution warehouse for Sony in Singapore procures parts from around the world to be used by factories in the Southeast region. It also collects products manufactured within its control area for delivery worldwide. In fact, its function is similar to the 'heart' of the distribution system by connecting the 'arterial system' that provides parts to various Asian factories with the 'veins' that collect the manufactured products or semi-finished goods. It functions as a strategic unit for Sony's global logistics: it oversees the district distribution system that involves parts procurement and product sales.

Source: Tokunaga.

At the same time, there is an increase in the exchange of components and semi-finished products between the other members, such as Malaysia and Thailand or Malaysia and Indonesia. The setting-up of a free trade zone in 1993 is undoubtedly giving impetus to this trend. In addition, Japanese affiliates located in ASEAN are increasingly providing a great many components to units located in Japan and NIEs. According to labour cost discrepancies and current automation programs, this area should become in the near future a foremost supply base for parts and subsystems to be incorporated in various electronic equipment and devices through the whole area. This should, in turn, enhance the ASEAN fledging regional integration.

On the reverse, the two other cores – NEIs and mainland China – disclose contrasting patterns outside an obvious integration scheme. On one side, supplies to Asian markets by Japanese affiliates located in the NEIs are dwindling as they are strengthening their export base status[16] toward North American and Western European markets. These latter are gaining importance from a meagre two percent in 1991 to 20% in 1994–96 [Eximbank 1993]. On the other side, Japanese units in mainland China are in the vast majority national market-oriented joint ventures. However, this trend abated from June 1995 with the implementation of measures aiming at the increase of foreign affiliates exports. The scheme was the following: if, for instance, a Chinese unit is foreign-controlled up to 65%, it should export 65% of its outcome [Far Eastern Economic Review 7/09/95]. Due to labour cost discrepancies and large skilled manpower resources, the Chinese plants should play a pivotal future role in supplying the units localized in neighbouring countries such as NEIs or (more crucially) Japan, because of high labour costs. This prospect could be another engine of regional integration.

Finally, current trade imbalances show the critical role still played by Japanese parent companies, notably through the supply of key components, as quality, delivery and stability of procurement are acute issues in production networks[17]. Similarly, recent studies disclose the technological catch-up strategies followed by Korean conglomerates which have imported from Japan a large amount of capital equipment and key components [Ernst 1994].

7.2 The Lock-in Perils for National Policies

Obviously, the international division of labour patterns achieved by Japanese production networks through Asia is putting constraints on industrial policies implemented in nearly all Asian countries except Hong Kong. There are, for example, relatively few technology transfers due to the closeness and the dual framework of the Japanese networks; supply linkages with local partners are also weak. Therefore, as these networks could freely move their different units from one place to another according to resource and capability

Table 11.3 The most important customer for existing and future Japanese-controlled production bases by region/country in electronics machinery

years	Japan (a)			NIEs (a)			ASEAN (a)			China (a)			Asia (a)		
	1992	1993	94–95	1992	1993	94–95	1992	1993	94–95	1992	1993	94–95	1992	1993	94–95
NIEs (b)	21.6	12.6	0	54.6	54.6	40	6.2	8.4	0	0	0	20	82.4	75.6	60
ASEAN (b)	21.6	22.8	23.1	16	7.1	23.1	30.9	40.7	38.4	0	0	0	65	70.6	84.6
CHINA (b)	–	20	13.8	–	8	10.3	–	0	0	–	56	69	–	84	93.1

Source: Japan Eximbank's 1993 Survey
(a) = Customer
(b) = Location of production subsidiaries

endowments countries, Asian countries could be locked into a specific segment or even subsystem. It could be, for instance, a standard assembly in Malaysia and Thailand, design and hard disks in Singapore or PC motherboards in Taiwan. This prospect would be consistent for countries with high profiles of foreign investment and/or trade strategies of maximum specialization. Industrial policies aimed at the upgrade of national capabilities could be inhibited inasmuch as electronics is in most Asian countries a rapidly growing provider of foreign currencies through exports. In addition, due to the high globalization of this industry Asian national electronics industries are hence largely penetrated by multinational firms, notably Japanese ones, which cover a much wider range of electronics segments than the American multinationals.

7.3 A Productive Rationale at Stake for the Japanese Production Networks and the Impact on Regional Integration

We cannot assume the future continuity of the current dual-pattern relationship between Japanese parent companies and their Asian subsidiaries. There are already evolving signs – the setting-up of regional headquarters in Singapore, an enlargement and deepening of regional integration for different stages of the process – that Japanese corporate networks are reluctantly changing their organization through Asian countries in reaction to new constraints.

8   ASIAN ECONOMIC INTEGRATION PULLED BY THE ELECTRONICS INDUSTRY DYNAMISM

Obviously, electronics play a pivotal role in Asian regionalization and encompass a broad process of division of labour on a vertical and horizontal level through several production networks. This structure is a powerful instrument of interdependence and complementarity through Asian countries. It is grounded basically on a regional procurements pattern of materials and components. The network arrangement was originally developed by Japanese firms at home and further transplanted in Asia. It is now a prevalent feature of the electronics industry: American multinationals, and even Korean and Taiwan ones, exhibit such a pattern in Asia. In this respect, Japanese production networks are already challenged by American networks, whereas the latter emerge at international level. The former unfolds a contrasted type of behaviour: openness to outsiders with a large amount of production outsourcing, technology and know-how transfer to local firms. Hence, they constitute a valuable alternative for Asian enterprises willing to upgrade their capabilities or jump on the bandwagon of globalization. Furthermore, Korean and Taiwanese networks are taking assurance in order to abate their technological and industrial dependency on the Japanese.

The ongoing shift made by Japanese networks in Asia from consumer electronics (where they still show a strong market share[18]) to electronic components and, to some extent, industrial electronics with less power market and technological leadership will affect the network dual pattern and induce more cooperation outside.

Rising investments made by Japanese makers of electronic parts have contributed to increasing the local content of Japanese assembling firms in these countries to supply to both Japanese and other markets (such as American and Asia)[19].

Furthermore, access to financial resources in the electronics industry has become a crucial point for the parent firms in Japan since 1991, due to sluggish markets and shrinking profits induced by the outburst of the speculative bubble. At this stage the parent firms captured the earnings of their Asian affiliates, which displayed high profitability compared not only to the Japanese units but also to North American and European affiliates. Sony, for example, used some tricky balance sheet devices to send home a large share of its Singaporean affiliate's profits. Nevertheless, it seems difficult vis-à-vis local authorities to maintain such a levy without a counterpart such as more autonomy or consistent technology transfer. Moreover, the hollowing-out or *kudoka* issue is gaining room in Japan and would imply in the future a radical reorganization of the whole electronics industry base and therefore its current articulation with overseas units[20].

Furthermore, cross-border production networks would remodel industrial policies exclusively based on national ground as they put an emphasis on interdependence and complementarity. Therefore they are able to restructure comparative advantage in a regional framework.

The electronics industry contributes to the shaping of Asian integration on both the 'intra' and the 'inter' levels. First, it articulates developed and developing countries through vertical and horizontal linkages. Second, it contributes to interface Asian regionalization with the world: finished products are still largely dependent on North America and Western Europe, as electronics components are increasingly becoming (display devices, hard disks or PC motherboards, for example).

Finally, even if the outcomes are already captive both at the region and/or industry level, nevertheless political agreements have now to be implemented to harmonise and regulate this pervading process. A qualitative threshold is mirrowing with the result to fade away the growth engine or produce several adverse effects. APEC meetings with loose aims apart, the decision achieved in 1992 by ASEAN countries to establish an ASEAN Free Trade Area within the next 15 years, starting in 1993[21], seems to be a salient feature. It will eventually constitute a new hub for regional integration and enhance other commitments throughout the Asian area.

Notes

1. M. Fouquin, Le développement du régionalisme commercial, Lettre du CEPII, November 1993.
2. Paribas Bank, Tropismes asiatiques, Conjonctures, April 1995.
3. In 1993, both represented 3/4 of the whole inward investment in China, Almanac of China's Foreign Economic Relations and Trade, 1994.
4. Japan in Asia, Financial Times Survey, November 15, 1995.
5. As Intel in microprocessors, Apple in PCs or Microsoft in software.
6. Although the trend was disrupted in 1990 and 1991 by the yen's depreciation it started to revive again in 1992 and from 1993 on, by the yen's appreciation [Kwan 1994].
7. Since multinational firms are heavily dependent on transport and communication, the lack or scarcity of phones, roads, rail services or air services can be enough to discourage investment made by these firms.
8. Source: Foreign Affairs Ministry.
9. Japan Electronics Almanach 95/96, Tokyo: Dempa Publications, 1995.
10. See the 'mini-Matsushita' model duplicated in each closed local market with a complete set of the parent Matsushita's product lines. As its name suggests this model was essentially dedicated to low-scale production.
11. 'Chinese rules trouble Japan's electronics firms', *Far Eastern Economic Review*, September 7, 1995
12. They feared a boomerang effect.
13. Similarly, this trend propelled outward direct investment from Taiwan to Asia.
14. Change of venue: Japan's big chip makers discover Indonesia, Far Eastern Economic Review August 24, 1995.
15. Due in part to its historical role as an important entrepot and services center for neighboring countries.
16. Through productivity and scale increase, automation programs and constant quality improvement of products.
17. For example, SMK, an electronic components firm, recorded a financial loss in fiscal year 1994 despite a steady increase of its turnover of around 20%. The explanation is given by the bad financial results of its Asian affiliates – they contribute to 35% of the whole outcome – as they import from Japan all of the key components (Tokyo Business, August 1995).
18. In 1992, 5 out of the 6 first worldwide producers for electronics consumer were from Japan. Sony ranked first and Matsushita second [Consumer Electronics Information Service 1994].

19. Inasmuch as, in some cases, there is a fully 100% of the production process located outside Japan.
20. Left behind Japan's electronics firms find something to make, Far Eastern Economic Review, August 31, 1995.
21. This schedule was shortened to ten years at an ASEAN ministerial meeting held in September 1994. AFTA will cover trade in manufactured goods and processed agricultural products. By liberalizing trade in the region, AFTA should encourage a more horizontal division of labour in industrial goods by making it attractive for multinational corporations to build production networks across national borders [NRI Quarterly 1994].

REFERENCES

Abo, T. (1995), Japanese Electronics Assembly Plants in East Asian Region: A Comparative Study of 'Hybrid Factories' in East Asia, the US and Europe, 12th Annual Conference of Euro-Asia Management Studies Association, Milan.

Besson, D. and Lanteri M. (1994), ANSEA: la décennie prodigieuse, essai sur le d!eveloppement en Asie, Paris: La Documentation française.

Borrus, M. (1995), Left for Dead: Asian Production Networks and the Revival of US Electronics, mimeo, BRIE, University of California, Berkeley.

Delapierre, M. (1991), 'Les accords inter-entreprises, partage ou partenariat?' *Revue d'Economie Industrielle* No. 55.

Ernst, D. (1994), The East Asian Production Networks of Japanese Electronics Firms: main features and new challenges, mimeo, BRIE, University of California.

Ernst D. and O'Connor D. (1992), *Competing in the Electronics Industry. The experiences of Newly Industrialising Economies*, OCDE, Paris.

Figuière, C. (1995), Les origines des structures productives japonaises, in *Japan Pluriel*, Arles: Picquier Publisher.

Hagedoorn, J. and Schakenraad, J. (1992), 'Strategic Technology Partenering and International Corporate Strategies,' in Hugues K. (ed.), *European Competitiveness*, Cambridge University Press.

Kwan, C. H. (1994), 'Asia's New Wave of Foreign Direct Investment', *Nomura Research Institute Quarterly*, Winter 1994.

Minami, R. (1986), *The Economic Development of Japan: A Quantitative Study*, London: Macmillan.

Mytelka, L. (ed.) (1991), *Strategic Partnership and the World Economy*, London: Pinter Publisher.

Park, Y. C. and Park, W-A. (1991), 'Changing Japanese Trade Patterns and the East Asian NICs', in Krugman P., (ed.), *Trade with Japan: has the door opened wider?* NBER, University of Chicago Press, Chicago.

Tokunaga, S. ed. (1992), *Japan's Foreign Investment and Asian Economic Interdependence*, University of Tokyo Press.

UNCTAD (1992), *World Investment Report: Transnational corporations as engines of growth*, Geneva.

UNCTAD (1993), *World Investment Report: Transnational Corporations and Integrated International Production*, Geneva.

Viner J. (1950), *The Customs Union Issue*, Carnegie Endowment for International Peace, New York.

Wade, R. (1990), *Governing the Market: Economic Theory and the Role of Government in East Asian Industrialization*, Princeton University Press.

World Bank (1993), *The East Asian Miracle*, Oxford University Press.

12 Cooperation and Strategic Alliances with Japanese Companies[1]

Jacques Jaussaud

Harsh global competition has led a growing number of companies to forge alliances with foreign partners. In their efforts to anticipate or adapt to this new environment, companies often lack the necessary means to act independently. Consequently there has been an increase in co-operation agreements between American, European and Japanese companies over the last two decades[2].

'Alliance', 'co-operation' and 'collaboration' are all terms which are often used to mean the same thing. But the term 'alliance' has the strongest meaning; it implies a deeper commitment and can be defined as the sharing of means to achieve a particular operation or project[3].

In their search for partners, Western companies are often led to consider co-operating with Japanese companies. The latter have been more inclined to be open to the outside world because their environment has deteriorated since the mid 1980s. The alliances between Western and Japanese companies are more numerous and characterized by a growing diversity.

Past conflicts have created durable fears of unfair behaviour on both sides. This paper will focus on the study of the special precautions which must be taken when defining alliance strategies with Japanese companies.

1 DIFFERENT TYPES OF COOPERATION

In the 1950s and 1960s the strict control over foreign investment in Japan and the fact that Japanese companies were lagging behind their Western counterparts limited the scope of possible co-operation. The main objective for Japanese companies embarking on such co-operation programmes was mainly to catch up with their technological lag. They tended to prefer acquiring simply the right to use Western technologies through licence agreements. With such easily implemented agreements they could preserve their autonomy.

When Western companies refused such licence agreements, a compromise could be found through the creation of joint subsidiaries to whom the technology was transferred. This was frequently the case in the pharmaceutical or electronics sector, in spite of the restrictions imposed on foreign participation in Japanese companies.

Japan has been a member of OECD since 1964. Under the pressure of this organization, control over direct investment relaxed in the early 1970s[4]. The creation of joint subsidiaries in Japan as a mode of co-operation between Western and Japanese companies was therefore facilitated.

In the 1970s trade frictions started between Japan and its partners. Sector by sector, as soon as Japanese companies reached the necessary level of competitiveness, they attacked the foreign markets as vigorously as the domestic market. Western producers bore the full brunt of these aggressive commercial policies, notably the practice of tight prices calculated, when needed, on the base of variable costs only. As Western producers were hardly present in Japan, they could not exert credible threats of retaliation on their aggressors' main market. The only short-term reaction was to make the conflict a political one. The 1970s were the decade of the steel industry and colour TV. In the 1980s the car industry, consumer electronics, office equipment and semi-conductors would be at the core of these trade frictions.

Impeded in their development by the unilateral implementation of quotas[5], 'voluntary export restraints' and anti-dumping duties, Japanese producers had to change their strategies. Local producers became aware of their comparative backwardness. Both parties started envisaging an alternative to this sensitive question[6]. Alliances with local producers in difficulty allowed some Japanese competitors to strengthen their position on markets in the process of closing. Some Western producers considered that working with a Japanese producer was a way to make up for their weaknesses.

Thus, in the 1980s Japanese steel producers supplied capital and technology to their American competitors. In the car sector, Detroit car makers got supplies of small car models from their partners, Isuzu, Suzuki, Mazda and Mitsubishi Motors, in order to counter Honda, Toyota and Nissan which were rapidly expanding on the US market. Ford tightened its links with Mazda, 25% of the whose stock it already owned.

In Europe, co-operation was somewhat less ambitious, except for the Honda–Rover alliance. From a simple licence agreement signed in December 1979 (for the Triumph Acclaim, derived from the Honda Accord) co-operation henceforth developed and allowed Rover to recover its quality control level. This led to the joint development of the Rover 800 (Honda Legend)[7]. In order to consolidate the alliance, a cross-shareholding agreement was signed in 1990 between Rover and Honda's British subsidiary, Honda Manufacturing UK Ltd.

Other significant examples can be found in technology transfer to Thomson (OKI Electric for semi-conductors and JVC for video tape recorders), or the creation of Fiat-Allis-Hitachi in civil engineering[8].

The rising yen from the autumn of 1985 onwards and the ensuing difficulties in the 1990s have further increased the possibilities of cooperation. Japanese companies were handicapped both by high wages and the strong yen due to the accumulation of a trade surplus in the 1980s. On the world's markets, Japanese products were threatened by competition from Newly Industrialized Countries (NICs) in Asia and from Western producers taking advantage of a strong yen. Foreign penetration was stronger in Japan. With harsh competition on their domestic market, a growing number of Japanese companies whose sales were no longer increasing suffered financial losses and announced drastic restructuring programmes. Since they had caught up with their Western competitors in many sectors, they have had to invest heavily in research and development in spite of the risks inherent in this kind of activity.

In this new context, Japanese companies are studying very carefully any alliance opportunity which could lessen their difficulties and reinforce their competitive position. R&D agreements have multiplied. For example, Toshiba forged a strong Multimedia[9] alliance with Apple in 1992. IBM, Siemens and Toshiba have launched a $1 billion joint programme for the development of new DRAM components[10]; Hitachi and Texas Instruments are developing a 256 Megabyte DRAM circuit; Sharp and Intel, NEC and Sundisk are developing flash memories[11] These new types of agreement have often led Western observers to fear that there might be further transfer of advanced technologies to Japanese companies.

Different types of co-operation are currently developing in every sector. Air France and Japan Airlines, both in difficult financial situations, have been exploiting jointly the Paris-Osaka New Kansai Airport line since Autumn 1994 in order to share the very expensive landing rights[12]. IBM and Toshiba are together producing liquid crystal screens for computers[13]. In distribution, new alliances with foreign partners are being forged. Daiei, Japan's first supermarket chain, is signing more agreements with Western producers (Agfa for films, Belgian brewer Bergenbräu) to tackle strong oligopolistic markets of consumer goods[14].

We should at this point make a distinction between partners who share the same objectives in their alliance and partners whose objectives are different but which are necessarily compatible[15]. When the objectives are common, they generally amount to cost cutting, risk reduction, or a combination of both, whatever the type of activity involved. This is the case in particular in R&D, electronics, or the car industry. Partners want to share both costs and risks. Through co-operation, global risks can be reduced as teams in different scientific environments work together. Such methods make it easier to find new ways to solve problems.

Cost sharing is necessary in a growing number of activities. In the development of new electronic components, each technological break-through involves enormous budgets. Results can only be optimized through massive investments in production capacities. The life cycle of each new generation of component is increasingly shorter. This is a serious handicap for the companies which are late in developing new products. Co-operation is essential for all companies especially in the semi-conductor industry. Even IBM has been forced to change its isolationist strategy in the early 90s. But objectives are often different as in the case of Boeing's alliances in the aerospace industry[16] or, more surprisingly, the selective opening of the Japanese car makers' distribution networks to the main American competitors[17].

The case of the civilian aerospace industry is particularly interesting[18]. Japan is still suffering from the handicaps caused by the dismantling of its aerospace industry after the Second World War, and by giving up the export of military equipment, a policy which is still effective today. After the commercial failure of the YS 11 transport aircraft programme developed and produced by Mitsubishi Heavy Industries, Kawasaki Heavy Industries, Fuji Heavy Industries, Shin Meiwa and Japan Aircraft Manufacturing[19], Japanese companies have opted to co-operate with foreign producers.

It is in such a context that Boeing has secured strong relations with the main Japanese aircraft makers since the early 1970s. Boeing gave part of the production of its planes (the 737 and 747) to them under licence and up to 15% of the 767. In 1990, a new step was made: Boeing allowed Japanese makers to be associated in the conception of parts of the new 777, and made them responsible for 20% of the programme[20]. Boeing was mainly trying to secure its market position in Japan, as local production is a significant selling point. That is the reason why European producers have been multiplying co-operation offers with Japanese producers who have remained very prudent for fear of hurting their American partner[21].

The objective of Boeing is mainly commercial, even if the long-term prospect of acquiring some Japanese technologies may represent a secondary objective. Japanese producers want to access the know-how of their partner in order to develop their own aerospace activity with lower costs and fewer risks. The same complementarity of objectives can be found in the creation of most joint production subsidiaries in Japan between Western and Japanese companies.

The growing diversity in the types of co-operation between Japanese and Western companies is a relatively new phenomenon. What special precautions should be taken when defining and implementing alliance strategies with Japanese companies?

2   ADAPTING STRUCTURES IN ORDER TO SAFEGUARD THEM AGAINST THE HAZARDS OF OPPORTUNISM

The intensity of some conflicts between Japanese and Western companies and the very way in which Japanese companies have handled these conflicts[22] explain why some Western managers fear there might be unfair practice on the part of their Japanese partners.

The intensive competition between Japanese companies in Japan and in the world, without justifying them, explains such opportunistic behaviour. During the twenty years of high growth (1952–73), the acquisition of Western technologies was a determinant but costly competitive asset. When a supplier refuses to yield its technology or imposes restrictions, it is very tempting to try and acquire it through other means, or to accept *ex ante* conditions which will not be respected afterwards. In the 1970s and 1980s the aggressive commercial practices of Japanese companies outside Japan were considered unfair. The regular imposition of anti-dumping duties on Japanese companies by American and European authorities reinforced this idea. Opportunistic behaviour may also have been reinforced by the difficulties met by Western companies in trying to win cases in Japanese courtrooms.

But most of the characteristics of the environment which could have favoured opportunistic behaviour have profoundly changed over the last few years. Under the pressure of the USA, the deregulation policy has progressively led to more openness in the administration, and the revision of the code of trade in early 1993 has made litigation simpler and has reduced costs[23]. An agreement has just been signed between the USA and Japan on industrial property[24]. In addition, the growing interdependence of the Japanese and Western economies and the greater commitment of many Japanese companies in exchange, co-operation or competition relations with Western companies have increased the costs and the risks of opportunistic behaviour for the latter.

Moreover the cases of opportunistic behaviour are not only limited to the Japanese companies, as is shown in the case of Rover being sold to BMW by British Aerospace, while most observers consider that it is Honda that has put the British company on its feet again. The hazards of opportunism seem to be universal in the business world; O. E. Williamson stresses the necessity of *organizing* transactions[25] to safeguard them against the hazards of opportunism.

Williamson's study enriches considerably the economic analysis of trade. We can usefully extend Williamson's analysis by considering the hazards of opportunism in co-operative relations.

Williamson stresses the fact that when the transactions imply on the part of the supplier or the client the realization of a specific investment, tangible or intangible, uncertainty over the future conditions of the environment and the risk of opportunistic behaviour leads both parties to organize transactions. As partners cannot anticipate all the cases and their consequences (bounded rationality) and as they both fear that the other party might take advantage of any process of adjustment (of prices, for example, to adapt to the evolution of the market) they organize an adapted *governance structure*, i.e. a relationship management structure. They define the role of each party involved in the process of decision making which allows for the revision of the exchange conditions and defines the process itself. Each party resorts more and more to a designated arbitrator[26]. The arbitrator may reconcile conflicting positions in order to safeguard the durability of the relationship, especially when specific assets are involved. In the definition of the process of decision making some variables are privileged, such as quantities rather than prices, as they are less likely to arouse suspicion on the part of each partner.

We can use this approach in the study of the cooperative relations between companies. Such relations imply specific intangible investment including the costs related to the preparation stages for collaboration (prospecting, negotiating, training) and the opportunity cost linked to the absence, at least temporary, of alternatives to the relationship which is being implemented. Added to this intangible investment there is specific *tangible* investment whose importance depends on the nature of the planned operations. This investment in specific assets is made in an uncertain context with opportunity risks.

It is therefore necessary to structure the relationship in order to ensure its continuity, to provide for the evolution of the environment and to reduce the hazards of opportunism. Let us take the example of Jalatte, a French security shoe maker. This medium-sized company, which belonged to the André group at that time, realized in the early 80s that its main US competitors were gaining ground on the Japanese market through alliances with the largest local producers. Jalatte was contacted by a small Japanese producer which feared it might be marginalized because its competitors were accessing US technology. Jalatte studied the opportunity of a licence agreement. This approach presented many risks: many licence agreements with Japanese companies have only led to Japanese producers becoming stronger and more competitive[27]. How was it possible to organize the relationship in order to reduce all hazards of opportunism while ensuring its durability?

In-depth discussions with the participation of Crédit Lyonnais, Jalatte's bank in Japan, made it possible to find an original and intermediate solution between the two modalities which are, according to the transaction cost theory, the *trilateral governance* (the recourse to a designated arbitrator) and the *bilateral governance* (structured bilateral relationship with *credible financial commitments* such as specific assets invested by both partners, reciprocal exchanges, or still better, creation of a joint subsidiary)[28]:

(1) Jalatte conceded to its partner a technology which was in between the one it was using at the time, like most of its local competitors, and the one the French company had just developed.

(2) The minimum total of annual royalties was guaranteed by the local branch of Crédit Lyonnais. The role of the bank was much more than that of an arbiter. With its expertise in the Japanese business world, its public image and its many contacts, the bank could be an agent in the reduction of the hazards of opportunism.

(3) The French company's export manager became chairman of a club of distributors of the products made in Japan with Jalatte's technology.

4) The export activity of the Japanese company was entrusted to a joint distribution subsidiary created by Jalatte and its partner.

The intervention of a third party (Crédit Lyonnais) and the setting up of light structures with precise objectives (distributors' club, joint subsidiary for the export operations) allowed the two companies both to reduce the hazards of opportunism and enabled them to be sensitive to the evolution of the environment and adapt to the precise conditions of the relationship between both partners.

In many cases the creation of a joint subsidiary is the sign of a strong commitment by both parties. Giving the management of the co-operation to an autonomous entity, owned jointly, makes it possible to entrust to it the responsibility of periodical adaptations to the evolution of the environment without having to consult the two partners endlessly. The main advantage that can be found in vertical integration[29] can also be found in an alliance.

But the management of a joint subsidiary is not easy. The balance of power between the two partners, especially in the case of technology, may change. The activity portfolios evolve and may even make the joint subsidiary lose some of its strategic interest for one of the partners[30]. The accumulation of difficulties invariably leads to a crisis, the solution of which is either the end of the partnership or its redefinition. A strongly structured co-operation with a Japanese partner should not remain rigid.

Another feature of the Japanese economy – which we cannot study here for lack of space – must not be overlooked in the definition of alliance strategies: the characteristics of the group structures in Japan[31].

CONCLUSION

The profound changes in the environment of Japanese companies (Japan has entered a phase of economic maturity) give new opportunities to Western companies. As cooperation is possible in a growing number of circumstances, should they systematically choose to co-operate with Japanese companies?

The selection of a partner is always difficult. The number of potential partners should therefore be increased, which implies also considering Japanese companies. Moreover, the competitive field of a company must be assessed on an industrial world scale, i.e. the North America-Europe-Japan Triad[32]. But Japan remains the weak point for most Western companies. A well conceived co-operation with Japanese companies may give them access to the financial, human and technological resources of these companies and open the doors of the Japanese market.

However, alliances are often more difficult to forge with direct competitors. Each party fears these alliances might be detrimental to its activities or that the partner might profit more from the results of the joint activities. The failure of the European computer alliance, Unidata, in the 1970s, or that of Pirelli (Italy) and Continental (Germany) in the tyre sector in the early 1990s are good illustrations of the problem. Such failures, according to Kenichi Ohmae, show the necessity of alliances between 'distant' competitors. We must not forget, though, that the distance between the markets of the Triad is rapidly decreasing and that a 'distant' competitor today may be 'close' tomorrow.

Notes

1. Translated from the French by Jean-François ALLAFORT, Professeur Agrégé d'Anglais, IEP, University of Bordeaux. Many thanks to Crispin GEOGHEGAN, Bournemouth University, for his helpful comments.
2. *Teaming up for the 90s*, Timothy M. COLLINS, Thomas L. DOORLEY, Business One Irwin, Homewood, 1991.

3. *La Conquête des marchés passe par l'art des alliances*, Deloitte Touche Tohmatsu International, *L'expansion Management Review, n°74, Autumn 1994.*
4. *Foreign enterprise in Japan, laws and policies*, Dan Ferno HENDERSON, Charles E. Tuttle, Tokyo, 1983.
5. For cars in some European countries, particularly in France from 1977 onwards, in blatant violation of the GATT regulations.
6. *Enterprises japonaises et enterprises occidentales, la gestion des conflits*, Jacques JAUSSAUD, *Japon in Extenso* n°30, march 1993, taken up in *Problèmes Economiques*, n°2354, 15/12/1993.
7. Faulkner David, *'The Rover-Honda Alliance'* in SCHOLES KEVEN, JOHNSON GERRY, *Exploring Corporate Strategy*, Prentice Hall International, 1993, 3rd edition.
8. *La cooperazione produttiva tra imprese italiane e giapponesi: il caso della joint-venture tra Fiat Geotech e Hitachi Construction Machinery Ltd.*, Francesco FORMICONI, *Quaderni di Ricerca*, March 1989, Instituto di Studi Economico-Sociali per l'Asia Orientale (ISEAO), Universià Commerciale Luigi Bocconi, Milano.
9. *Apple and Toshiba forge Multimedia Alliance, Tokyo Business Today*, August 1992.
10. *Super Chip Alliance, Tokyo Business Today*, September 1992.
11. *IC World turns Upside-Down, Japanese Chips on the Defensive, Tokyo Business Today*, July 1993, *La Tribune Desfossés*, 05/07/94.
12. *La Tribune Desfossés*, 19/05/94 and 26/05/94.
13. *La Tribune Desfossés*, 24/06/94.
14. *The price revolution*, Hiroshi FUKUNAGA, Kyoko CHINONE, *Tokyo Business Today*, October 1994.
15. Cf. *Japan in Extenso*, n°35, March 1995, our article (note n°1)
16. *L'industrie aérospatiale japonaise*, Tadashi KAGEYAMA, *Japon in Extenso*, n°19, March 1991, and *Japan Economic Almanac, 1992, 1993 and 1994 editions.*
17. *Nissan Affiliates to sell Ford cars*, Hidenaka KATO, *The Nikkei Weekly*, 17/10/1994 and 26/09/1994.
18. Though 80% of the aerospace industry's turnover in Japan is made with military orders from the government. Cf. *Aerospace and Defense*, Akihiko HARA, *Japan Economic Almanac*, 1992.
19. Only 182 models of this plane were sold between 1965 and 1972 when the project was abandoned. Heavy losses were absorbed by the MITI which was associated in the project.
20. *Japan Economic Almanac*, 1992, 1993 and 1994 editions.
21. Boeing has been preferred to the French-Italian consortium ATR (Aérospatiale and Alenia) in order to study the feasibility of the Japanese 100-seat plane YSX project. Cf. La tribune Desfossés, 04/08/1994.
22. *Entreprises japonaises et entreprises occidentales, la gestion des conflits*, J. Jaussaud, op. cit.
23. *The corporate governance controversy*, Fusahiro TANAKA, *Tokyo Business Today*, August 1993.
24. *Le Japon et les Etats-Unis signent un accord sur les brevets, La Tribune Desfossés*, 18/08/1994.
25. *The Economic Institutions of Capitalism*, Oliver E. Williamson, The Free Press, Macmillan Inc., New York, 1985.

26. It is the case for the International Chamber of Commerce, Paris, in many international contracts.

27. Cf. *Le Japan, premier constructeur automobile mondial*, J. Jaussaud, *Japon in Extenso*, n°22, December 1991, or for the machine-tool sector, see *Les modalités de pénétration des marchés étrangers*, J. Jaussaud, in *Le Commerce international aujourd'hui*, Les Cahiers Français, n°253, October–December 1991.

28. O. E. Williamson, 1994 op. cit., chapters 3, 7 and 8.

29. 'The advantage of vertical integration is that adaptations can be made in a sequential way without the need to consult, complete, or revise interfirm agreements'. O. E. Williamson, 1985, op. cit. Chapter 3, p 78.

30. *Le cas de Rhône-Poulenc au Japon*, Gilles Barbier, Vice-Président, *Japon in Extenso*, n°18, December 1990.

31. *Alliance Capitalism, the Social Organization of Japanese Business*, Michael L. Gerlach, University of California Press, 1992.

32. *Triad Power, the Coming Shape of Global Competition*, Kenichi Ohmae, The Free Press, 1985.

13 Japan as a Base for Establishing Markets Throughout Asia: the Case of French Industrial Glue Manufacturers

Christine Di Domenico and Sami Slim

The frenetic levels of consumption and massive infrastructure requirements of Asia-Pacific countries are a regular focus of attention for Western economic and financial magazines. Day after day, industrialists in the construction, foodstuff and automotive sectors claim to place this region of the world at the top of their strategic priorities. It is true that the prospect of equipping and nourishing almost a billion new consumers from now to the year 2000 is enough to call the senior officers of every firm into action. The manufacturers of glues and industrial adhesives concentrated in the Triad countries, where the markets served are already mature and highly competitive, are also in search of new outlets. This intermediate industry, positioned downstream from chemicals, supplies all industrial sectors from construction to packaging, from manufacturers of domestic electrical goods to transport. The downturn in economic activity which hit these client sectors one by one after 1990 went on to shake the world of glues and adhesives, now experiencing a succession of mergers, acquisitions and reorganizations without precedent. At a time of production plant relocation, the chance to follow their industrial customers in their internationalization policy seemed attractive to many adhesive mix preparers.

However, the establishment of durable business activities in Asia requires the adoption of coherent strategies, specific to each type of segment served. A certain number of these segments are already global, whereas others require a specific, local approach. The principal thesis advanced in this article is that the glue industry, which is moving towards activity *on an international scale*, can benefit from the commercial and technological influence of Japan: here is found the perfect bridgehead for the conquest of a *new economic space* like the Asia-Pacific zone. First, we will evaluate the dynamics of this industry, on course for a survival race towards *technological intensification*. Subsequently, we will demonstrate how the Japanese archipelago can provide an excellent platform for expansion through its efforts in the fields of quality standards and of environmental protection, thus pursuing its integrative role within a region in search of prosperity and of technological independence. Through the logic of company multinationalisation of the kind developed by Dunning and Mucchielli, we shall consider what strategies for Japanese market penetration can be envisaged for this industry.

1   OVERVIEW OF THE INDUSTRY

1.1   A Concentration Within the Triad Markets

The worldwide consumption of glues and adhesives represents a huge market worth about 13.5 billion dollars (roughly 70 billion francs). The President of the Japanese chemical group Toray Industries Inc., Yoshikazu Ito, recently put[1] the annual production at about 17 million tonnes throughout the world (of which 1.2 million tonnes was in Japan). Since industrial adhesives play an integral part in the development of new materials and in the emergence of new technologies, it is not surprising to find their production concentrated in the most industrialized countries.

The annual world consumption of glues and adhesives per inhabitant is estimated at one kilo on a world scale. This rises to six kilos for the Triad countries alone.

In spite of the lack of reliable statistics in this field, one could reasonably estimate that the ten leading world manufacturers today supply about 38% of the total adhesives market. And the first twenty leading suppliers meet about half the current worldwide requirements (48%) (Henkel Market Research (1992)).

American supremacy with 40% of the world market (HB Fuller, Loctite, Borden, Morton) together with Europe which in turn has 35% of the market (Henkel, Unilever-National Starch & Chemicals, Total-Bostik and Elf Atochem-Ceca) with 10% in Germany alone, stands out clearly in this classification. Only one Japanese glue and adhesive manufacturer can be listed among the first ten world leaders: Konishi (at the 6th or 7th place), but even this firm only exports 2% of its turnover.

The Japanese manufactures overall currently make up 10% of the total market, the rest being divided between the other producer countries.

Table 13.1   The economic power of the Triad countries in 1989

	E.U.		USA/CAN		JAPAN	
Population (millions) of inhabitants)	326	6.3%	275	5.3%	123	2.4%
GNP (billion $)	3800	24.9%	3884	25.4%	1520	10.0%
Production (million of vehicles)	13.1	37.0%	7.9	22.4%	8.4	23.8%
Glue and adhesive market (billion $)	4.6	35.0%	5.2	40.0%	1.3	10.0%

Source: Henkel market research

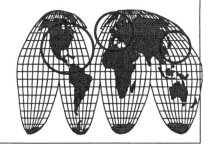

13.9 % of the world population generates :

- 60.3 % of the world GNP
- 85 % of the world glue and adhesive market
- 84 % of the world automobile production

1.2   Structural Profile: Major Groups Rub Shoulders with SMES

The glue and adhesives industry is difficult to define as a result of the great diversity of basic products, the variety of applications possible for the same chemical solution (additives, binders), together with the heterogeneous nature of firms in this sector (fully-integrated multinational chemical concerns, small local producers only making mixes)[2].

It therefore transpires that in this branch of activity diversified chemical groups are found (through a department or through subsidiaries: one case among others is the French Total Chimie and Bostik; another is Elf-Atochem with Ceca) that coexist with small independent firms whose activity is made possible through the presence of narrow regional markets and low requirements in terms of fixed operating assets.

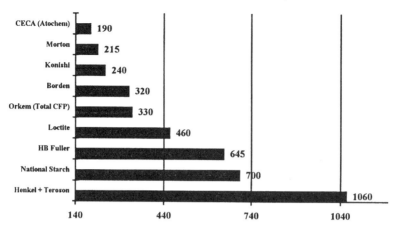

Figure 13.1 The ten world leaders in adhesives in 1989

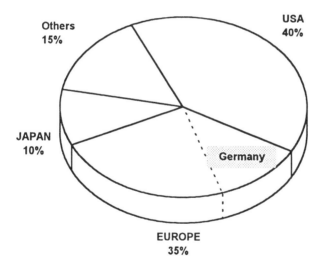

Figure 13.2 Regional distribution of the world adhesives market in 1989

These SMEs are generally specialized in a limited number of markets, and do not produce basic raw materials, unlike the large producers referred to above. Groups are also found among the major producers who have been for some time involved in glue production, since it complements what they manufacture (the American 3M is one case). In France, the sector is

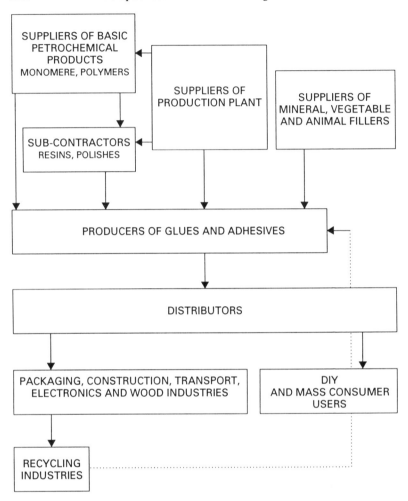

Figure 13.3   The glue and adhesives sector

dominated by multinational firms (Henkel, HB Fuller, Locite, Unilever-Nsc, Ceca and Bostik) and the level of concentration is already high in terms of market share.

This structural complexity in the industrial glue industry reflects the variety of user needs: hundreds of different applications, from the standard product to the made-to-measure. In fact, it is not unusual to develop a one-off glue for each customer. Glue producers, positioned downstream from the chemicals branch, supply all the industrial sectors, ranging from construction to car and aeronautical manufacturers, and including electrical/electronic equipment manufacturers as well as packaging.

The downturn in economic activity at the beginning of the 1990s has made glue producers modify their strategies, putting the emphasis on the degree of dependence of this intermediary industry, which displays little movement of capital investment in relation to its branch and to the networks which coexist with it.

2   AN INDUSTRY BECOMING AN INTERNATIONAL ACTIVITY

2.1   The Industry Life Cycle

In spite of an undeniable tendency towards *concentration* in each of the Triad markets (USA, Europe and Japan), this industry still shows certain features which belong to *fragmented* environments. Furthermore, the low levels of growth recorded in most of the segments in the geographical areas, as well as the minimal number of potential applications which remain to be mastered in the realm of assembling, are symptomatic of an industry in its *maturity* phase.

This said, technological development and substitution are far from being stabilized. In fact, technological innovation remains above all a means of staying in competition: the launch of new technologies such as urethane hot-melts and low-temperature-melting hot-melts (mainly due to recycling constraints and production rhythms) are having little effect on overall demand. This is due to major substitution effects between technologies for similar applications and identical customers. Furthermore, customer requirements are changing rapidly, leading to modifications to the profession and structure of the industrial glues and adhesives sector. As a result, from now on the customer will demand an improvement from the supplier in the technical content of the products (non-polluting, non-toxic, multipurpose, ease of application, speed of drying) together with free and immediate technical assistance. The same customer operates with low stock levels, requiring frequent and irregular delivery, giving rise to very high distribution costs (this is especially the case with Japan).

Intensification of technological content appears to be the only possible answer to these constraints. In terms of future development, industrial adhesives are capable of improving the structural qualities of products (lighter, more flexible or shock-resistant), as well as a perfect appearance (finish): two essential criteria in the final consumer's appreciation of a manufactured product.

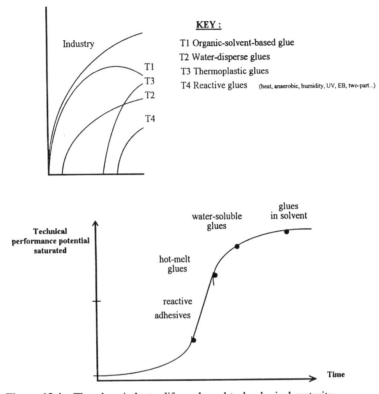

Figure 13.4   The glues industry life-cycle and technological maturity

2.2   The Search for New Markets

The pressure for swift amortization of investments and R&D costs is pushing multinationals – now taking the biggest market shares in all highly-industrialised countries – to participate in a wave of mergers and acquisitions, and to make alliances with other national or foreign partners[3].

Three dimensions are involved here:

(1) The degree of concentration of the industry ($\approx$ the number of competitors),
(2) The level of the industry's maturity ($\approx$ position of products in life-cycle),
(3) The degree to which the industry is globalized ($\approx$ firm globalization).

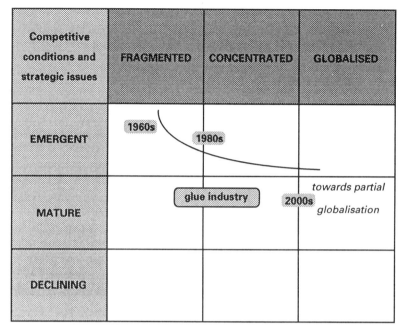

Figure 13.5   The glue industry: towards globalization

It is possible to visualize the development of the glue and adhesives industry among the nine industry types (Porter [1985] see below).

In reality, the race for innovation, for concentration and for the international development of industrial glue producers forms strategies to the constraints of a two-dimensional structural profile: fragmentation and maturity (see table). It can be seen that a company genuinely capable of growth and innovation will be forced to buy out competitors or to diversify (diseconomies of scale), while broadening their offer or even while making process innovations (as and when the industry reaches maturity). Other firms, without these capacities of growth and innovation, will be able to compensate by international development and/or by acquisitions.

There are three reasons for the internationalisation of certain segments:

(1) following and accompanying the development of customers who are internationalizing,
(2) exploiting a competitive technological advantage (patent or manufacturing secret),

(3) in the case of the biggest producers, a culture and internal dynamic favourable to internationalization in the face of globalization, or the result of a desire to be present and to be known abroad.

Each of these reasons will now be examined in detail.

(1)   Following Customers

The need to keep major customers whose business has taken an international turn, squeezing concessions from glue manufacturers at the same time (cf. the period of negotiation and of supplier selection which precedes the introduction of a new product in a Japanese-style network) has also made it possible to strengthen commercial links in the country of origin (closer partnership) and to ensure growth in the worldwide market.

The two main advantages of this type of internationalisation lie in the certainty of finding an immediate outlet through the existing customer (the building of a local factory can be envisaged without too much risk if the customer's business is well-established), and in the setting-up of a 'strategic platform' from which the company can conquer new markets in the host country (the customer 'guaranteeing' the supplier's development financially, in a certain way).

Up to now this type of opportunity has been limited only to those suppliers of major industries such as automobiles, construction equipment, or personal hygiene (nappies, sanitary towels), who benefit from a strong partnership agreement in their country of origin. The leading Japanese manufacturer Cemedine applies this process in penetrating international markets. It followed Toyota and Honda to the USA and into Thailand, now holding major contracts from the 'Big Three' US automobile manufacturers.

(2)   Exploiting a Technological Competitive Advantage

The glue producers who have successfully developed this type of approach in the course of their international expansion are very highly-integrated major producers of glue. It is rare that the majority of manufacturer/preparers (who at the very most buy their raw materials and develop a mix to meet a specific customer need) have a technology advanced enough to directly lead to international expansion.

(3)   A Distinctive International Dynamic

For the major producers, who find it increasingly more difficult to expand their market share at home, world markets remain a priority target. One can

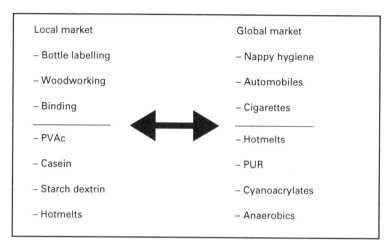

Figure 13.6 Structure of the industrial adhesives market

recall the global strategy of systematically setting up foreign operations adopted by American firms in the 1960s and the 1970s, for complete product families in each new national market. This attempt, fruitless for a long time, has enabled them to acquire precious information about the 'multidomestic' nature of this industry.

At a time when entry barriers are being strengthened, particularly by the partnership race to which European and Japanese firms are applying themselves, both in Europe and in the USA, it appears that producers who have already begun their multinationalization will reinforce their positions. This industry globalization can be continued, bearing in mind:

⇒ the chance offered by customers to follow them in their internationalization
⇒ the opening of new markets for modern consumer products (China, India, Russia)
⇒ the opportunity for licensing agreements in these new markets.

3   THE ATTRACTIVENESS OF THE ASIA – PACIFIC REGION

3.1   Strong Growth and Frenetic Levels of Consumption

According to the most recent report from the Asia Development Bank (ADB) published in April 1995, growth in Asia, despite a slight dip, will continue to

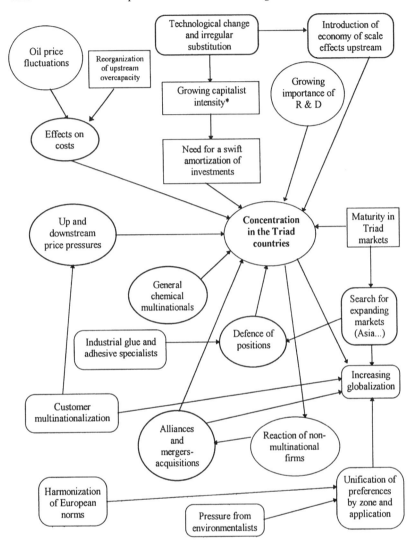

*e.g. Bostik and their pilot plant for applicability and performance testing

Figure 13.7   Development dynamics in the industrial glue and adhesive sector

outperform all the other regions in the world for the next two years. The ADB has forecast a growth of 7.6% and 7.4% for 1995 and 1996 respectively, whereas the rest of the world is hovering around 3% (*Les Echos*, 7–8 April 1995). With annual growth at 8.2% last year, Asia was well above the world

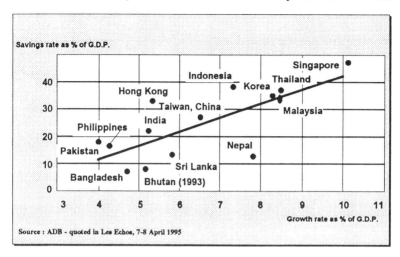

Figure 13.8 Savings and growth go together

average of 2.1%, thus making the most of recovery in Europe, Japan and the US. The authors of the report recognize that growth in international trade, and the huge investment flows (both external and internal) injected into these economies, have boosted exports, in particular those of Southeast Asia.

The ADB also notes that the region will continue to prosper in the next few years. The growth rates of South Asia (India, Pakistan, Bangladesh, Nepal, Sri Lanka), which are currently in the starting blocks, will certainly overtake those of Southeast Asia (Thailand, Malaysia, Indonesia, Vietnam), which are the current leaders. Despite the austerity programme initiated by the government in 1993 and the devaluation of the yuan, to slow down growth, China still grew by 11.8% in 1994[4].

All these countries benefit from high and stable levels of savings (between 7% and 47% of GDP), which avoids too heavy a dependence on external debt. In addition, for those households that really save, the purchase of something of real value can be made with less difficulty. The high savings rates show firms that consumers are optimistic and wish to improve their material comforts as soon as possible.

The Chinese have thrown themselves into 'consumerism' with vigorous enthusiasm. Despite considerable inequalities, consumption in China should triple in the next decade. For Jardine Fleming, a Hong Kong firm, more than 1.5 million people throng the main street of Shanghai every day. Shops are open twelve hours a day, 360 days a year, and shoppers splash out $50 million daily.

Table 13.2 Household equipment in cities (as %)

	1985	1993
Furniture	–	34.1
Washing machine	48.3	86.4
Refrigerator	6.6	56.7
Electric cooker	19.0	66.7
Colour TV	17.2	79.5
B. and W. TV	66.9	35.9
V.C.R.	–	12.2
Hi-fi	–	5.7
Scooter	1.04	3.5

Source: Statistical survey of
(Quoted in *Enjeux* February 1995)

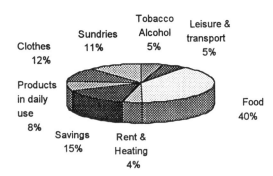

SOURCE: Xinmin Wanbao, 1994

Figure 13.9 Budget of an urban household

Over the last few years, the structure of consumption has changed. Bicycles, watches, radios and sewing machines have been replaced by colour TVs, VCRs, hi-fi and household goods. According to the French Daily *Enjeux Les Echos*, in February 1995, 26 new malls in Beijing offer ready-to-wear clothes, perfume and luxury goods known throughout the world. The Japanese toy manufacturer Bandai says parents in Japan spend more than 30,000 yen ($300) annually on toys for their children.

How can such frenetic levels of consumption be explained when even the most optimistic hypotheses put Chinese revenues at one twentieth of those in

Population

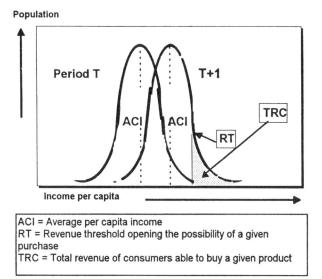

ACI = Average per capita income
RT = Revenue threshold opening the possibility of a given purchase
TRC = Total revenue of consumers able to buy a given product

Figure 13.10 The revenue effect

Japan or the US (Chinese G.N.P per capita was only $461 in 1993)? The explanation is simple: it is the revenue effect.

Car sales in Malaysia offer a good illustration. An increase of 40% in per capita income between 1987–91 was accompanied by a 290% increase in car sales, primarily in Kuala Lumpur.

In the next few years demand is likely to explode, in industry after industry. According to the New China state agency, more than 50 million Chinese households already have an annual revenue of more than 50,000 yuans ($16,200). With this they can buy the cheapest cars built in China: Daihatsu or Suzuki.

Kenneth Courtis, Director of Economic Forecasting for the Deutsche Bank in Tokyo, reckons that Asia, excluding Japan, will account for two-thirds of growth in global car sales this decade, according to *The Economist's* Survey of Asia of 30 October 1993. By the end of the century, between twelve and sixteen new car plants will have been built, each with a production capacity of about 200,000 units a year. 75% of the plants will be Japanese, with sales of more than 550,000 units as from 1998. In China alone, car production should triple by 2000 to about 2 million units.

Honda is investing $1.5 billion over 5–6 years in India ($280 million in 1995), to produce between 350,000 and 600,000 vehicles a year. Honda's

Table 13.3   300% increase in Chinese car production by 2000

	1994*	2000**
VW/Changchun	47,000	200 à 300,000
VW/Shanghai	110,000	200 à 330,000
Citroën/Wuhan	10,000	150 à 300,000
Peugeot/Canton	20,000	200 à 300,000
Daihatsu/Tianjin	50,000	200 à 300,000
Chrysler/Pékin	35,000	150 à 300,000
Suzuki/Chongquing	52,000	70 à 300,000
Subaru/Guizhou	5,000	50 à 80,000
Vehicles assembled	329,000	1,220 à 2,040,000
Vehicles imported	150,000	80 à 200,000
Total market	479,000	1,300 à 2,240,000

Source: Peugeot S.A.
*Forecasts **Installed capacity
Quoted in 'Enjeux', February 1995

aim is to counter the aggressive tactics of Daewoo from Korea, which recently signed a contract with one of India's largest industrial conglomerates. The suppliers of adhesives to these two giants can anticipate their long-term future in India with a certain serenity, particularly as this delocalization will encourage other manufacturers to invest in India. This investment logic is likely to be repeated in numerous client sectors, on condition the manufacturers have taken the trouble to build up a solid client-supplier relationship based on trust and

3.2   Go via Japan to Bounce Back in Asia and in Europe

After pioneering the economic take-off in Asia over the last few years, Japan now dominates the rest of Asia with its level of technology and the size of its direct investments (accelerated since 1991 by the rise in the yen). Mr Ozawa, a Japanese economist, has emphasized the linkage between the different phases in the industrialization of Japan and the corresponding staggered phases in its investment abroad, particularly in the rest of Asia.

On one side the Japanese, masters in the art of innovating to please both spoilt and demanding customers, who want to double their efforts in fundamental research by the end of the decade (Les Echos, 11/10/94; on the other, the four Asian dragons, China and (soon) Indochina, seeking technological independence, a strategy of vertical integration, as they taste the delights of consumption and economic prosperity. Japan manages to impose its technical standards and industrial norms through the quality and volume of the manufactured goods it sells throughout Asia, despite the risk of their being in turn copied. Japan's industrial norms (in sanitary and anti-pollution terms for the chemical sector) thus enable it to pursue its policy of integration into the whole region (See table on Investment Clusters).

However, as Japan consolidates its domination over the region, it also becomes a launching-pad for its partners in the Triad to penetrate other Asian markets. An opportunity exists, for example, for Western industries to supply Japanese export-oriented industries. But is Japan the right launching-pad for specialty chemical activities such as the production of industrial adhesives and glue?

Japan has always been perceived as protectionist, geographically distant and with a business philosophy that has little in common with the founding principles of GATT (now replaced by the World Trade Organization). Despite strenuous efforts on the part of the authorities to prise open the Japanese market, this perception still remains valid. Japan represents a market of 125 million people living in an area 23 times smaller than the US. Japan possesses a highly competitive industrial sector that exports worldwide, backed up by a stock of leading-edge technologies that evolve constantly.

Since the middle of the 1980's, Japan has gone through fundamental change: obstacles to imports have been considerably reduced, and the number of niche opportunities has risen. Japan has also become much more internationally-oriented. Setting up a subsidiary in Japan is no longer an impossible obstacle course, provided one can offer a leading-edge technology that can overcome the barrier of certification (Japanese norms are known to be among the toughest in the world).

The Japanese market is a demanding and highly competitive one that forces firms to constantly improve the quality of their products. This is crucial in enabling firms to succeed in markets of the advanced industrialized countries, in developing countries, and in high-growth Asian markets.

Japan also gives firms the opportunity to do some environmental scanning of the competition to identify potential challenges, both in other markets and on the French domestic market. The strength and scope of Japanese industry also enables firms to find partners to develop joint ventures in other Asian markets.

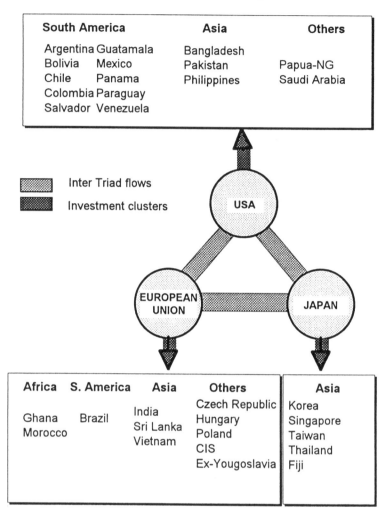

* Economies in which one of the 3 members of the Triad dominated incoming FDI :
1986-89   SOURCE : U.N.

Figure 13.11   Investment clusters* in the Triad

The Japanese chemical industry, ranked no. 2 in the world, is not sufficiently international, with only 10% of production being exported. Their chemical firms are fragmented (6000 firms, equivalent to the whole of Europe), do not have a critical mass and have, as a result, been hard hit by the drop in demand and by increasingly aggressive foreign competition. Prices are now the only factor of discussion in sales negotiations in the present crisis, and producers have been forced to cut costs dramatically.

The growing number of joint ventures and acquisitions made by foreign groups in Japan is an indication of the growing desire of Japanese firms to seek international link-ups to protect jobs and ensure survival. In addition, many firms that use speciality chemicals notice that quotas for foreign products are gradually disappearing. French firms whose products had already aroused a technical interest among potential Japanese clients have seen sales grow by leaps and bounds. The chemical industries of the two countries are in many ways complementary. While the Japanese market in general presents difficulties that are well-known, this is not so much the case in the chemical industry, as for other sectors.

Similarities between the two industries are numerous: the absence of petroleum and the need to develop fine chemicals (organic chemical products with a high value added, most often obtained from a particular know-how in certain synthetic or separation processes). Also, both countries develop speciality chemicals that are needed by all semi-finished or finished product sectors such as ink, paint, varnish, industrial adhesives, materials, electronics, cars, steel, agricultural products, food, personal health and animal health.

However, Japan still lags behind in the technology of fine chemistry, thus offering opportunities for foreign firms to exploit their lead to technology and know-how. If foreign investors make the most of the opportunities open to them in Japan, they should be able to exploit the zone of influence these firms have in the rest of Asia, and simultaneously reinforce their own positions in Europe. This is the case for the French firm Plato (part of the Fournier group), which is positioning itself as a supplier to several Japanese car manufacturers (e.g. Toyota, well known for the rigour of its tests and specifications), for its pressure-sensitive adhesives. This segment has a bright future ahead of it. Once it is recognized as an authorized supplier to the European subsidiaries of Japanese car manufacturers, after two years of stringent testing it will have a window of opportunity for the rest of Asia, as Toyota and its competitors are delocalizing across S.E.Asia.

3.3   The OLI Paradigm and Ways of Penetrating the Japanese Market

Since 1977 J. Dunning has developed what he calls the OLI paradigm, which takes into account three levels of analysis simultaneously: the firm, the industry and the country. At each level three appears a greater or lesser propensity towards multinationalization.

The O in OLI stands for *ownership advantage* – the internal advantages possessed by firms. Each firm has its own unique firm-specific advantages which give it a competitive advantage relative to other firms. These firm-specific advantages take the form of the possession of intangible assets, such as:

- product differentiation, trademarks
- large size, reflecting scale economies
- managerial, marketing or other skills specific to the organizational function of the firm...

The L is for *location-specific advantage*. This is more closely linked to the notion of the comparative advantage of the host country; it includes concerns such as the geographical and cultural distances between markets, and the level of government intervention in business...

The I is for *internalization advantages*. This concerns the advantage a firm may acquire in organizing itself internally in response to its market.

All three conditions are required for foreign direct investment.

In the table below we apply the OLI paradigm to the adhesive industry. In each column we rank items in order of importance.

Mucchielli has attempted to build a general model to identify the factors that influence delocalization. His three levels of analysis (firm, country, industry) are clearer than the somewhat eclectic theories of Dunning.

The specific advantages of MNCs can be linked to Michael Porter's concepts of the competitive advantage of firms in terms of cost and differentiation. Localization advantages are based on the more general notion of the competitive advantage of nations, taking in to account other factors such as the size and dynamics of the national market. Mucchielli suggests a kind of *convergence* (TC if total) or *divergence* (TD if total, PD if partial) can arise between these advantages, both in terms of the firm and the environment of its home base. In Table 13.5 below, the signs + and − indicate competitive advantage or not.

Firms committed to continual innovation in competition with their rivals are always on the prowl for possible strategic alliances, both in research and in development. These link-ups bring what Mucchielli calls 'specific alliance rewards', where costs linked to competition or duplication of research are eliminated, enabling firms to reach the critical mass required for R&D with a fair and lower risk. As a result knowledge is shared and the sector's competitive environment changes.

This theoretical discussion can be proved in practical terms by Japan's frantic search for foreign partners to ensure some firms' survival. Examples are more numerous for the paint and ink sectors because sales volume is greater. Sartomer (a subsidiary of Total), present in Asia for the last 20 years,

Table 13.4 The adhesives industry: advantages in multi-nationalization

'O' Specific advantages of French suppliers	'L' Advantage of setting up in Japan	'I' Advantage of internalisation
MNC (Multi-national corporations)	(1) Country with a lead in technology and in market share in the Pacific Rim and on the relevant workers.	MNC
(1) Technological lead in formulators.		(1) Lower transaction costs (in the case of a production subsidiary).
(2) Previous multi-national activity in Asia (reputation and managerial experience of joint-ventures).	(2) Japanese norms are accepted throughout the region.	(2) Less uncertainty (inventory).
	(3) Japan's role in facilitating integration into Asia.	(3) Better control of supply (quality and quantity) and improved environment scanning (both commercially and technically).
(3) Culture of respect for the client with a total commitment and a long-term vision.	(4) Low quality of input and infrastructure in neighbouring countries.	(4) Control of outlets.
(4) Access to raw material markets (vertically integrated producers like ELF or TOTAL) particularly in the Asia-Pacific region.	(5) Local presence of numerous potential targets for acquisition. Presence of potential partners in technical and sales terms.	(5) Possibility of agreements upstream (Japanese networks).
	(6) High quality infrastructure.	SME
(5) Possess own structure to understand national differences, purchasing behaviour, R&D and decentralised sales operations (adhesives is a multi-domestic industry).	(7) Very competitive environment acting as a stimulant in the learning curve for firms committed to continual innovation.	(1) Less risk of fraud on patents. (2) Possibility of agreements upstream (Japanese networks). (3) Better control of supply (quality and quantity) and improved environment scanning (both commercially and technically).
SME (Small and medium sized enterprises)		(4) Transport and communication costs.
(1) Technological lead in formulators.		(5) Perceived distance in terms of language and culture.
(2) Culture of respect for the client.		

is one of the leaders in photo-reticulatable systems in Ultra-Violet and in electron beams in the US. It has just signed an agreement for production and sales in a joint venture with a local firm in the sector.

Table 13.5   International strategies, comparative and strategic advantages in the adhesives industry

Competitive advantage of the firm (France/Japan)		Comparative advantage of host country (Japan/ France)		Method of entry	C / D
Demand of production factors	Product supply	Supply of prod. fact	Product demand	FDI	
1. +	+	+	+	National production and sales	CT
2. +	+	−	−	FDI ex-Japan	DT
3. +	+	−	+	FDI ex-Japan for re-import	DP
4. +	+	+	−	Export	DP
5. −	−	+	+	FDI entering Japan	DT
6. −	−	−	+	Import	DP
7. −	−	+	−	FDI entering Japan for re-export in Asia	DP
8. −	−	−	−	Foreign production/ foreign sales	CT

Strategic advantage
of the firm in the race for continual innovation

... Situation 7. (−−/+−) with a strategic advantage +	Licence agreement in Japan
Situation 7. with a strategic advantage −	Export
... Situation 5. (−−/++) with a strategic advantage −	Incoming FDI (JV or acquisition)
Situation 5. with a strategic advantage +	Int. Cooper. agreement (R&D)

Obviously the method of entry into a market will differ according to the size and degree of vertical integration of the manufacturer concerned (See 'Choice and local set-up' below).

For big MNCs like Total or Elf, being present in Japan on the adhesives market can be explained by the ambition to be recognized as an authorized supplier to large well-known firms such as Toyota. Secondly, firms need to be continually updated on technological and sales innovations, and finally there is the ever-present possibility of the acquisition of a local producer. For SMEs there is the same necessity to be recognized as an authorized supplier. Being present in Japan (through strategic alliances) is based on the fact that patents and trademarks are much more respected in Japan than anywhere else in Asia. However, SMEs are confronted with numerous difficulties. A long-term commitment is necessary (e.g. two years of tests before Plasto can become an authorized supplier) which involves considerable sums of money.

In both cases, becoming an authorised supplier in the most demanding market in the world enables a firm to strengthen or reinforce its position in the rest of Asia or Europe, through an enhanced reputation and a stronger portfolio of clients.

3.4 Choice of Local Set-up

So as to satisfy the needs of a market that is fragmented globally, there are four alternatives for entering the Japanese market for adhesives and sealants. The choice lies between a licensing agreement, a joint venture, a production subsidiary and a strategic alliance. Export (on condition that environmental regulations and customs duties are favourable) is not an option, because it is perceived as being a limited commitment in the long-term (not being taken seriously). Exporting does not give a firm a sufficient understanding of local needs, let alone the level of service that well established firms can offer.

Licensing Agreement

For small or inexperienced firms this method offers immediate entry into a new market. Control over production and product marketing is slight. If the firm is following its clients in their process of internationalization, this can be a useful option in the short term to satisfy client needs. This method of entry is also appropriate for testing client receptiveness with a minimal risk.

Joint Venture

This kind of link-up with a suitable partner, where both sides are looking for new markets, can work well. Common vision and values tied to a common commitment to quality underline the chances of success with joint ventures. Sometimes conflicts occur when the local partner promotes his own products rather than those of the JV. As in licensing agreements, the solution lies in close monitoring and control of the partner. Companies that have succeeded worldwide have all used licensing agreements or joint-ventures to develop their business internationally.

In multi-domestic industries like adhesives, *majority joint ventures* open the door to a wider international portfolio of activities. Advantages include a more efficient allocation of resources between countries and lower costs of entry to foreign markets. The right partner will of course contribute his local knowledge of business and administrative constraints and contacts. The top three adhesives manufacturers worldwide, Henkel (Germany), National (USA) and Fuller (USA) are well established in Japan and have established links with Japanese firms for the transfer of technology and joint-ventures.

Local Production Subsidiaries

All the manufacturers interviewed pointed out that whenever possible it was preferable to set up a local production unit to supply the particular market concerned. Multi-domestic industries encourage internationalizing firms to gain a foothold in large foreign markets. The acquisition of a local producer, when financially possible, seems to be the preferred strategy of most manufacturers. However, starting off in Asia with a local subsidiary seems a high risk approach, unless a guaranteed market is in place (following an existing client), given the highly competitive nature of the industrial adhesives sector.

It is worth reflecting some time before taking a decision on the method of market entry. Time should be taken to analyse the market one wants to enter, as well as local regulations concerning joint ventures and foreign patents. Local financial conditions are also important as well as the number of potential local partners.

New forms of international investment should not be forgotten. There are agreements between MNCs, cross-participation in shareholdings, and joint subsidiaries set up to share the spiralling costs of R&D. Other objectives are the search for greater economies of scale and the need to share information on local market conditions.

Source: based upon the results of the Adhesives & Sealants Council's Survey, 1992 (USA)

3.5   Difficulties in Implementing a Local Set-up

In all the cases mentioned above, export is not a satisfactory answer. FDI (foreign direct investment) in the form of a production subsidiary or a joint venture are the best ways of getting round the multitude of imperfections in the market.[5]

We include below some of the drawbacks of the 'Japan' solution to setting up in Asia, linked to the problems of implementing the set-up. Some pitfalls are more threatening:

- The fact of offering licensing agreements often means you create your own competition.
- Thanks to cultural and linguistic barriers, many Asian countries maintain an indirect control over access to their markets.
- The all-pervasive influence of the big Japanese firms can be a drawback.
- Regional markets remain small and thus do not permit significant economies of scale.
- The globalization of operations means there is a certain risk of technical talent moving elsewhere.

The example of Total and its reorganisation of Bostik illustrates how the local improvement of formulae is a 'must' that can seriously handicap firms that consider it unnecessary. The specific needs of local clients and the availability of chemical raw materials forced Bostik to adapt. It is thus crucial to have the necessary production facilities to modify the chemical formulae. The firm as a whole can benefit from this expertise.

There can also be problems of a logistic nature that affect firms setting up in Japan. The 'just in time' system of production with minimal stock is widespread in Japan. The distribution system is very different from that of its neighbours (and from European ones as well), and this can present some problems for foreign producers, as expertise acquired in Japan may not be sufficiently useful in other countries in Asia. As far as the transfer of processes or of technology to Japan is concerned, some modifications are always required for industrial adhesives.

Climate also has to be taken into account. For example, with the local levels of humidity, resistance to acid rain is diminished. This is another reason why export may not be the most appropriate method of entering the market.

Numerous trials and tests are needed over a period of about two years before one can say one is firmly established in Japan. During this time local Japanese producers will test the quality of material proposed by foreign manufacturers. In addition, the foreign firm should have an efficient after-sales network of sales technicians to promote the product with the existing clientèle. Of course, this does not only apply to the industrial adhesives sector.

What is most important in Japan, regardless of the price, is the mix between an interesting technology, a guaranteed high level of quality and guaranteed regular deliveries. The products that best answer these requirements are adhesives and sealants for insulation with a high added value. They are structurally sound, they can be applied by robots and they have a short drying time, necessary for rapid industrial applications. They respect the environment, including water-based adhesive with a rapid drying time, hot-melt adhesives that can be recycled and pressure-sensitive adhesives.

Given their lead in technology, the European manufacturers that have tackled the problem of the level of organic solvents in their products can find partners in Japan interested in technology transfer. Alliances need to be set up differently depending on the size of the firm and the sector concerned.

Adhesives for the construction, packaging and car industries, which have the most widespread applications, offer boundless opportunities for French producers (the lumber industry offers similar opportunities but is in decline). Currently this market is dominated by Konishi and Cemedine but is in a process of rapid change. Small Japanese firms suffering from the pressure of the competition could well be attracted by the chance of transfer of technology from abroad.

The sector of adhesives for Do-It-Yourself centres (DIY) is well established in Japan. Future growth should be slow but regular. The leader is Toagosei with 80% of the market for quick-set adhesives, followed by Konishi and Cemedine. None of these firms is planning significant sales promotion in the immediate future.

CONCLUSION

The outlook for the industrial adhesives sector revolves around the future for its clients. Currently the highest growth rates for user industries of adhesives are to be found in Asia.

Choosing Japan as a launching-pad for the rest of Asia is best explained by the need to find synergies between the technological lead held by European firms compared to the Japanese, and on the other hand the attraction of rapidly emerging markets. This of course compensates for market saturation in Europe. The recommended entry strategy for a French firm is thus to make contact and co-operate with a Japanese producer, of which there are many in the adhesive sector.

Secondly, after two years it may be worth creating a full subsidiary. Importing the finished product is a hazardous exercise, as Dupont and ICI found to their cost. The reasons for this setback were the following:

- Transport costs are exorbitant.
- The requirement to respond rapidly to changes in the rules for certification (fixed by the government) – e.g. adhesives for the construction industry.
- It is essential, in common with Japanese producers, to have regional sales offices, covering the whole of Japan. In this way it is possible to respond rapidly to customer requirements. These offices need to be sufficiently well organized to be able to give clients detailed technical information on product ranges and specifications.
- Client – supplier relationships are close, particularly in the car industry. Clients are not systematically on the look-out for new suppliers (Japanese networks).
- The market is highly competitive. Japanese will only import adhesives that are scarce in Japan, or those that are of higher quality than the local available product.
- Imports from the Southeast Asian subsidiaries of Japanese firms are on the increase.
- When in-depth tests for certification take place – e.g. for the construction industry – producers have to react immediately to the result of the tests.

Once a European producer has gone through all these stages, the chances of increasing market share in the rest of the Asian economic area are more or less guaranteed. Japan has a very decisive influence, particularly in the adhesive user sector.

In conclusion, this original approach to the Asian market via Japan seems particularly appropriate considering the leading edge technology of the products.

Notes

1. International conference at Kyoto in 1992, jointly sponsored by the Japan Adhesive Industry Association and the Japan Sealant Industry Association, the two syndicates of industrial glue and sealing joint producers
2. EUROSTAF, *L'Industrie européenne des Colles et Adhésifs*, No. 25, DAFSA 1978. This file has apparently not yet been updated, but several observations are found here which are still highly pertinent today.
3. T. Atamer & R. Calori, *Diagnostic et Décisions Stratégiques*, DUNOD 1993: this work is useful to make comparisons with another specialised chemical sector: paints. p. 502–509.
4. The efficiency of the government measures is hampered by a household's expectations on inflation (more than 30% p.a.)

5. The very nature of an industry (nature, fragmented, multi-domestic) has encouraged multi-national producers of industrial adhesives to adapt to local conditions (tailor-made service for the client) and to manage a more or less integrated network of subsidiaries. Unlike other high-tech products like lasers or computers. M.N.Cs have found market structures already well established in target countries (thanks to the existence of local suppliers). But while clients had similar applications, the differences in regulations, the environment, human expertise and the number of tests to be carried out, meant that formulations had to be adapted to local conditions. These local differences meant that exporting was never really an answer.

REFERENCES

Books and Magazines on Economics and Business Policy:

Atamer, Tugrul and Calori, Roland, *Diagnostic et Décisions Stratégiques*, Dunod, 1993.

Bidault, Francis, *Le Champ Stratégique de l'Entreprise*, Economica Gestion, 1988.

Dunning, J. H., *International Production and the Multinational Enterprise*, George Allen & Unwin, London, 1981.

Morvan, Yves, *Fondements d'Economie Industrielle*, 2nd edition, Economica Gestion 1993.

Mucchielli, Jean-Louis, *Alliances Stratégiques et Firmes Multinationales: Une Nouvelle Théorie pour de Nouvelles Formes de Multinationalisation*, Revue d'Economie Industrielle, n°55, 1 er trimestre 1991.

Ozawa, Terutomo, *Japanese Multinationals and 1992*, in Burgenmeier, B. and Mucchielli, J-L, *Multinationals and Europe 1992*, Routledge, 1991.

Porter, Michaël E., *Competitive strategy: Techniques for Analysing Industries and Competitors*, New York: The Free Press, 1980, Choix Stratégiques et Concurrence, Paris: 1982, 1985.

Sachwald, Frédérique *et al.*, *Les Entreprises Japonaises en Europe: Motivations et Statégies*, Institut Français des Relations Internationales (Travaux et Recherches de l'IFRI), Masson 1993.

Sazanami, Yoko, *Globalisation Strategy of Japanese Manufacturing Firms and its Impacts on Trade Flows Between Europe, Asia and North America*, Mimeo, March 1992.

General Books on Japan:

French Embassy – Service d'Information et de Presse et Maison Franco-Japonaise, Bureau Français, *Le Japon 1994*.

Revue *France Japon Eco, Vie et Affaires au Japon*, n°46–52–53–56–57, Chambre de Commerce et d'Industrie Française du Japon.

La Documentation Française – Collection des Rapports Officiels, Ministére de l'Economie, des Finances et du Budget, Ministère du Commerce Extérieur, D.R.E.E. – Bureau Analyse et Prévision, *Exporter au Japon, Atouts et Défis*.

Centre Français du Commerce Extérieur, Direction de l'Approche des Marchés Extérieurs, P.E.E. de Tokyo, *Un Marché: Japon*, °25, 1993.

Karl van Wolferen, *L'Enigme de la Puissance Japonaise*, 1990, Editions Robert Laffont.

Hidetoshi Katô *et al.*, Ouvrage collectif d'intellectuels Japonais, Hihon no Kokoro, *The Spirit of Japan, Views of Japan from Japan*, September 1987, Nippon Steel Corporation.

Specialised Sources:

Chemical Week (U.S.), March 1993 and 1994.

Eurostaf, L'Industrie Européenne des Colles et Adhésifs, n°25, 1978, DAFSA.

Information Chimie, n°335 (February 1992), n°354 (December 1993/January 1994).

Industrie et Techniques, n°746 (February 1994), n°756 (January 1995), n°758 (March 1995).

Japan Chemical Week and *Japan Chemical Daily*, 1989, 1990, 1991, 1992, 1993, 1994.

The 1992 Kyoto International Conference's JAIA Report.

L'Usine Nouvelle, n°2416 (24.06.93), n°2425 (23.09.93), n°2431 (04.11.93), n°2437 (16.12.93), n°2449 (24.04.94), n°2469 (08.09.94), n°2472 (29.09.94).

Index

ASEAN (Association of South-East Asian
    Nations) 25
Asia and EU antidumping provisions 67–8
Asia and EU antidumping provisions –
    discussion of some concrete cases 68–71
Asia–Pacific Economic Cooperation
    (APEC) xii, 25
Asian economic integration and the role of
    Japanese Corporate networks 191–3
    the case of the electronics industry 193 ff

BOT projects in China and India 89–90
China
    an assessment of political risk in 151–4
    economic reforms and political
        authoritarism in 146–9
    environmental concerns 113–14
    evolution of political risk 144 ff
    FDI in 93, 101–8
    FDI in and economic integration of
        East-Asia 121–9
    human resource management: the Japanese
        experience 163–7
    integration into the regional economy
        92 ff
    investments of the Diaspora 129–33
    Japan and trade relations with 97–101
    macroeconomic reforms in 157 ff
    new role in the regional economy 109
    reform of the pricing system 162–3
China and India: performance of the
    giants 86–8
China's 'Township and Village
    Enterprises' 85
China's Special Economic Zones and Open
    Coastal Cities xv
Chinese market
    decision process of organizational buyers in
        the 173–6
    industrial procurement practices of
        Taiwanese firms in 172 ff
    organizational procurement and the
        Concept of Country of Origin 177
comparative advantages and disadvantages of
    Japan, Indonesia and the 'four
    dragons' 13–18
comparative advantages and disadvantages of
    other Asian Countries 18

Deng Xiao Ping and 'The Open Door
    Policy' 84, 85

East Asian Economic Integration: the first
    indicators 25–32
EU antidumping rules 63, 64 ff
EU Policy towards Asia xii–xiv, 62
exchange indicators 3–11

Fabian Society and the London School of
    Economics 82
Foreign Direct Investment (FDI) 24, 25, 26,
    32, 33

GATT/WTO 63
globalization and regionalization 24, 25

IMF estimate of growth in Asia xi
IMF and India 83–4
impact of Asian growth on the global
    economy xi–xii
Indira Gandhi 81, 83

Japan
    business cycle and trade dynamics 38, 48
    development assistance 32–3
    evolution of bilateral opening rate 41, 48
    trade with East Asia 38 ff
Japanese companies
    cooperation and strategic alliances
        with 208
    types of cooperation with 208–12

Mao Tse Dung 84

NAFTA xv, 25
Nehru 81–3

Professor Mahalanobis and Indian economic
    experiment 82

Salman Rushdie on India's 'Midnight's
    children' 81
Sydney Webb (Fabian Society) 82

The Great Leap Forward and the Cultural
    Revolution 84
The Indian intelligentsia of the 1930s 82

transaction costs 212–15

World Bank estimate of growth in Asia xi
world glue industry 219–27
world glue industry
  attractiveness of the Asia Pacific
    region 227–32

attractiveness of the Japanese market 218
Japan as a base for market expansion in the
  region 232–5
WTO antidumping code 64–6

Yuan Shi Kai 84